"Ruary is not only a notable dragonfly expert but perhaps more importantly the greatest ambassador these insects have had in the UK ... This lovely book catalogues his journey and charts his many successes. It cements his status as one of Britain's greatest living naturalists. One dragonfly on his shirt led to all this ... thank goodness it pitched there!" CHRIS PACKHAM

"I like to think I know a little about dragonflies, but Ruary is the expert." BILL ODDIE

"The work [the Dragonfly Project] has done has been tremendous." ALAN BOWLEY, WOODWALTON FEN NATIONAL NATURE RESERVE

"25 years not out has been a tremendous innings and what a valuable set of achievements during that time." NJ MOULD MVO MRICS, DUCHY OF CORNWALL'S OFFICE, HIGHGROVE

"[The Dragonfly Project] has given dragonflies the glittering profile they deserve." TREVOR LAWSON, *DAILY TELEGRAPH*

"Ruary is not only an expert on dragonflies but a gifted storyteller whose enthusiasm inspires as it entertains. This is a fascinating, informative and extremely readable book." MALIZE MCBRIDE

"Radio at its picture-painting best." RADIO TIMES, PICK OF THE DAY, FOR RUARY MACKENZIE DODDS ON BBC RADIO 4'S *NATURE*

"A fantastic legacy to the world of dragonfly knowledge and appreciation." MIKE & LINDA AVERILL

"A fascinating memoir... Zen and the art of pond watching." ANDREW CALLANDER

'Order of the Geek' Award BBC *SPRINGWATCH*

To Rachel
With Very Best Wishes

Ruary

The
Dragonfly
Diaries

The unlikely story
of Europe's first
dragonfly sanctuary

Ruary Mackenzie Dodds

Saraband

Published by Saraband
Suite 202, 98 Woodlands Road
Glasgow, G3 6HB, Scotland
www.saraband.net

ISBN: 9781908643551
ebook: 9781908643568

Printed in the EU on sustainably sourced paper.

Editor: Craig Hillsley
Additional editing and layout: Laura Jones

The cover artwork is based on the Dragonfly Project logo
Original artwork © Kari de Koenigswarter and Berit de Koenigswarter

Contents

For everyone who lent a hand

Part One

Catching the Bug

1980 to 1990

Chapter 1

I'm standing on the towpath of the Grand Union Canal at Denham, holding a camera, alone in the sunshine, trying to relax from my super-pressurized job in Kensington. I'm here to get a dose of fresh air, soak up the calm, maybe take a few arty photographs.

A dragonfly lands on my shirt, and three things happen, lightning fast. *One*: I don't really like insects, but I'm completely comfortable with this amber-black thing sitting above my heart. *Two*: I actually look at a dragonfly, properly, for the first time in my life. It's beautiful. I feel a strange sense of wonder. *Three*: the dragonfly says, 'Why not photograph dragonflies?' and vanishes in a whirr of wings.

I'm left with the oddest feeling, much stronger than just an idea about photography. It's … I don't know. Something a bit like a *déjà-vu*, but not. An intuition?

I live in central London but I'm always seeking out quiet places: parks, woodlands and especially canals. Canals are like veins of peace; glass-smooth and thin, slipping discreetly past noisy factories and under busy streets. Bits are ugly, bits are dangerous, but the part I'm in right now threads through a mile-long fragment of countryside somehow left behind in the middle of all the bricks and concrete.

The Grand Union at Denham is bounded to the south by the roar of the M40, and to the north by trains heading to High Wycombe and beyond. It's a little area of leafy, watery quiet. The banks of the canal are lined with old oaks. Keeping company with the canal is the River Colne, and there are several broad gravel pits, worked out now and filled with water. It's the combination of canal, river and placid lakes that makes the place so attractive.

Anyway, I started to photograph dragonflies. Things have changed a bit since 1985. I'd have a digital camera now, and I wouldn't have to wait for prints to come back, but I'd still need a sunny day, a great deal of patience, and clothes I didn't mind getting seriously dirty. I'd still have to be ready to crawl and I'd probably end up with wet shoes.

After many attempts, the first successful picture I got was of a damselfly, not a dragonfly. When I took the photo I didn't know the difference between the two, but now I do: when it lands, if it leaves its wings out flat like an aeroplane, it's a dragonfly. If it folds them neatly back, along what I kept calling its fuselage until I learned it's the abdomen, it's a damselfly. Of course, as with most simple definitions there are exceptions, but just being aware of that difference means I already know more about Odonata than 99.9% of the world's population. Odonata is the proper name for the Order that includes both dragonflies and damselflies.

Kari, my partner (we're married now), got that first success. She didn't actually do any crawling or camera stuff, but her hawk-eyes spotted a tiny blue triangle in the grass. We were wandering through a field close to the canal later that summer. It had begun to cloud over. We'd decided we were out of luck when suddenly Kari pointed. I dropped to my knees and crept forward, warily as a cat. Into the viewfinder came an insect the colour of lapis lazuli, half of each elegant wing stained a deeper blue. I was transfixed. I've used that picture of a Banded Demoiselle (*Calopteryx splendens*, its Sunday name) again and again, on interpretation boards and in talks. Every time I see it, I feel the sense of wonder and victory – and something else, something hard to define – that shot through me on that quiet morning. Did I really take that in Denham, Middlesex? Did we only have to take the Central Line to West Ruislip then walk a bit? Not have to trek into the Brazilian jungle?

Hawk-Eye Kari had spent ten years of her adult life in New York. Like me, she wasn't interested in insects, but, almost as soon as I got the dragonfly-photography bug she showed an extraordinary ability to spot them. Genetic maybe; her grandfather, Charles Rothschild, was a pioneer of nature conservation, her mother Pannonica was named after a moth, and her Aunt Miriam was one of the world's leading authorities on fleas.

I never knew Charles Rothschild; he died in 1923. But I knew Nica and Miriam well. I met Miriam first. She wasn't exactly an ordinary person, and her home at Ashton Wold wasn't an ordinary house. They've gone now. I still go back, but only in my head. And in my heart.

SATURDAY, MARCH 22ND, 1980: LONDON

(Five years earlier)

I don't feel very well, but I'm ignoring it. Kari and I are in a little Citroën Dyane heading for Ashton Wold, on our way to see Kari's Aunt Miriam. I don't know much about her. Kari's very fond of her and wants us to meet. I'm told she's a flea expert, a serious fighter for wildflowers, and fellow of the Royal Society. Clearly not a lightweight.

The journey from London in the underpowered Dyane seems to take years but at about midday, we turn into a scene so twee it could be a film set: thatched houses ring a village green, and at the top is a thatched pub, the Chequered Skipper. We've arrived? Wrong. We drive through the village to a lodge and a gate, beside which is a sign:

NOTICE: NO PERSON IS PERMITTED TO TRESPASS
IN ASHTON IN SEARCH OF INSECTS.

We head up the private road. Later I hear this is called the 'drive', but that's a nonsense: it's nearly two miles of the bumpiest track imaginable, with potholes as long and as deep as trenches. The Citroën's suspension is built for French *pavé*, but as we crash and sway uphill I'm sure other cars soon fall to pieces under this treatment.

Eventually we reach Ashton Wold at the top. The track leads through lines of overgrown laurels and we run parallel to what is obviously the outside of a walled garden with potting sheds and a tired-looking Fergy tractor. Then we veer off round the service side of the house, so I can't work out the actual size of the place, but it's certainly big; and I like the look of its mullioned windows. As we swing round the bend I notice, in a copse beside the track, a moss-covered mountain of stone blocks topped by five upside-down cast iron baths, each with four fat little legs in the air.

We leave the car at one end of a small courtyard and go through a large white door at the other. The loud bang as it closes behind us echoes down the long, bare, whitewashed corridor ahead. At once we hear the sound of distant barking and a patter of many paws on parquet, and as we round the corner into an even longer much more elegant corridor, a pack of shelties – led by a small black mongrel – is hurtling towards us. I'm usually all right with dogs; not with this lot. They're after our ankles. On subsequent visits, I know to dodge smartly into the kitchen on the right and slam the door behind me, but not now.

'Come here!' yells an imperious female voice. 'Come here, I say.'

I look at Kari.

'She means the dogs,' says Kari, hopping sideways.

The seething, fanged mass of brown, white and black fur subsides and trots reluctantly back down the corridor into a distant set of rooms.

'Kari?' yells the voice again. 'Is that you?'

'Hello, Miriam,' Kari calls.

'With you in a minute. Help yourself to a drink. Sunday! Moonie! Come here!'

Kari and I walk into the library. As with the word 'drive', 'library' is a misnomer. It's a vast, bright, oak-panelled room, walled by ceiling-high bookshelves. At one end is a mighty mantelpiece with a Stanley Spencer painting of lilacs above it and a roaring fire below. Ranged round the fireplace are three massive sofas, each covered with a white throw and each showing signs of considerable doggy activity. At the other end of the room stands a concert-size Steinway and, under an enormous leadlight window, a long table piled high with brand new books: art, architecture, biographies, novels, scientific journals and Jewish politics. In the middle of the room is another table on which is a giant vase of (real) lilacs, and, nestled in the porchway looking out to the garden, another table with an array of drinks that would impress the most jaundiced of barmen. It includes vodka. I hover, uncertain. Kari taps the top of the vodka bottle.

'A big one,' she says. I obey and hand her a thumping glassful. She works at the same outfit as I do. She's Head of Marketing. I've watched her keep pace with very hard drinkers. Personally – and uncharacteristically – I settle for a glass of sherry.

I see the wellingtons first; they're white; I haven't seen any like that since my doctor father played Santa Claus at his local hospital in Lincolnshire. Then I see the dress, a beautifully cut billowy silk affair, white and violet. Then the scarf, also violet, tied so as to reveal sweeping curls of silver hair. A pale, almost translucent face; a sharp nose; high cheekbones; very piercing, fleeting eyes; and a sudden powerful presence.

'Hello,' says Miriam. 'Who are you?'

'I ...'

'Oh yes, I remember. Kari rang. Have a drink.'

'I have one, thank you. Would you ...?'

'No. Have you seen the snake's head fritillaries? On the tennis court. Go and look. Stay on the path. Lunch at one.'

We go out through the garden door and down pale spacious limestone steps to a terrace, then down more steps to another terrace and, brushing aside overgrown white lilacs, down yet more steps to the tennis court. It isn't a tennis court. I'm getting used to this. Yes, it has been, but now it's a yellow carpet of cowslips, dotted with purple fritillaries, with a tiny path weaving diagonally across it to a long rampart facing south. I leave Kari, bent over, gazing at the wildflowers, and tiptoe down the path. In the corner it leads to a hidden stairway. At the bottom is a wrought-iron gate to another overgrown garden. I can see a lily pond, and, on another terrace, a ruined thatched dovecote. There's the faintest air of sadness.

I turn and look back at the mansion. It's half-hidden by untrimmed trees, but, with its golden stonework and its mullions, it looks like a very large Edwardian version of a Sussex ironmaster's house, albeit strangely truncated. I discover later that, back in the Fifties, Miriam had all the roofs taken off, the entire middle floor removed, then the roofs put back on. As the masons took the stones down, they numbered each one and piled them all in that copse close to the house, then put the baths on top.

Kari calls me back and makes me crouch down to look at a snake's head fritillary. On its tiny, grape-red, bent-over bell of petals are minute brown flecks, repeating uniformly like a fleur-de-lis wallpaper pattern in miniature. We go back up to the house. As we walk back into the library, Miriam is on the phone.

'Well, you can tell the Lord Chancellor he'll have to cut his speech,' she says, and puts the phone down. I've heard her before, when she's rung Kari at our London flat. She never says goodbye. She swings round.

'Look here, there's no food. Margaret's not here. We'll have to go and scrounge.' The black mongrel is now gazing adoringly up at her. 'Come on, Sunday,' she says.

She leads the way into the dining room; another massive space, also oak-panelled, but a lighter shade, almost white. In the centre of the room is a grand table. I count fourteen Chippendale chairs round it. In a long daffodil-lined alcove by the window there's another table. The smaller one can accommodate at least a dozen, too, but it's set for three. There are two sideboards: the nearest has ashets of cold duck, cold roast beef, cold ham, smoked mackerel, peas, tomatoes, salads of different sorts, beetroot, potato salad, fennel and celery. Miriam's idea of scrounging. On the far sideboard stands a small army of pickles, mayonnaises, mustards and sauces. I glance at them appreciatively.

'I hope you like quail's eggs,' says Miriam. 'Pour the wine, will you? None for me.'

The wine is a sparkling white, Pétillant Deux-Sèvres.

'You'll never guess what Sid's done,' says Miriam, turning to Kari, and so begins a long conversation about the farm and the family. I tuck into the eggs, and then the duck.

'Have some more, Ruary,' orders Miriam.

'I'm fine, thank you, that was delicious,' I say.

'Oh, go on,' she says testily. 'There's tons there.'

After the meal, we go upstairs, through the spacious billiards room, to the bedroom we've been allocated. Separate beds. It's crammed with portraits and photographs of the family. I lie down and begin to feel unwell again. I shouldn't have eaten that vast lunch. It gets worse. I start to sweat. Eventually I tell Kari I won't be able to come down for tea.

'You've got to,' she says. 'Tea's important.'

'I can't. I'll throw up.'

'Miriam hates sick people.'

'Well, we'd better go back to London, while I can still drive. I'm really not right.'

'I'll go and tell her,' she says.

Kari goes downstairs, breaks the news, and an hour later, after I've built up strength, we repack and go out to the car. As we load our stuff, Miriam appears from the walled garden. She sees me, continues coming towards the house, but gives me a very wide berth, taking care to keep at least fifteen metres away.

SATURDAY, OCTOBER 11TH, 1980: ASHTON WOLD

After an enormous lunch – roast duck and Château La Cardonne claret – Kari and I go through that wrought-iron gate I saw on my first visit, past the lily pond, through another iron gate and into the deer-field. Under a dark sky, we're walking down to Ashton Water. I haven't been there before and we're with Kari's cousins – Miriam's children – Charlotte and Charles. They both have auburn hair, very bright against the greyness of the day. They have their own flats within the house, and Ashton is their home when they aren't working in London.

We head downhill through woodland trampled by deer to a lake that looks like something out of Africa: bare, muddy and pocked with thousands of hoof-marks. There's the Top Pond upstream of it with the same devastated look, and between them stands a small ten-sided building with a faded duck-egg blue door, the observation hut. The thatch is badly damaged. As well as a conical thatched roof, it has thatched walls and odd-shaped, many-paned broken windows on one side only, all looking out over the lake. I peer in through one of the jagged glass rectangles: nothing except a pile of hay, an empty bottle and a broken three-legged chair, lying sideways on a perfectly laid wooden floor that even through the dust and grime looks good enough to dance on.

The lake has two little islands and is surrounded by old willows, some so tall as to have dropped whole boughs that have fallen and reared up again as separate trees. The water is a flat brown. Even at that moment, as we walk round the margin of the lake, talking of nothing in particular, our voices echoing over the silent still surface, I have a strange feeling. This lake is calling to me.

Chapter 2

SATURDAY, NOVEMBER 22ND, 1980: NEW YORK

I'm not sure I want to return to Miriam's. I haven't especially enjoyed my first experiences of her, or Ashton itself, despite that moment by the lake. Miriam is a very strong personality and I don't really know how we could get on.

It's Nica – Kari's mother, Miriam's sister – who makes me go back. Kari and I have been together just under a year now so it's time to meet 'The Jazz Baroness', as Nica is known in the newspapers.

When we land at JFK, there, in her silver drophead Bentley S1 Continental, is Nica to meet us. She's smaller than Kari, has long, still-dark hair, a striking angular face, and staggeringly beautiful, almost violet eyes. She wears a flowery silk shirt and inexpensive slacks.

I'm packed into the back of 'Sputnik' and off we drive. In the front, Kari and her mother launch into a long conversation about the family. I've taken a bit of trouble to prepare for the visit, looking at maps and so on, and, as they talk, it soon becomes clear that the Empire State Building is dwindling fast in the rearview mirror. Tentatively I lean forward. 'Oh', says Nica, 'you're right,' and promptly U-turns the Bentley into three lanes of suddenly nose-diving sedans and blaring monster-trucks.

That first night I'm taken to the Village Vanguard. Nica stops beside a parking spot right outside and asks me to take over, get the car nearer the kerb.

'Sputnik doesn't have power-steering,' she says.

I glance at her slim arms, the Bentley's big steering wheel and the beefy Checker Yellowcabs leaping and thumping past over the huge potholes that pock every New York roadway. I've never driven a Bentley before, let alone one this rare, let alone in the madness of New York traffic.

'You go on ahead,' I say, swallowing. 'Does this key lock it as well?'

'Oh, thank you. No need.'

No need to lock it? In New York? In 1980? Where I've been warned that, on the Subway, you have to look as if you're the one with the meat cleaver? Where, earlier in the evening, I'd been in a store on 14th Street and the cops had chalked white rings round the spent shell-cases in two of the aisles while a a puddle of blood congealed on the sidewalk outside?

Nica is already at the door of the club, but she senses my thoughts and turns to me.

'Really. It's fine.'

I slip into the soft red leather driving seat and Sputnik turns out to be as fabulous to drive as its looks; the car virtually parks itself. I hurry into the club. Nica and Kari have waited for me at the door. I watch while the crowd parts as if a queen has arrived. The set has already begun. Barry Harris is at the piano. We're ushered to a table right at the front.

I realize within seconds that to talk while bebop musicians are playing is ignorant bad manners, as rude as chattering through a Bach recital. Nica listens to the music with an intensity that's almost shocking. There's a whisky in front of her but she hardly touches it. Her face says everything about whether or not she approves of the musicians' work. She reaches for a Chesterfield occasionally. Each time, the lighter-flame reveals those amazing eyes.

When the third set finishes, I'm struck by the blend of affection and deep respect all the musicians in the club have for her. And, so far as they're concerned, if you're with her, you must be all right.

And what's this about The Bible? There are several references to it by people in the club, and, as we leave, 'Hey, Nica, got The Bible?' asks one of the two black guys keeping an eye on the Bentley on the sidewalk.

'Someone always guards it,' says Kari.

Nica makes the two men double over with laughter, but doesn't produce The Bible. I'm none the wiser.

Kari hops into the back of the Bentley and I sit beside Nica as we make for the Lincoln Tunnel, heading back to the Cat-House, her home in Weehawken. Without taking her eyes off the road she reaches under her seat. The Bible turns out to be a leather-bound volume; I open it reverentially, then laugh. It contains a large silver flask.

'Try it,' she says.

I sip. It's delicious.

'Chivas Regal,' she says.

The tunnel is deserted. Nica's an excellent, confident, fast driver. Among other more clandestine activities, she drove staff cars for the Free French Army during WWII. She stops gently questioning me and, one hand on the wheel, a Chesterfield in the other, she swings round to talk to Kari.

'You really ought to get with Miriam more often you know,' she says. 'Both of you.'

Already I can see Nica is a very different person from her elder sister. She couldn't care less about convention and she looks right inside you.

I notice the speedometer is just touching 120 mph. I look again to make sure; it really is.

SATURDAY, APRIL 9TH, 1983: LONDON

Nica's over on a very rare visit from the States. Naturally she wants to go up to visit her older sister Miriam at Ashton. They'd spent long summers there as children. There must be so many memories. Nica wants Kari and I to come.

I drive us from London in the Dyane, a very different form of motoring for a Bentley-owner like Nica, but she's interested in the car's suspension and the extraordinary way it goes round corners. She says it puts her in mind of a jeep. She should know. We discuss poetry, then limericks. In view of Nica's age and station, I recite a polite one:

> *There was a young lady from Bude*
> *Who swam in the sea in the nude.*
> *A policeman said "What a M...*
> *...agnificent bottom!"*
> *And smacked it as hard as he cude.*

The Jazz Baroness grins at me, is silent for a moment, then replies:

> *A girl called Dynamite Lil*
> *Tried gelignite for a thrill.*
> *They found her vagina*
> *In North Carolina*
> *And bits of her tits in Brazil.*

Which leads from bad to worse. We pause at a shop to buy a bottle of vodka and by the time we arrive at Ashton we're friends.

Kari and I go up to Ashton more regularly. We begin to be incorporated into Miriam's family. Some of the people who come and go in the huge meeting place of a library could only be described as legends. Many of them are generally scientific and generally something to do with animals: Professor Sir Vincent Wigglesworth, Robin Chancellor, Sir Andrew Huxley. But there are exceptions like the enormous, immensely witty lawyer Sir John Foster, whom Miriam obviously adores. There is also a trickle of super-intelligent guests, among them Isaiah Berlin, the Neubergers, John Gurdon, Rupert Sheldrake and Adrian Wolfson, and one or two regular friends, including a wealthy American businesswoman, an Israeli publisher and a duchess.

What constantly surprises me is finding myself treated as an equal. Almost invariably I'm actually listened to and taken seriously, which of course encourages me to concentrate and participate. I contribute little, but I'm excited and stimulated by this succession of astonishing people. One or two visitors remain indifferently grand, including a local lord who really does walk about with his aristocratic nose in the air. In these surroundings it's easy to see that his sort are hiding behind a carefully constructed image of their own importance, birthright and station. Kari often reacts differently to me when we meet new arrivals. In some cases I become very enthusiastic, keen to talk long into the night, only to find Kari almost wordless. Her judgements are usually, annoyingly, right.

Exhilaratingly, children are allowed to barge in and take over whenever they want, and to call all adults by their first names, including their own parents. I love Miriam's mischievous sense of humour and begin to relax into the fast, free-wheeling life at Ashton, very different to that of my own family, and my work in London.

I get the feeling that, quite apart from Miriam and Kari, I'm at Ashton for a reason, although I'm not sure what. Is it something to do with the lake?

Chapter 3

SUMMER, 1985: LONDON

Following the Banded Demoiselle incident, I go out to Denham several times. At first, it's about perfect shots. There are problems with getting good images: dragonflies fly too fast, and, even when they land, they position themselves in the most awkward places so that you have to crawl towards them in order to have even the remotest chance. They have a brilliant notion of exactly when you're about to press the shutter, and they're gone. It's also difficult to get a good shot of the whole insect, including the wings.

I end up obsessing about things like 'depth of field'. But when I get a good picture, there's a wonderful sense of victory. There's also a sense of something else, I can't work out what. The word 'therapeutic' comes to mind. Anyway, soon I begin to see that there are several different types of dragonfly. Information about them is very hard to find, but I buy the only two books on dragonflies available at the time. Others books exist but are either impossible to find, even in London, or are out of print.

Of the two books I buy, one is a 1985 softback reprint of *Dragonflies,* a Collins New Naturalist hardback, written by Corbet, Longfield and Moore. It tells me, in a very readable way, a vast amount about dragonfly biology and behaviour. But, though the 1960 edition had colour plates, my reprint has black-and-white versions. This is the only way – so Collins have told the authors, and so they tell us in the book's introduction – that the softback will wash its face at all. I read it from cover to cover and, sure, the biology and behaviour is fascinating, but what I need is a way of identifying dragonflies; and it's the second book that helps me with that. Basil and Annette Harley of Harley Books have just brought out *The Dragonflies of Great Britain and Ireland*, by Cyril Hammond. It's a big hardback book, awkward to cart about in the open air, but it serves me wonderfully well.

Denham Lock is now one of my favourite spots. Just above it, the river flows under the canal and I can nip between the two, just as the dragonflies do. I see that some damselflies prefer the flowing water of the river, in particular the Banded Demoiselles, whereas some of the dragonflies like to perch on reeds above the calmer water of the canal. My New Naturalist book tells me that this is characteristic of certain dragonflies: some like flowing water and some like stiller stretches and ponds.

One particular dragonfly puzzles me, a red one. It perches above the canal on a rush stem and from time to time it shoots into the air only to return to the same perch once more, which is handy for getting reasonable photographs, but what is it? It can only be one of two species, I decide, either the Common Darter or the Ruddy Darter. Ruddy Darter! What a name! And its Linnean Sunday-name is so elegant, too. How would you feel if your name was *Sympetrum sanguineum* and people called you Ruddy Darter? I think it's the Ruddy-thing that makes me concentrate on learning the scientific names for dragonflies, and, later, when I meet a Swedish entomologist up at Ashton, who frowns confusedly at the words 'Ruddy' and 'Darter', I discover that using the international Linnean name is the only way to be sure we're talking about the same thing.

But here at Denham, is it a Ruddy or a Common? I open my Hammond at the correct page and, instantly, the dragonfly itself lands on the book, exactly beside Cyril Hammond's larger-than-life coloured illustration of it. It's a Common, a *Sympetrum striolatum*, not a Ruddy. Common? For something as beautiful as that? With its rusty-red body, great slashes of yellow down the sides of its thorax and its black and yellow legs? And its take-off speed so fast that, even before you see it move, it isn't there?

It's through these two books that I learn that dragonflies are in trouble. The preface to my edition of *Dragonflies* says, "Changes in farming patterns and technology have led to increased drainage. This has threatened nearly all our rarer species so that the need to protect their remaining habitats becomes increasingly urgent. The destruction of thousands of farm ponds and ditches containing permanent water has also caused large-scale reduction of populations of the more abundant species. Their continued existence can no longer be taken for granted."

Time and again, as I crawl about in the undergrowth to gaze at these beautiful insects and try and capture them on film, these words ring in my head. How could it be possible that such amazing creatures be under threat? I read that dragonflies have existed for hundreds of millions of years. How can a group of insects like that be at risk of vanishing?

At this point I have no contact whatsoever with anyone else remotely interested in dragonflies. Yes, when I go up to Ashton I find myself among squadrons of scientists and experts on various aspects of natural history, but scarcely anyone – bar a handful of entomologists who specialize in other groups such as beetles, butterflies and of course fleas – mentions dragonflies. Except Miriam who says off-handedly that she and her son once wrote a scientific paper about some esoteric aspect of them, but she says no more.

In 1986, another dragonfly book appears: Bob Gibbons' *Dragonflies and Damselflies of Britain and Northern Europe*. It states baldly that "in 1637 there were 3,380 square kilometres of wetland in East Anglia. Now, three hundred years later, there are 10. And this phenomenal rate of habitat loss is paralleled in almost every temperate country." If you're a dragonfly, that's catastrophic. It seems that, in the roughly 350 million years or so that they have been around, we newly arrived humans are by far their biggest problem.

So I start my own form of action. I work at the Canning School, and we train foreign businesspeople to do their jobs better in English. I give talks to them in the evening, sometimes on Trafalgar, sometimes on Waterloo, sometimes Hastings, sometimes IK Brunel. Anyway, now I write out seven little white prompt-cards and begin to harangue the participants on dragonflies instead. I find I can make people not remotely interested in natural history pay attention.

I tell the slightly cynical audiences about my first memories of dragonflies, as a six-year-old aboard a cabin cruiser on the River Cam near Cambridge. And then about that electric moment at Denham. It's that image of the Banded Demoiselle – suddenly flashed up onto the screen behind me – that catches them. Then I explain how my focus gradually shifted from photography to the dragonflies themselves: how I discovered the difference between dragonflies and damselflies, how I learned about their astonishing life history. Do they realize, I ask them, that, typically, a dragonfly lives under water for three years before climbing out and flying for about eight weeks? That a damselfly lives for a year under water and has a mere four weeks or so flying? Some dragonflies can live up to seven years under water, I tell them.

And then I throw little glass tubes around the room, each one containing an exuvia, the cast skin that a dragonfly leaves behind when it climbs out of the water and turns into the beautiful insect we all recognize. I say how dangerous a stage this is, as the dragonfly unsheathes itself and expands its abdomen and wings, totally vulnerable to being eaten by waterfowl. I tell them about how newly-emerged dragonflies fly away from water to eat and grow strong, ready to fly back to the war-zone that is the water, where they fight for territory and females, where they copulate – in the most astonishing way – and guard the females as they lay their eggs and so begin the cycle once again.

I show them a photograph of a battered Golden-ringed Dragonfly, taken in my garden in Scotland – I don't usually mention that I was inadvertently naked at the time – and use it to explain the three amazing things that really excite me about dragonflies: their colour schemes, their eyes, and their wings. This, I say, is an old dragonfly, but how old are they as a group? And I tell them that they were around 150 million years before dinosaurs and are still here now, that they probably ruled the skies for 200 million years before birds appeared, that they used to have wing-spans of up to 70cm.

And then I say that they have only really been in trouble for the last million years, more especially in the last thousand years, perhaps most of all in the last three hundred years. In other words, because of us. And I mention Cornelius Vermuyden in East Anglia and how he surveyed the 3,380 square kilometres of land with a view to draining it and now there are a mere ten square kilometres left. And in the last forty years Britain has lost four of its forty-three species.

Then I ask the question I imagine most of the audience really want to know: are dragonflies useful? I give details of dragonflies consuming mosquitoes worldwide and tsetse fly in Africa, and how they're wonderful indicators of water quality. And so on. I begin to campaign for some sort of action to help dragonflies. But my appeal is woolly. I have no idea where to begin.

I talk and talk and talk about dragonflies. I amuse and interest my audiences, usually. In some cases they're touched. On three occasions, I'm approached afterwards by senior managers that offer to help; perhaps they can get funding from their companies, they say. In all three cases, the moment news of proposed finan-cial assistance reaches the ears of their British subsidiaries, there's a shocked and angry reaction: why, they ask, have their budgets been cut, only for this sort of off-the-wall suggestion to be made?

Time and again I go to the pub afterwards and bask in the comments about how interesting my talk was. And then comes a moment, as I'm heading down the lamp-lit street after yet another talk, surrounded by cheerful foreigners, my coat collar turned up against the wet London night, when I stop. And bid them good night. And go to a quiet pub by myself. And sit gazing at my pint, a bit angry, wondering what I can actually do to help dragonflies, I mean do something concrete, rather than just talk about them. Then I remember Ashton Water.

Chapter 4

Kari and I are up at Miriam's again. I walk down to Ashton Water alone. The afternoon is absolutely still, the willows on the east bank are motionless and the lake is like a mirror. But it's not a picture of English beauty; just now it looks like something out of Africa, its edges a mudbath, used exclusively by the thirty or so Père David's deer. These massive animals, originally from China, are as big as 'Monarchs of the Glen' and spend much of their time wading about in water, though at the moment they must be up in the woodland; I can neither see nor hear them.

Because of the deer, the smaller pond just above Ashton Water, the Top Pond, looks like an enlarged Somme shell crater. But if the lake itself were fenced off, surely something could be done. It could be made attractive for dragonflies. Couldn't it? I have a very strong sense that something is willing me on. I've already talked about it with Kari. She thinks what I have in mind is achievable – a bit mad but achievable – and she'll help. There'd be no point in going further if she hadn't said that. I sit down on a log and begin to ponder.

I'm divorced. Still reeling from my mother's death when I was fifteen, and having to deal with a helplessly alcoholic father and the sale of everything we owned, at twenty-one I married the first woman with whom I'd had a serious relationship. I think it was a normal, fairly happy marriage. There was much laughter and four lovely children, thirteen years of ups and downs, distractions on both sides, but as we got older we slowly grew apart, and I suppose I'd always known that one day I might meet my real soulmate.

It happened. I had to make a decision, the hardest and most painful I'll ever have to make; and live with the consequences. I'm still living with them. But I strongly suspect that had I decided to do the decent thing and try to keep the marriage together, I'd have followed in my father's footsteps pretty soon.

Quite what Kari saw in me I'm still not sure, she being the tri-lingual daughter of a French ambassador and the fruit of a union between two distinguished Jewish banking families, me being the younger son of an unambitious Lincolnshire doctor. I sup-pose there's a vague parallel, in that she'd spent time in Mexico, Peru, Indonesia, France, England, Switzerland, Spain and New York; in other words nowhere for long, so nowhere was home. I'd always been a bit confused about where home was too, as my Scots parents talked of Edinburgh as home and never regarded Spalding, in Lincolnshire, as such. Spalding was my home though, whatever they said, at least until everything fell apart, when sud-denly nowhere was home. There are two other parallels, as both our families disintegrated, and both of us were kept loyal to our parents by reliable and loving nannies.

As for education, neither Kari nor I took it very seriously. Both of us had experienced at an early age how facts can be bent. At seven I'd been sent off to a sadistic boarding school in Fife where, in history classes, the successes of the brilliant, intelligent, adaptable, honourable, hard-working Scots against the dastardly, snobbish English were drummed into us. Aged nine, I'd been transferred to a much friendlier school in Norfolk, where, in his-tory, the Scots were unpredictable bit-part players if they were mentioned at all. Kari had seen differing interpretations on his-tory, too, at her schools in Mexico and Peru. If that could happen to the past, why trust anything a teacher said about the present? Or the future?

Kari's fluency in French, Spanish and English stands her in very good stead at Canning. Her mother tongue is French, as I know from when she adds things up under her breath. And occasionally her English lets her down. 'Sleep? I went out like a log.' 'I'd take that remark with a ton of salt.' 'It was not a rip-raging success.' 'I'm just off for forty minutes' wink.' 'Is "Gay Gordon" the dance where you set to?' And so on.

Anyway, 1980 brought a monumental change. I had in fact made a major life-change before – not to be compared with divorce – but, in 1975, aged twenty-eight, after ten successful years with Michelin, from sales clerk to Company Secretary of a UK subsidiary, I quit. With the moral support of my then-wife, I joined a smaller, riskier, more exciting, creative set-up: the language-training outfit called Canning.

I'd already been giving evening lectures at Canning for a year or two – Trafalgar, Brunel and so on – when one night a very tall elderly Swiss participant asked me to join him for a drink in the Kensington Palace Hotel after my talk. René Buser was Managing Director of Ciba-Geigy in Spain, and had a powerful, peaceful presence. He would be perfectly frank, he said. He knew all about successful young company men and, whatever I thought, I wasn't one. He advised me to join Canning. This was his fourth visit to Canning. He didn't need to study English. He just came for the kick these witty, intelligent, open-minded young men and women gave him. Joining Canning wouldn't be the final step for me, and he didn't know what would be, but I'd learn a great deal from the huge range of people who came to Canning from all over the world. 'And Canning,' said René, 'will be, how to say, a step-stone?' So ten years later, when that dragonfly landed on my shirt, I'd already made – maybe *undergone* would be a better word – two major changes in my life. Now, sitting on the log, gazing across the lake, I wonder if perhaps I'm readier than most for yet another change.

I stand up, suddenly hungry, go back up to the house for tea, and, over the cucumber sandwiches – I've been warned to avoid the seductive, sometimes-not-so-fresh egg ones – I talk to Miriam about the possibility of fencing off the lake, making it attractive for dragonflies.

'You?' she says. 'You're not serious. When have you ever shown any interest in natural history?'

'I'm really serious, Miriam. Dragonflies are in trouble. I'm sure it would be a good place for them.'

'I don't believe you.'

'Miriam, it'd be a wonderful way to generate interest, to get the public involved.'

'Oh, the public, too.'

'At least let me …'

'No. Let me think about it.'

So that's that, I assume. But, next time we drive up, I'm scarcely in the library before Miriam says, 'I've arranged for you and Kari to have tea with a friend of mine in Swavesey. On Sunday afternoon.'

'Well, Miriam, on Sunday we were planning to …'

'His name's Norman Moore. I want you to talk to him, if you're still serious about the lake.'

'I certainly am.'

'Well, Norman knows more about dragonflies than almost anyone else in the world. He lives in a farmhouse over at Swavesey. He was something very high up in the Nature Conservancy Council and he's used his retirement money to dig a pond in a field behind his house. For dragonflies.'

Miriam doesn't need to tell me who Norman Moore is. He's one of the authors of the Collins New Naturalist dragonfly book. I already worship him from afar. But I know nothing about his pond; and now it seems I'm going to meet him. I find myself slightly short of breath.

Kari and I have bought a big black Bentley, a little older than her mother's and not as grand, but still a Bentley. The Citroën had been crushed – with me inside – hit full-on by a drunken, one-eyed, uninsured Irishman with his foot jammed onto the accelerator of a Pontiac. When I came out of hospital, pneumothorax and other things more or less repaired, Kari insisted we needed something more likely to withstand drunk drivers in Pontiacs.

A friend who knows very much more than me about car mechanics looks at the Bentley and remarks, 'You have not acquired it. It has acquired you.' We nickname it 'The Beast'.

We take The Beast to Swavesey on the Sunday. I have trouble getting it into Norman's drive. Like most really great men, Norman is cheerful, friendly and down-to-earth. He sits me down at a red formica table and I see that there's a piece of blue paper under his hand. During my ten years as a manager with Michelin, I developed a habit of reading upside down, usually other people's paperwork on their desks, but I can't see what Norman is hiding. I assume there were upside-down readers in the Nature Conservancy Council, too.

He asks me several questions about dragonflies and my intentions vis-à-vis Ashton Water, and presumably I pass some sort of test because he suddenly slips the paper across the table and asks me to read it. It's an application form for membership of the British Dragonfly Society. As soon as it's signed he takes me outside, shows me his pond, and tells me that what was a field three years ago now boasts fourteen species of dragonfly.

Of course technically he's cheating, but I know enough now to see what he's doing. He's using the word 'dragonfly' to mean the whole order Odonata – including both its sub-orders, namely real dragonflies (Anisoptera) and their cousins, the more delicate damselflies (Zygoptera). But everybody else does it, especially when they want to show off how many species they've seen at a site, so …

Norman says the key thing is a variety of native water-plants. He lists seventeen types and I dutifully note them down. If, he says, I can put in the plants, then the dragonflies – and damselflies – will come by themselves. He knows Ashton Water; it gets plenty of sunshine and is well protected from northerly and westerly winds. He thinks my idea might work. I laboriously reverse the Bentley round and out into the road, drive back to Ashton and we go in for a drink before supper.

'Norman was wonderful, Miriam, he …'

'You'll have to write it down. What you have in mind. And give it to me.'

So I do. Its title? *A Happier Habitat for Dragonflies at Ashton Water*. Three sheets of carefully typed persuasion, including a diagram (scale: 1mm to each of my strides) and a list of plants; messed up, smallpoxed with Tipp-Ex, then retyped and redrawn in desperation. Dated 24-11-86 and sent off.

Ignored.

Or so I think.

Chapter 5

The waterfall is behind me, down below, in the deep crevice that is the Pass of Lyon. Its sound brushes through the trees. I'm walking up the rough road that leads to my thatched grey stone cottage, bought in January, intended as a haven from the mad life of London, and, I suppose, the place where eventually, permanently, I will come to rest. It even has roses round the door.

Sunlight and leaf-shadow shift across the broken tarmac in the rutted track ahead. To my right, over a tumbledown dyke studded with sycamore and ash trees, there's a broad sheep-filled field. To my left, behind a long wall of nettles, the woodland slopes upward. The wind stirs the nettles, menacingly close to my left arm. Wait. Stop. What's that?

On a nettle-stem, a dragonfly is perched. A big one, its wings spread wide, its long black abdomen ringed all the way down with gold. I stare at it. It doesn't move. What's that brown tube at its bottom end, about 2cm long, like an extra length of fuselage?

I go closer. It's a piece of reed. She must have been laying eggs in the mud of a burn, and somehow got this thing jammed onto her ovipositor, the curved device at the bottom of her abdomen that she uses to lay her eggs. It's shaped like the tail-skid of an early biplane.

She doesn't move as I look at her. She's a Golden-ringed Dragonfly, *Cordulegaster boltonii*. This is the first time I have ever come this close to one of these magnificent insects, as big as any in

27

the UK. I curse the fact that I haven't got my camera. Just a minute – I could run up to the cottage and fetch it.

By the time I get back I'm absolutely sure she'll have gone, but no, she's still there. I take the photograph; the shot will be marred by the length of reed, but it'll still be a wonderful image. I can't understand why she hasn't flown.

And then I realize: I have a job to do. I reach forward and pull the piece of reed. It doesn't move, and nor does she. I reach again, take a firmer hold and very gently tug. Her six legs clamp her firmly to the nettle-stem. The reed comes free. She's perfectly intact but still she doesn't move. I take another photograph, a gem. And then, quicker than thought, she's gone.

Since then, every summer, Golden-ringed Dragonflies zoom into my little cottage garden, zing round, perch awhile, then disappear. A reminder. Each time I see one, I perk up a bit.

SATURDAY, NOVEMBER 21ST, 1987: LONDON

Still nothing definite about permission to start work down at Ashton Water. Miriam's son, Charles, who lives abroad now, is being consulted. But I'm invited to the Annual Indoor Meeting of the British Dragonfly Society in Leeds. Other than Norman, who tells me he's going and says I really ought to go too, I know no one.

I set off from King's Cross early on Saturday morning. I've never been to Leeds and when I arrive it's exactly as I expect, grey and wet. The rain increases as I make my way uphill to the university. There are small arrows directing me through the concrete modernity and into the original red brick building. I plod damply along stone-floored, brown-tiled corridors dutifully following the markers. Then I hear a distant, instantly recognizable roar.

As a Director of Courses at Canning, my ears are highly attuned to social noise. What I'm hearing sounds like a full-on, sherry-fuelled, smoke-filled, Friday-evening Canning participants' party. But this is a wet Saturday morning in Leeds. I head for the noise, imagining a large group of university students with outstanding post-Friday-night stamina, carousing somewhere between me and the BDS meeting point. No. It's the BDS themselves, in full swing, smokeless, on coffee and biscuits. I suppose if you're daft enough to come to Leeds on a wet November Saturday to talk about dragonflies, there's very little point in being inhibited.

I sit through fascinating presentations, although as a presentations trainer I wince at some of the cack-handed performances with the technology. And I find myself sitting in a battered easy chair at lunchtime, sharing sandwiches with Norman Moore. There's another distinguished looking, silver-bearded chap sitting on Norman's other side. I'm introduced to Professor Philip Corbet. I nearly faint away. He's another of the authors of the Collins New Naturalist book. Philip puts down his sandwich, shakes my hand, has difficulty speaking with his mouth full, and laughs.

I wonder how to make myself useful and end up helping with the BDS shop. Jill Silsby, a substantial, Surrey-voiced lady who would make an impression on any gathering and is the Society's Secretary, is in charge. A bespectacled man called Bill Wain introduces himself and purchases a glaringly yellow sweatshirt with a black dragonfly silhouette on it; I wonder whether to get my sunglasses from my bag. I couldn't wear one of those.

As I gaze across the room I decide only the British could be as enthusiastically potty as this. After more talks, mostly concentrating on the study and conservation of dragonflies – although Jill Silsby shows us mouth-watering images of exotic Far Eastern species – I'm given a lift back down to the station by another bearded chap, Brian Eversham, who has just made a short speech about struggling to produce an atlas of dragonflies. An atlas of dragonflies! Amazing! I take the train back to London in a trance, delighted to have found like-minded souls.

I decide to renew my attack on Miriam. Nothing doing. Yet.

Chapter 6

SATURDAY, FEBRUARY 6TH, 1988: DENHAM

It's a glorious morning. The sun has hauled us out of bed in Kensington and sent us out to Denham; it's warm enough to be May. We're sitting on the heavy timber arm of a lock-gate, letting the sunlight ease away the cramped coldness of winter, eating sandwiches.

'Too early for dragonflies,' I say. 'We'll have to wait till the end of April.'

Kari turns and looks at me. 'Why are you obsessed with just the last bit of their lives? What's wrong with larvae?'

'They don't fly. They're not beautiful. They're boring.'

The moment I say the word 'boring' about an insect, I realize I've forgotten Kari's natural-history genes. They didn't really show themselves until she came from New York, and it wasn't insects that activated them, it was wild flowers. Early on in our relationship, I used to drag her for walks along the canal above Old Oak Common. As we strolled along I'd airily gesture towards wild plants.

'That's a daisy. That's a dandelion. That's scarlet pimpernel. That's speedwell.'

In fact, my knowledge was minimal, basically what my mother taught me as we wandered about the Lincolnshire landscape. But soon, on our canal-side treks, Kari was stopping and looking hard at plants. She bought a book, Dietmar Aichele's *A Field Guide in Colour to Wild Flowers*, which seemed to ignite something in her, and very soon things changed.

'More dandelions over there, look,' I'd say.

'Well, I agree they're compositae, but I'm not sure they're dandelions.'

'Oh right,' I'd agree, defeated. 'Anyway, this is Herb Robert.'

A long silence, with Kari bent double – she does yoga – staring at the plant I've just pointed out. It's not really a stare; it's more of a totally focused beam of absolute concentration. She started doing this when she got the wildflower thing. It was a bit disturbing at first, standing there with Kari tipped right over, completely still, frowning slightly, eyes only inches from whatever she was looking at, book in hand, long dark hair touching the ground.

Her childhood interest in art has also rekindled recently. She's about to send off a painting of a Bee-eater to Nica for Valentine's Day. Anyway, now she straightens up.

'No, sorry, it's Bloody Cranesbill.'

She goes off to Southwark college in the evenings after work and gets an O-level in Botany. Her classmates come from very tough backgrounds but they obviously like her and make no comment about my picking her up after classes in the old Bentley. She does all the work for an A-level, including a field trip to Aberystwyth, but stops suddenly ('They're not interested in the plants at all now. It's just bloody chemistry.'). She begins to draw flowers. We go to botanical drawing exhibitions. She takes a botanical drawing course at Kew Gardens, then does a course in still life painting at Richmond College, all this in addition to her very tough full-time job at Canning. Before each course we talk things through; it means time away from each other. With experience gained from previous relationships we're careful to take time to let each other say exactly how we feel. Pretty much.

But when I take an interest in dragonflies, she finds herself pulled in. With me it's the power, the beauty, the speed, the acrobatics that fascinate; with her, it's the detail. Her blood has made her an entomologist. And now I've just called an insect boring.

'Don't be so stupid,' she says. 'What about the way larvae feed?'

'Oh, I'll give you that,' I say. 'That mask is amazing.'

In my talks to business people, I've had difficulty explaining the larval stage. I have no photographs of larvae. Kari and I spend that February afternoon crouching by a shallow bit of one of the gravel pits, hoping to get a shot of one. As yet, we don't know that the best way to find larvae is to use a colander or a sieve and shoogle along the undersides of banks.

So, for my lectures, Kari draws me a larva, with its astonishing labial mask extended. Can you believe it? It was completely acceptable in 1988 to be able to say to people, 'Of course I don't have an underwater camera, so I have a drawing for you.' There are hundreds of larvae photographs nowadays, some with the mask in action. It's like an arm, complete with an elbow in the middle, stuck onto the larva's lower lip. Normally, it's folded under the mouthparts but when it sees prey – a mosquito larva for example – the mask can shoot out. And it has claws on the end to grab its victim. Dragonfly larvae really are underwater monsters.

And just as with plants, Kari's powers of observation are outstanding; aided by her hand lens and her microscope, she's soon able to identify each of the thirty-nine species of British odonate (that's the adjective) larvae. I know that damselfly larvae can be told apart from dragonflies by their three fin-like gills at the back, but whenever I really need to know something about the larval stage of dragonflies and damselflies, I ask Kari.

WEDNESDAY, NOVEMBER 30TH, 1988: LONDON

Kari's in New York again, seeing Nica who's ill and needs a heart-bypass operation. The phone rings. It's Kari. Nica has gone. Never woke up from the operation. I board a plane and spend a week mostly cooking meals for the family at the Cat-House while they deal with the thousands of mourners. The Memorial Service at St Peter's is huge and heart-rending. Someone says she was 'such a gas'. She really was. So different from Miriam, who tends to shy away from matters metaphysical or spiritual, whereas Nica would dive in. If Miriam is strong on the outside, Nica was strong on the inside. It's only really as music and tears flow that I realize how important Nica was to me – and to Kari, too – in terms of our development, and the extent to which she set a very clear example of how, through refusal to accept norms, you could grow. And how, if something serious was inside you and you ignored it and just took the safe route, you weren't living up to yourself. And how Nica silently expected us to find what it was in ourselves, and to get on with it.

SATURDAY, FEBRUARY 4TH, 1989: ASHTON WOLD

Kari and I have just arrived from London, in time for lunch. It's cold and miserable, but there's a blazing fire in the library. Miriam strides in.

'Look here, Ruary, do you still want to do something about dragonflies down at the lake?'

'You know I do, Miriam.'

'Well, go down this afternoon, have a look, then come back and talk to me. There's a Scented Briar somewhere on the north bank. You need to find it. Rub the leaves. They smell of apples. I don't want it grubbed up by some clumsy oaf.'

'Right, Miriam.'

'Now, Kari, I want to talk to you about the wildflower meadows. Come through to my study.'

They disappear next door and I pour myself another – larger – sherry. There's really no need to go down. I know exactly what I want to do; it hasn't changed since 1986. I can't believe there's actually a chance that now it might happen.

We walk down to Ashton Water anyway. During previous visits, I've been discreetly stockpiling bits of broken fencing, branches and lengths of old timber just in case. So now, in the rain, we start pacing out how to protect a section of the north and west banks. My real aim is to get permission – and funding – to fence off the entire lake, but I'll need to win my spurs first by proving that plants will regenerate, and that dragonflies will re-appear once the Père David's deer are kept away from at least part of the lake margin.

I find the Scented Briar, and it does indeed smell of apples.

Kari makes a note: "Ruary has barricaded off all along the section of wood leading towards the boathouse, and has built a fence across the path. A Canada Goose (*Branta canadensis*) was nesting in a hole on the thatched roof of the boathouse and doesn't seem to have been disturbed by all the banging. She had seen us several times before and maybe realized that we mean her no harm. In any case she never once left her nest when we were near. I helped by barricading off the other side of the lake, and then we both built a fence to the water. The reason for all this activity is that Ruary would like to turn Ashton Water into Britain's first Dragonfly Sanctuary. The fencing/barricading is needed to keep out the Père David's deer. They not only eat all the vegetation on the shore, they walk into the water and eat all the reed (*Phragmites australis*) and other aquatic plants causing the water to become turbid and damaging the 'swamp plants' and emergent zones. Ruary saw what he thought were approximately seven Greylag Geese (*Anser anser*) swimming in the lake. They only stayed about an hour."

Kari's use of the word barricade is literal. We only have a few posts and rails, not nearly enough to do the job. So, seeing as the key thing is to keep the deer out, what we need to do is to make entrance to the area impossible for them. That means collecting masses of broken branches and boughs and piling them up in lines at each end, high enough and thick enough to deter deer. It takes a great deal of work by the two of us, but finally the north bank looks as if it's set to withstand a siege.

Two weeks later, we drive up to Ashton again and head down to the lake, anxious to see if the barricade has held. It has. And Sid Jackson, the Farm Manager, has left us a heap of posts, rails and nails; exactly what we need to make things more secure. Not only that, but waterside plants have already begun to regenerate. And … we spot our first Blue-tailed Damselfly! *Ishnura elegans*, such a beautiful insect, instantly spottable by the very obvious neon blue mark at the bottom of its black abdomen. It also has – appropriately – Ashton blue sides to its thorax. Ashton blue is a delicate blue-green and it's used for all the doors and windows on the estate. It's the colour, very faded, on the door of the observation hut. It's not dissimilar to the duck-egg blue I used to paint the undersides of my Airfix Spitfires.

Then we see several more Blue-taileds, darting among the rushes. And Kari finds the first exuvia, the technical name for the cast skin of a larva, in this case a damselfly that has climbed out of the lake and is now almost certainly one of the adult Blue-taileds currently nipping about. We go up to tea with the news.

'I'll get Hilary to drive us down tomorrow,' says Miriam. 'I want to see what you've been doing, Ruary. Can you both be ready at eight?'

Hilary, one of Miriam's two helpers, has the white Volvo waiting promptly next morning and we set off. I had no idea that it was possible to drive down to the lake, but here we are. Miriam marches about, and is pleased to see the plants have started to re-grow. I ask her for permission to open out an area of woodland for dragonflies to hunt in. It's important to have somewhere sunny but sheltered from the wind for bigger dragonflies to spot prey easily in flight. She agrees to our clearing a section of alder and elder trees inside our protected zone.

We have the makings of a Sanctuary for dragonflies. I add another lecture prompt-card – it's pink – to my seven white ones.

Chapter 7

The phone rings.

'Hello.'

'Is that you, Ruary?'

'Yes, Miriam.'

'Look here, I want you both to come to Woodwalton Fen tomorrow morning. Quite a few important people are coming. Do you know where it is?'

'I'm afraid ...'

'Well, I'm no good at directions. It's hard to find. Look it up. Can you be there at eight?'

'Well, Miriam, we were planning to ...'

'Eight in the morning, I should say. Wear wellingtons. See you there.'

'I'm sorry, Miriam, we ...'

But the phone has gone dead. So, of course, at eight the next morning, we do see her there. We get up absurdly early, drive north from London and thread our way along the flat Cambridgeshire roads in the sunlight. We park beside other cars on a bank above a long straight fen dyke, walk across a bridge, down a long grassy track, squelchy underfoot, deep into an original fen landscape of scrub and willow. The ground shakes slightly at every step. We turn a corner and face a dark wooden bungalow, thatched, entirely raised in the air on thick concrete stilts. Miriam's white Volvo is parked outside and she's sitting in the passenger seat with the door open.

'There you are. Well done. My father built it. Go on up. Get some coffee.'

It turns out that Charles Rothschild bought Woodwalton, a substantial chunk of fenland, in the early 1900s and offered it to the National Trust. Aware that in order to protect species, habitats themselves needed to be protected, he'd already donated thirty acres of pristine fenland to the Trust over at Wicken Fen, near Ely. But the Trust turned the offer of Woodwalton down, allegedly saying that it would 'only be of interest to entomologists'. After all, nature conservation was a very new concept back then. The refusal led Charles to set up the Royal Society for Nature Conservation, the forerunner and now umbrella-body of all the Wildlife Trusts. So here we were, standing in a piece of conservation history.

We climb the steps into a hubbub of obviously eminent naturalists. Those who don't have beards have spectacles. Some carry nets. At least two are wearing shorts and sandals. There's a profusion of straggly grey hair and they're all shouting at each other in outdoor voices. There's tea, coffee, beer and splendidly thick, soggy bacon sandwiches. Kari, a vegetarian (like Miriam), grimaces and says, 'I'll just have coffee, then. She could have said he was my grandfather, couldn't she?' Kari's not a morning person. I tuck into the sandwiches and open a bottle of beer.

On the way round, trailing in the footsteps of natural history's great and good, Kari suddenly cheers up.

'See that?'

'That? With the large yellow flowers? Yes. So what?'

'It's *Senecio paludosus*.'

'Right. Is it?'

'My grandfather introduced it at Ashton but it didn't survive.'

She swings round and points at an immensely tall Jack-and-the-beanstalk plant with pathetic little daisy-like flowers on the top.

'Unlike this one.'

'Ah,' I say proudly, 'that's *Sonchus palustris*.'

I know it, because it's still doing fine at Ashton Water, and when I take visitors from up at the mansion round the lake,

Miriam has asked me to stress – as they gaze disappointedly upwards at spindly nothing-much bunches of daisy-like flowers at the top of immensely long stalks – that it's almost certainly the rare native variety and was not introduced from Hungary by her father, Charles. I'm beginning to realize that species introductions of any sort are not really acceptable in conservation circles. No discreet slipping-in of unusual dragonflies into Ashton Water, then.

Woodwalton is a mecca for dragonflies. Norman Moore has been recording here for years. Kari and I crouch and peer at a Ruddy Darter, perched on a reed on the far side of a dark deep-looking dyke. It shines like a bright scarlet jewel in the sunshine, poised for instant take-off the moment it spots a mosquito or a midge.

Dr Paul Whalley has introduced himself and is standing beside us. He's nearly as enthusiastic about dragonflies as we are and knows a great deal about their prehistory. Momentarily, we zoom back almost 350 million years. He reminds us that some species had – relatively speaking – huge wingspans, up to 70cm. He produces a small close-focusing monocular, points it at the dragonfly and squints through it.

'You'll end up getting one of these sooner or later,' he says, 'if you're serious.'

He's right. I buy one shortly after and it serves me well. We climb up into a tall hide and watch a pair of Marsh Harriers glide over the reeds. Whatever we'd planned to do in London is long forgotten. We drive back to Ashton for lunch.

That afternoon, sweat-soaked from clearing a new path down at the lake, I come up to the mansion for tea and get into con-versation with an Israeli scientist. I explain that I'm setting up a dragonfly sanctuary.

'And what is your method?' she asks.

'Well, I barricade off the land around the lake to protect the margins from deer and to encourage damaged vegetation to regenerate, and I put in a variety of local native water plants to create attractive habitat. I'm hoping the dragonflies will arrive of their own accord.'

A silence.

'Hmm,' she says. 'Well, I suppose there is some merit in the naïve approach.'

I'm beginning to think that, if I'm really serious – in the way Paul Whalley means – I'm going to have to put more time in. There's no question of stopping full-time work. I've still got my two youngest children, Catharine and Richard, to support. But what about taking a sabbatical from Canning? Can I afford it? And would they countenance such a thing?

SATURDAY, OCTOBER 21ST, 1989: PERTHSHIRE

Kari and I are on a brief holiday at my cottage. Ever since I bought the house, whenever we've had serious issues to discuss, about our relationship, or our future plans, we take a walk along the river up the glen. The road curves round through a tight pass, cliff on one side, sharp drop in the other, the sound of the waterfall coming up from below. Then, at this time of year, we walk through a long, twenty-minute tunnel of tawny autumn oak, ash and beech before coming out into a view to the south. We always stop briefly and gaze away southward across the succession of misty hills, and then down into the sheep-dotted, alder-speckled, drystone-dyked twist in the valley below us.

I've talked the possibilities through with Miriam and she's very encouraging about the whole idea and quite happy for the kids to come when they can. They'll love it. I've done the sums. An unpaid sabbatical is do-able. But asking my fellow directors and partners for four months away at Canning's busiest time amounts to a statement of disloyalty. Well, perhaps not as extreme as that, but at least an indication that I don't entirely believe my whole future lies with the company. It'll mean time away from Kari, too, albeit in comfort at Ashton.

By the time we reach home again, we've decided. I'll do it. If I can.

Chapter 8

Our directors' meeting is scheduled for 9.30am, but my first call comes just before 7.00am. I listen, still dripping from the shower, as William, with a voice like gravel, describes what sounds like terminal pneumonia.

Somewhere in a Kensington hotel, a very important German banker is grooming himself, ready for a week of intensive one-to-one language training. He's expecting a fully-briefed professional trainer, well versed in the complexities of international banking, to meet him at our Gloucester Road branch at 8.45am. Unfortunately, that professional trainer is William. I now have a hundred and five minutes to find a replacement for William and get him, or her, briefed.

Still dripping, I put the phone down and have a think. There are six other banking specialists in the company: two are on missions abroad, one is on holiday and the other three are about to start their allocated tasks, two in London and one in Bath.

I look at my operations plan; it's an A3 chart, thick with pencilled-in details and littered with rubbings-out and alterations. It contains precise details of the week's activities of sixty trainers, across our five branches. I see that one of the banking specialists, Annette, is scheduled to work with the Financial Director of an Italian pharmaceutical company at our Kensington branch. Could she handle the German banker instead? And could Jim, currently slated to prepare for a sales trip, handle the Italian? After all, he used to run our Milan branch.

I ring Annette, to tell her that her carefully planned week has entirely changed. She'll have to brief Jim about the Italian, contact the croaking William for details of the German banker, and head for Gloucester Road, not Kensington. No reply. She's set off.

I ring Jim, tell him the news. He's furious. Don't I realize how important this sales trip is, how crazy it is if he spends the week training and not selling? But he eventually agrees. I put the phone down and breathe out. I've had trainers break down and cry at moments like this. I myself have, when it's been done to me.

Years in the job tell me this won't be solved simply by finding Annette. I dress hurriedly and cycle to our head office in Earls Court. As I come along the corridor, my phone's already ringing. The Course Director at our Olympia branch has lost one of his trainers to stomach trouble. Can he have some help? I direct courses too, so I know how hard this is going to be. I tell him he'll have to take over the training himself today; it isn't easy to put it gently.

I replace the receiver and wonder if I've done the right thing. It rings again immediately. It's Annette. She set out for work but has gone home again, feeling awful. I look at my watch. 8.35. The Italian financial manager will be on his way to our Kensington branch, and, over at Gloucester Road, the German banker will already be rapping the elegant door-knocker.

I'm not going to have time to prepare for the directors' meeting …

By 9.25am, the situation is under control, despite strong words and considerably increased heart rates in parts of west London. There are now five minutes before the meeting; that's two minutes to check my mail, two minutes to remind myself of what I'm going to say, and a minute for a pee.

I'm nervous, yes, but I know I'm doing the right thing. I run upstairs and make it with half a minute to spare.

It's a long meeting and I can't concentrate. I'm anxious about the item at the bottom of the agenda under AOB: it reads, "Ruary, Summer 1990." I catch myself again and again staring at the ceiling, still trying to find the right words. How to explain what I really feel? How to show them that I'm aware I may be committing hari-kiri with my career? And how to save face for everyone in the room, as I admit that, for me, there's actually something more important than being a director of this close-knit family-style company, something more important than fifteen years of loyal service, something more important than security and a pension.

Then Donald, the senior partner, leans forward and says, 'Ruary, over to you.'

I begin: most of them, I say, know of my hugely increased interest in conservation; I've become very concerned about dragonflies and I've learned they're in trouble. I tell them I want to set up a Sanctuary for dragonflies and it's going to take time to organize. I say I have the backing – moral, not financial – of Miriam Rothschild, an eminent entomologist. She's prepared to let me set up the Sanctuary on her son's land. She's not getting any younger. Neither am I. To be offered support like hers is rare. To refuse it would be like being offered help by David Attenborough and saying one had other commitments.

I tell them that I propose to take a sabbatical, four months away from the company, unpaid, (I don't mention that I've spent hours itemizing every penny I've spent over the previous six months to see whether I can afford it), during the busiest time of our year, leaving in mid-May and coming back in mid-September.

For a split second, I remember revealing my plan to my brother a few days before. He'd contemplated his mug of tea, then said, 'Well, Ror, I know what my company would say if you suggested that. They'd say, fine, take your sabbatical. Just don't come back.'

I assure my colleagues that my loyalty to the company is as great as ever and I'm anxious to remain a major contributor. I remind the collective frowns that I've discussed the thing with key colleagues and they all feel they can deal with the administrative difficulties.

I stop talking. There's a heavy silence. Less senior people in the room are waiting to see which way others will jump. Awkward questions start, long faces, graver looks. Phrases include 'no suitable replacement', 'considerable difficulties' and 'unfortunate precedent'. Two of the partners look very unhappy. It's not going well.

Then Donald, the senior partner, speaks. Everyone's surprised. He normally sits there, tipping his chair back, saying nothing. People who don't know him sometimes come to these meetings, mistake him for a figurehead, shoot their mouths off, think they've won, then, at the very end, find themselves blancmanged by his barrage of gentle, incisive, unrelenting questions.

Now, he startles the meeting by tipping forward and saying, 'I think it's a great idea, Ruary.' The mood instantly changes. A few more questions, technicalities, and I'm there. The meeting finishes and I stand up and offer to buy anyone interested a lunchtime drink in The Hansom Cab.

In the pub, I expect to be questioned about my plan to surrender so much time and money – and perhaps my career – to dragonflies, but the conversation quickly reverts to shop-talk. I sit quietly and gaze at the dusty cab suspended from the pub's ceiling. These people have done something most company directors would never countenance; they've allowed a key person to vanish and then to reappear as if nothing had happened. They've just made me stupendously happy. I'm forty-three; I've been in continuous employment under a regiment of bosses since two days before my eighteenth birthday; and now I'm being allowed to be with dragonflies for four months, *four whole months.* The conversation turns to departmental budgets. I nod sagely and grin at my pint. I want to dance on the table.

Chapter 9

SATURDAY, DECEMBER 9TH, 1989: ASHTON WOLD

Now I know for sure that I'm getting my sabbatical, I go to work at Ashton Water with renewed effort. I need to create a proper route round all four sides of the lake, so I begin sawing a path through bushes, brambles and trees.

'Mind what you're doing with the elders,' says Peter Scott, the gardener.

'Any particular reason? Not alders? Willows? Hawthorns?'

'Just the elders.'

'Because?'

'When you cut down an elder, even if you cut off a branch, knock on it three times before you do it. Or it's bad luck.'

I disregard Peter's advice; stupid, superstitious nonsense. Two weeks later, just before Christmas, whilst clearing an area on the north side, I'm tugging an elder branch and it whacks back and hits me in the face. There's a lot of blood and I think I've gone blind; I haven't, but a small splinter lodges permanently just below my left eye. Bloody but unbowed, I pile broken branches, whole trees even, into the water at points where I think the deer might penetrate my defences.

Miriam writes that she'd be pleased to have a survey of drag-onflies across the whole of the Ashton estate next summer, not just at the lake. That's a very tall order. In any case, how to record what I see in a systematic way?

I visit my friend Steve Brooks at the Natural History Museum in London. We squeeze into his tiny office and he tells me about the Transect Walk system.

'Take a 1,100m length of water margin,' says Steve. 'Imagine you're walking along a corridor with walls of glass about five metres either side of you. Count the dragonflies between the walls.'

'Can't I divide it up into sections?' I ask.

'Sure, provided you cover exactly the same ground.'

'It's going to take up a massive amount of time. The estate is 5,000 acres.'

'Ah, well, you won't be able to do it every day. You'll need good weather conditions.'

'What are the criteria?'

'Do it between 11.00am and 3.00pm. No more than a light breeze, say 10 mph. Make sure you can see your shadow. And you need to fill in one of these.'

He hands me a form. It's called an RA70. It looks complicated.

'What? One of these for every transect walk?'

'Yep.'

I begin to see that my summer days are going to be extremely busy, even if I concentrate solely on transect walks. Steve and I go off to the pub, talk about tanks and planes and forget all about dragonflies. But I know what's involved now. I'll need to measure out possible walks, test them, and time them to see if I can do them all without collapsing.

SATURDAY, JANUARY 21ST, 1990: ASHTON WOLD

Up early and at the lake by six. Driving up from London on Friday nights is becoming part of our routine now, one that will last several years. Kari and I stand in the Saturday morning sun, look at the red sky and eat cold toast. We're still tired from the late journey last night, although Miriam gave us a royal welcome and plied us with La Cardonne, smoked salmon and cold pheasant smeared with honey.

Two of the transects I've selected are down the hill on the River Nene, at Ashton Mill. I've chosen these because it means

I can include flowing water in my dragonfly survey. I've learned that some dragonflies like still water and others prefer flowing. Of course there are lots of dragonflies that couldn't care less and will set up territories and lay eggs in almost anything. But down at the Mill, there's the relatively slow-moving millrace and the faster moving Nene itself. There's no flowing water anywhere else on the estate.

Today, I park in the small courtyard outside the Mill. It used to be Miriam's Fish Museum. Kari and I came with several members of the family near the end of last year and had a rather depressing look around. On one of our first visits to Ashton in the early Eighties, the Museum had been going strong, but for some reason it faded and died. Through the white gates to the left, I can see various farm exhibits still there, gathering grime.

I walk down the passage on the right, over the mill outfall and look over the wall. The soft cream limestone of the former miller's house is reflected in the placid water of the millpond. I sense a sudden stillness inside me. Something is going to happen here, I've no idea what. And then I walk off up the millrace thinking about water margins and suitable lengths and landmarks for transects.

The sudden power of that moment is blotted out by a happy lunch up at the house, Miriam surrounded by her family and friends. She has a knack for making friends with those of her grown-up children, which means she's often in the company of much younger people; and she somehow enables them to be uninhibited yet behave. Drunkenness is not appreciated, though visitors are never short of drink. Miriam herself very rarely even sips alcohol. That evening, nine of us sit long into the night, gathered round a roaring fire in the candle-lit dining room, drinking champagne, challenging each other, arguing and laughing.

Next morning, breakfast consists of chocolate cake, quail's eggs and more champagne provided by David, a cousin. The spirit of wealthy, generous weekend Bohemia is alive and well in Northamptonshire. I raise my glass and thank my lucky stars. I also feel a strong desire in some way to repay my good fortune.

SUNDAY, JANUARY 22ND, 1990: ASHTON WOLD

I'm sick and tired of chasing Canada Geese away. I've loaded my small revolver and now I open fire, marching round the side of the lake, popping at them. They look at me as if I've gone mad, as if they know it's only a blank pistol, which it is, and continue to munch the plants. I give up for the time being; in any case, I don't want to disturb one special goose, quietly sitting on eggs on the little island in the middle of the lake. At least she's not on the wrecked thatch on the boathouse roof, as she was last year.

And the deer are still wandering into the water, keeping it a mudbath. Our barricades have stopped them coming onto a section of the bank because they can't swim round the boathouse, but really the whole perimeter needs to be fenced off. I discuss the problem with Miriam.

'Will you allow me to fence the whole lake off, Miriam?'

'Who's going to pay?'

'If I can get grant money?'

'Well, yes and no,' says Miriam.

'Which means?'

'You'll need to leave some of the lake accessible for the deer, just in case the Top Pond dries out. They need to get into water.'

Yet another obstacle thrown into my path. It's taken three years to get thus far, and now I've got to work this one out. I go down and study the problem. How on earth can I leave part of the lake open whilst preventing the deer from barging in? I decide to postpone any decision until I've got a grant for the fence as a whole.

I make contact with the Worldwide Fund for Nature in Godalming, explain my intention to set up a Dragonfly Sanctuary accessible to the public, and am amazed at how well they receive the idea. I explain I need just under £1,000 for 230m of wooden posts and rails. I fill out forms, send in detailed plans and costings, and then go and visit them, taking a couple of hours off work in London late one afternoon to do so. I've damaged my ankle heaving something large at the lake, and hobble through the darkness from Godalming station to their headquarters. They take pity on me, give me the grant, and a lift back to the station.

It's a terrific feeling to have the support of an outfit like WWF. I nail their large panda logo to the door of the observation hut, order up the timber, and go and plead for help with Sid Jackson, the Farm Manager. I've done quite a bit of driving in posts with a sledgehammer in my time, and 230m is a very long prospect.

I carry on pacing out possible transect walks. It feels strange to be pacing out likely transects in the cold and the rain, sometimes even – due to lack of time before dashing back to London – in the dark, all the while knowing there's not the slightest chance of seeing a dragonfly until the end of April at the earliest.

FRIDAY, APRIL 6TH, 1990: LONDON

I get a call from the estate office: my timber has arrived. We drive up after work. It's a calm night. I can't wait until the morning, so I stuff a sandwich made for supper into my pocket and walk down to the lake in the moonlight. There's a bulky shadow standing beside the observation hut. It's a trailer, loaded with posts and rails. I pace about in the gloom, munching tomato and cucumber, double-checking my measurements, overcome with excitement.

Next morning, four of us get cracking: Kenny Head and Bill Maher from the farm, Peter Scott from the garden and myself. Bill brings down a JCB – I've frantically hacked a path for it – which, in his expert hands, pushes the posts into the ground as quickly as shoving a knife into soft butter. Kenny and Bill are very good-natured and encouraging, although I'm fairly sure they think the whole thing is potty. I struggle with the art of hitting six-inch nails into timber. By the end of the day, as I lie exhausted, flat-out on the empty trailer heading up the hill, there's only 30m left for me to finish; and by Sunday evening it's done. Except, that is, for the 40m-gap I've had to leave for the deer.

Chapter 10

There's a sheen of ice on the grass, and the deep orange sun strikes the tops of the poplars and turns the churned-up tracks left by the JCB into darkest brown. Steam rises in wisps across the lake and, away in the trees to the south, a woodpecker drums. Peter Scott says that if you hear a yaffle calling, it means rain, but today there isn't a cloud in the sky. A kestrel, high up, watches us. Typically, Kari is bent double by the waterside; already this morning, she's identified two types of sedge.

I'm sitting on a battered but elegant garden bench, an Edwardian one, with lovely curly ironwork; I dragged it the half-mile down here yesterday, leaving scoop-like scuffmarks along the dry earth track. I'd been exploring the woodland close to the mansion, and found a little ruined boiler-house, used long ago for heating the water in the original elegant swimming pool, now deserted and overgrown with buddleia. Beside the rusting boiler, among other dusty junk, I spotted this bench, on its side, jutting upwards, with a heap of mouse-chewed sacks on top. We'll sand it down and paint it Ashton blue. I've asked Miriam and obtained permission to use it. I'm always careful about this; she has an extraordinarily efficient local intelligence service, not surprising considering she was a codebreaker at Bletchley Park during the war.

It's extraordinarily warm, with the lightest of westerlies rippling the lake's surface into golden sparkles. The air is tinged by a mud-sewage smell. Yesterday, with the fence in place, I dragged the now redundant anti-deer branches and tree-trunks out of the water, and the resulting black pond ooze still hasn't settled.

I work all day, clearing a path through the fallen willows, along the west bank, until it's almost dark and bats are flitting over the water.

TUESDAY, APRIL 10TH, 1990: ASHTON WOLD

I've had my eye on two blue kayaks down at Ashton Mill, ideal for observing dragonfly activity from the lake itself. I saw them whilst visiting the defunct Fish Museum with Kari and various family members last year. A quick word with Miriam, and they're ours. I later discover they actually belong to Miriam's daughter, Rosie. Knowing her mother's ways, she's graceful about the inadvertent theft and encourages our work.

I go down to the estate office, pick up an enormous bunch of keys for the Fish Museum and borrow the battered blue transit van that belongs to the estate. It's my first visit inside the mill building alone, and, as I roll the big sliding side-door open, once more I get a strange feeling of – what? Foreboding? However, it's instantly swept away by a terrific fright from the burglar alarm and a frantic search for how to turn it off.

I slip the kayaks into the back of the van; they're too long and stick out behind. I've checked out the route that the JCB took and reckon I can get a Transit down to the lake, across the fields and through the woods. I hurry the Transit through the village and up the 'drive', with the kayaks leaping about in the back, yank open the big gate in the deer fence and whisk the van downhill; three discreetly successful miles. I unload the kayaks, drive back up to the mansion, use the van to purloin an enormous ladder from the garage, rumble down to the lakeside again, fix pulleys and ropes in the tall ceiling of the observation hut, rig the kayaks a new home, return the ladder to the garage, the van and the keys to the estate office, walk back down to the lake, and stand inside the hut, looking up, triumphant, at the kayak's sleek black bottoms slung from the roof.

I can't resist trying one. I lower it down, sling it over my shoulder and carry it to the lake. In the boathouse, I wobble into it and bash my way out through the reeds into open water. The Canada Geese are obviously surprised, but don't take off.

Miriam hasn't yet been persuaded to come down and see the fence, but this evening she arrives in the white Volvo, eschewing my newly-created JCB/Transit track, driving straight down the footpath as before, brambles squeaking along the car's sides. The Volvo emits its 'you've-forgotten-to-put-your-seat-belt-on' alarm all the way down. Miriam ignores it; which is ironic, as she maintains she invented the seatbelt. She pads about in her white wellies. 'It's wonderful,' she says. She looks at the 40m-gap between the two fences but says nothing.

SATURDAY, APRIL 28TH, 1990: ASHTON WOLD

We arrive early and go down to the lake: first swallows, first cowslips, first cuckoo and, coincidentally, first cuckoo flowers. At midday, filthy from undergrowth clearance work on the west bank, we head back up to the mansion.

Professor Derrick Denton from Australia and Professor John Gurdon, a pioneer of stem cell research, are among several guests who arrive for lunch. Washed and tidy, we sip gins and tonics on the lawn beforehand. We're in little groups of twos and threes, in the sunshine on the terrace outside the library. Miriam and I are talking to Jean, John's wife. Miriam mentions my work at the lake and I talk about the problem of deer penetration via the water.

A woman with her back to us, who has obviously been listening, turns suddenly.

'Have you tried lion dung?' she asks.

It's Tessa Smith from London Zoo. I almost drop my glass.

'Deer are terrified of it,' she says.

Jean, very taken with the idea, gently talks Tessa into seeing if she can get me any. Jean is clearly not a person who, once she has decided to help, gives up. She takes me aside and assures me she'll stay on the case.

Lunch – grander than usual – is accompanied by bottles of 1975 Lafite. Miriam watches several people's reactions when they taste the wine. Astonished at its luscious glory, they discreetly check the labels.

'Sorry,' she says, twinkling behind her spectacles. 'The '47's gorn orf.'

One or two less discerning guests, too busy impressing each other, don't notice the wine's quality and shove it back like Ribena. Miriam glances at them, picks up her water glass and looks out of the window, inscrutable.

I make some unintelligible notes about her stories:

"Smelly sock for farm manager."

"Duke of Huntingdon owed debt to M.'s grandfather. Thus Ashton."

"Man who thought touching M. would bring fortune and good luck."

"Russian Jews, now in Israel, transported through Hungary. Appalling."

"The nude on the battleship."

"The cowgirl with a boa constrictor, ten greyhounds and a lame Muscovy duck."

SUNDAY, APRIL 29TH, 1990: ASHTON WOLD

It's early. We're in one of the bedrooms at the back of the mansion. Twin beds, very pink, a loo and a little kitchen close by. The pigeons are cooing in the trees outside. 'Take two cows, Taffy. Take two cows, Taffy. Take…' they say. At least, that's what Miriam insists they say.

I wash, have a cup of tea and head straight out. Kari is slower in the mornings. As soon as I'm outside, the stillness and the morning fragrance bring me to a standstill. I'd planned to go down to the lake with a wheelbarrow full of rattly tools, but, with such calm, it's unthinkable.

As I walk slowly across the sunlit field, the sky is ringing with the songs of thrushes, blackbirds and wrens. The blackthorn blossom is over now, but down by the whitening hawthorns, I find myself very close to the deer. The breeze is blowing from the west and I'm approaching from the east. The whole herd munches unconcernedly, until at last a doe turns and sees me. She freezes and stares, then makes a low rumbling groan; but it's only when she barks, loudly and firmly, five times in quick succession, that the herd begins to move. Even then, they shift without the usual clattering of hooves. Young bucks pause to take a longer look, and gently slip away.

The lake is full of Canada Geese, floating like a fleet at anchor in the golden drifts of mist. Bloody birds. Time for a kayak. I paddle angrily out of the boathouse as a clutch of Mandarin Ducks hurtle into the air. The geese stare, dumbfounded but unmoved. I empty all six chambers of the little blank revolver at them. It makes not the slightest difference. They actually look slightly supercilious. Only by yelling and oaring straight at them do I succeed in getting them to take off in a great squawking and flapping of wings.

Later, to my delight, I find my first damselflies of the year. They're all Blue-tailed Damselflies, the same species as we first found last year, such lovely delicate things, with those powder blue blobs on the ends of their slim black abdomens. As before, most have Ashton blue thoraxes, but some of these have other colours; red, apple green, purple. My book tells me these are females, 'rufuscens', 'infuscans' and 'violacea' respectively. What lovely names! Apparently, the thoracic colours can change with age.

I dash back for my camera and get a couple of good shots. Crouching stock-still on the dew-damp turf to get the photographs, in the silence I hear the sound of a ball being bounced on a cricket bat from the pavilion up the hill, and the distant church clock in Polebrook strikes nine. Kari joins me and slowly patrols the reeds. She finds several exuviae and takes them up to the observation hut for identification. Her work will confirm which species are actually breeding in the lake. She clearly has the same obsession with dragonflies that I do, only for her it's the larvae that fascinate. As she reminds me, that's how dragonflies spend most of their lives. But, to me, they just don't hold the same magic as the adults: no stunning flying, no sudden speed, no flashing beauty. There's that ferocious labial mask, though, and the way they breathe through their backsides …

I pick up the strimmer and set to work clearing a meadow, ready to plant Oxe-Eye Daisies; they attract greenfly, suitable prey for damselflies. My body really enjoys the effort and it's great to finish, sweating, and see a broad open space where this morning there was just a tangle of rough ground.

SUNDAY, MAY 13TH, 1990: ASHTON WOLD

A big insect, yellow-brown, definitely not a damselfly, flashes down the north bank of the lake and disappears behind the boat-house. Camera in hand, I creep after it. Our first proper dragon-fly? I spot it in among the bushes, photograph it, and go closer. I obey the maxim 'Keep shooting, it's only film,' but of course every celluloid shot adds to the cost. It's a female Broad-bodied Chaser, *Libellula depressa*. I gaze at it in wonder. It's got a fat mahogany abdomen with little lemony crescents down the sides and it looks a bit like a hornet. Its wings are slightly milky, which tells me it's only just emerged. Kari eventually finds the exuvia. Yes! Our first dragonfly at what is now Ashton Water Dragonfly Sanctuary.

Tonight will be the last time we join the Sunday-evening tide heading back to London. Half a week of one-to-one work with a German who makes rubber seals for expensive cars, then, on Wednesday afternoon, my sabbatical starts. I wonder what it will be like to be free. Will it feel free? What about the kick I get from leading a team? Or the gratitude of a group of businesspeople at the end of a week's training? Or the satisfaction of fitting all the trainers into the right places and a Monday morning working perfectly? Have I ruined my chances of a partnership in the company? Will messing about with dragonflies feel lightweight? Or even meaningless? I'm a bit afraid.

Part Two

Finding Sanctuary

Ashton Wold, Summer 1990

Chapter 11

Waking, I realize that for the first time in decades I'm absolutely free, free to work exactly as much or as little as I want. It's ridiculously early, but the sun is blasting through the mullioned windows, and the thought of freedom throws me out of bed. I feel a bit guilty about Kari, stuck at work in London.

I've been allowed to stay upstairs in a wing of the mansion, in what used to be the servants' quarters. It has its own separate entrance, so I can come and go as I wish. Being an Edwardian Rothschild house, this space would delight many modern middle-class families. It's bigger than our flat in London. But it's shabby, the walls are peeling, the carpet is sticky with over-use, and the place reeks of camphor from the seed store downstairs.

I love it. I've set up my typewriter and filing system in the long corridor whose windows look down into the Kiftsgate-rose-entwined courtyard below. Charles Rothschild's barograph, given to us by Miriam and brought back to life once more, is ticking away on the window-ledge, slowly scrawling a heavy black line – rising steadily – round its cylindrical graph-paper chart.

I go out, pad through the woodland, slip through the gate, cross the empty deer-field and head down the grassy track towards the lake. My footfalls are soundless; only the trill of a wren breaks the calm. The hawthorns are so full of bloom they look like clouds. Thirty or so Père David's deer are at rest in the Top Pond. This morning they react instantly and, as one, they swish out of the water and disappear into the far wood in a clicking of heels. It sounds like sixty pairs of slingback stilettos crossing a street.

I watch a tern with a slightly damaged wing, swinging over the lake, diving repeatedly. Then I look for exuviae on the north bank: nothing. But that doesn't mean nothing's there. When dragonflies emerge from the water to transform themselves from larvae to adults, the process can take hours and, as they haul themselves out of their larval skins, pump up their wings and extend their abdomens, they're extremely vulnerable. It's a perfect time for birds to pick them off. So emerging dragonflies are masters of the inconspicuous.

I turn back to the observation hut, whose dusty panes I peered through on my first visit to the lake ten years ago. Before I go in, I stop myself and stand and give it a proper look. It's now my headquarters. It was designed by Charles Rothschild when he first came to Ashton. The Rothschilds had owned Ashton since 1830, but it was Charles who constructed Ashton Water – with its smaller Top Pond above – as a duck reserve. A duck reserve in 1900 must have seemed the height of eccentricity to his peers. His elder brother Walter had a duck reservoir at Tring but, like everyone else, he used it for shooting.

Here at Ashton, the thatched boathouse was built as soon as the new dam began to hold back the water of the Polebrook, then the whole area was ringed with an elegant deer fence whose curved-top gates still stand open, rusty and forlorn, a hundred yards off. But the observation hut was an afterthought: there's a photograph of the lake with the boathouse completed and an empty space where the hut will shortly be. Charles must have decided he needed somewhere dry from which to watch the waterbirds he hoped to attract. It's ten-sided, with a conical thatched roof and – most unusually – thatched walls. Four of the sides have tiny-paned bay windows, linked together so as to give a continuous view from the inside whilst rendering any interior movement almost invisible from the outside. Peter Scott, the gardener, has come down in his own time, evening after evening, and lovingly replaced all the little smashed panes. The estate has agreed that the roof can be re-thatched and I'm arranging for a local man, Barry Watts, to come. The tall round-topped finial that crowns the roof is completely rotten but as yet I have no answer for a replacement.

I climb over the little fence – I'll make a stile for it soon – and go in. I got the kayaks in here a few weeks ago, but when I first tried to get in, it took all my weight to shift the heavy door at all, and even then it would only allow me to squeeze in sideways. With its elegant U-shaped handle, it still sticks, but only halfway now. The bottom of the door has scraped years of curved marks on the wooden floor. Both door and finial are painted in very-faded Ashton blue.

It's no ordinary hut; it has parquet flooring, which I've swept. Despite years of complete neglect and marks of water ingress here and there, it remains in excellent condition, smooth as a dance floor. One at a time, I've carried two long heavy trestle tables, crude and full of splinters, down from the cellars under the mansion. And, in an outhouse, I've found two varnished wooden folding chairs from some defunct marquee company and brought them down, too. A large dragonfly identification chart is now pinned on one wall-panel, and, on others, details of the life cycle and behaviour of dragonflies. There are notebooks, clipboards, tanks, a torch, and a candle in one of those pale green austerity-ware eggcups. Charles Rothchild's black butterfly net, with its short club-shaped handle, hangs from a hook.

The original broken three-legged chair is still here after ten years and is now propped against the wall, acting as a small table. But if I sit on one of my two new chairs and look through those little panes, I can watch activity on either waterspace. It would have been much easier in Charles's time; the willows have grown enormous now and partly block the view.

As I sit and look out, very proud of my new fence stretching away into the distance, I realize why the hut has its tall coni-cal roof. It makes a dome inside that magnifies outside sounds. Right now I can hear a moorhen scolding her young. A jay is bouncing along the top of the fence towards me, completely unaware of my presence.

Charles and his friends would have sat exactly where I'm sitting, watching the ducks and geese fly in. His friends included almost all the prominent naturalists of his time: Jordan, Meinertzhagen, Wollaston, Harris, Drowne, and Charles's own brother, Walter. I sense Frohawk, the artist, on the other chair, sketching quietly; and Charles himself, right behind me, telescope in hand, approving of the place's new role. The hut is telling me it needs to be shared with others.

Chapter 12

Down to the lake for what I know will become routine, checking
and noting all the weather conditions: cloud cover, air pressure,
wind direction, wind speed, air temperature, water temperature.
I've made a lead-weighted sea-going thermometer so, using a
kayak, I can lower it down on a string and check deep-water temperature. I note that, at 17°C (62.6°F), the water's warmer than
the air. And then a search for exuviae. It's important to find exuviae quickly because, though they're clamped sufficiently firmly
to vegetation for adults to emerge from them, they can be washed
into the water by rain, or simply fall off within two or three days.
Some of them are upside down. I make notes.

In the course of my hunt, I find four teneral Blue-tailed
Damselflies. 'Teneral' means newly emerged, and they're often
spottable by their glistening wings and pallid colours. All dragonfly species only gain their full coloration some time after emerging. There's obviously plenty of life there in the water. It's very
satisfying.

I climb on my mountain bike – it's called Moonshadow, ever
since a midnight bike-ride round Richmond Park – and make my
first trip down to Ashton Mill to do the two transect walks I've
paced out. I discover that, though I may have an all-terrain bike, I
don't have an all-terrain backside, at least not one capable of with-
standing the enormous potholes of the 'drive' between the village
and the mansion.

By Ashton Lock, there's a weir, and in the roar of tumbling water and the sugar-sweet smell of river foam, there are fluttering clouds of Banded Demoiselles, just like the one I photographed five years back at Denham. I think they're the most magical of British damselflies, deep iridescent blue with big dark patches on their wings. They love flowing water, and these ones are flickering in the sunlight among the big club-rushes at the foot of the weir. I am entranced.

The distance between my chosen transect walks is proving a problem. It's hard to cycle down to the Mill, then up again, then along to the far end of the estate. Even though I started at 5.00am this morning, I'm not sure how I'm going to do it. I must try and get more sleep tonight, but I feel a new energy seeping through me.

FRIDAY, MAY 25TH, 1990

Another beautiful start. The clouds have cleared away. Swallows are skimming across the still-steaming lake and damselflies are in action already. It's mirror-calm, the tiniest of ripples reflecting sunshine up the reeds. The wind has gone round to the west, bringing the noise of trucks from the Oundle bypass, and, from Polebrook, the smell of baking bread. I look for the moorhen and her chicks that I disturbed whilst struggling to get a photograph of a lovely blue male Broad-bodied Chaser yesterday close by the boathouse. They've gone.

I glare at the Canada Geese, floating serenely on the far side of the lake. Time and again, I've arrived exhausted from a hard week in London, come down here and driven them off. And here they are again.

Broken Wing the tern has just been for breakfast, circling over his own reflection, with the occasional nippety-squawk. His wing looks completely better. He's been coming every day, and, every day, I stand waiting for his sudden graceful dive into the water. He dives, surfaces, takes off, circles, then drops, again and again, a perfect little show. He's eating fish; good news, as they eat dragonfly larvae.

It's the end of my first full week away from London. I've worked like hell, up early and into bed late, but I've done all the transect walks, all the weather checks and all the exuviae hunts. It's been fantastic. And there have been unexpectednesses: in dry hay beside the lily pond up near the mansion, I saw two grass snakes, green and yellow, entwined; my first ever. I'd no idea they were so stunning. When they finally noticed me, they uncoiled themselves like two whips, slid into the water and swam elegantly away among the lilies.

One day, cycling back up from the Mill, I just had time to hear a roar behind me, see a maroon estate car, and spot a big brawny hand lifted in salute before I was enveloped in a cloud of white dust and brought to a choking standstill: Sid Jackson, the farm manager, at speed.

Down by Ashton Lock among the clubrushes that afternoon, I looked up from a circus of blue damselflies to see a blond boy and a dark-haired girl, both in their school uniforms, waltzing very slowly and closely on the lock bridge. I didn't move till they'd kissed and strolled away.

SATURDAY, MAY 26TH, 1990

There's a frost on the grass and the steam from the lake is rising a metre high, drifting west. Today, I don't have to take the boat to the geese. They clear off as soon as I approach, and I hear them make landing calls away towards the River Nene. I saw up and drag away a fallen fir tree on the west bank, hack out spaces where we can monitor emergence more easily, and mark damselfly exuviae and leave them in position. They vary in height above the water.

Broken Wing's wing hasn't mended. I thought it had, but this is a different tern. It arrives and circles and dives, and while I gaze up, Broken Wing himself appears. They fly together, squawk to each other briefly, then Broken Wing takes over the show and the intact one flies off. One good tern ...

Close to the boathouse, two blue Broad-bodied Chaser males clash in combat for a moment, then vanish. Their battle for the territory seems to have ended in a draw. I see the first buttercup of the season. The Mandarin Ducks now have a fleet of chicks.

Using Kari's grandfather's net, I've just caught my first blue damselfly. It fights and I don't want to hurt it. I let it go. I'll never make a scientist.

SUNDAY, MAY 27TH, 1990

High cirrus but another lovely start. I see a muntjac deer slip off into the undergrowth. The Canadas are gathered on the Top Pond. I find my first anisopteran exuvia. Anisoptera are proper dragonflies; it means 'not-the-same-shaped-wings' in Greek. Damselflies are Zygoptera, Greek for 'same-shaped wings'. It fits exactly. When you look at a dragonfly perched, you see its front wings are different from its back wings. If you look at a damselfly as it folds its wings along its abdomen on landing, all four wings are so similar and so neatly parked that it looks as if they have only one wing.

The order Odonata has two basic sub-orders, Anisoptera and Zygoptera, in other words dragonflies and damselflies. The way I remember it is by thinking A to Z, A being the bigger jobs, and Z being the smaller more delicate ones. 'Dragonflies' is such a confusing word because sometimes it's used to mean just dragonflies, and at other times it's used to mean the whole lot. If you ask an odonatologist how many species of dragonfly he or she has at their pond, the chances are they'll proudly give the number for both dragonflies and damselflies. You can quickly cut them down to size by asking whether that's just dragonflies, or both dragonflies and damselflies; although I hadn't dared do that to Norman Moore when I first visited his pond.

Today, there's a lot of territoriality and mating among the Broad-bodied Chasers. To my astonishment, a male Banded Demoiselle appears. Presumably he's just taking a look because they're very definitely a flowing-water species. It's interesting, though, that he's taken the trouble to come over from the River Nene. Even delicate damselflies are explorers.

Kari, up here for the weekend, has been continuing our list of lakeside plants begun at the start of April. We watch the deer standing in the Top Pond. Two stags clash antlers, throwing up sheets of muddy spray. We glimpse an old buck looking wistfully at the lake.

MONDAY, MAY 28TH, 1990

The frustration of searching for exuviae: seemingly endless hunting for them in the undergrowth. They're so infuriatingly well concealed. It's hardly surprising that dragonfly and damselfly larvae choose carefully where to emerge. With geese, duck, tits and warblers all looking hungrily for food for their young, the risk of being seen and eaten is massive. It's astonishing that any survive at all. I poke a finger at a possible; it moves and turns into a spider. Then I spot another obvious one, kneel down, and find it's a curled-up dead leaf.

I've spent the whole day down here at the lake, from sitting quietly, gloved and scarfed in the early dawn, to stripped to the waist in the heat of midday. I've hacked a visitor-friendly path through the boathouse brambles, and hauled out fallen, tangled poplar branches from the north-west corner to give the reed a better chance. I've rigged up a hammock under the trees on the north bank, and despite a siesta in it, I'm shattered.

Back in London, Kari has been doing some smart negotiating. She has presented a case for doing her very demanding job at Canning in four days rather than five, thus saving the company money and giving her more time, essentially to be up at Ashton with me. Not surprisingly they've agreed and so, as from next week I can take her to Peterborough station on Monday mornings and collect her there on Thursday evenings.

FRIDAY, JUNE 1ST, 1990

We've identified eight species of dragonfly and damselfly here this summer so far. Last year we only found five throughout the whole season.

There are martins spinning over the lake this morning, much more talkative than swallows. The white of the May trees has gone, but the colours of summer are coming. Wild roses and elder flowers are fully out, and scarlet pimpernel has appeared. The ground is black in places with tadpoles; it's almost impossible not to tread on them. Sitting looking out of the windows in the observation hut, I'm disturbed by what sounds like an approaching four-engined aircraft, suddenly right behind me. It's a queen hornet, a wonderful, terrifying, intelligent beast. I leave the hut and, thankfully, very shortly afterwards, she does too.

On my bike-trip down to the Mill I pause in the village and chat to Sid. We share childhood stories. We were both born in Spalding, in the billiard-table flat lands of south Lincolnshire. He tells me that as a lad he fell asleep one evening at the controls of a big yellow Caterpillar crawler tractor while ploughing close to the tidal River Welland. He woke to find the machine heading down the long glistening slope of mud into the river, headlights shining on the black water coming closer and closer below. He yanked one track into reverse, put on full power and sat praying as the big machine slithered slowly down and round. He was inches from the dark wavelets before the thing began to crawl agonisingly slowly back up towards safety, its lights pointing at the sky. He said they were the longest minutes of his life.

Hasty transect walks, then back to the mansion for paperwork, phone calls and typing up a press release. It's important to get as much publicity as possible.

Chapter 13

TUESDAY, JUNE 5TH, 1990

Apart from the sound of a distant lorry, the world is awash with birdsong. The sky is quite still, like rippled gunmetal. A gull is working the lake, its movements heavy compared to the agility of the terns. A heron takes off, shoving a discordant exasperated squawk into the harmony. Right above my head, a thrush is imitating other birds' songs. Do birds have a sense of humour?

The exuvia search has been fruitless and freezing today. On the north bank, rabbits watch a fox pass, one of their kind hanging out of its mouth. They pause only briefly in their nibbling, presumably aware the fox is no longer a threat, for now.

I spend the morning clearing willow debris, and the afternoon sawing trees. I'm stopped in mid-saw by a pretty little coo-ee from a baby moorhen. I've completely exhausted myself again.

THURSDAY, JUNE 14TH, 1990

Where's my bloody pondweed? Gone. That's a whole day's work, vanished. I've begun to spend time cycling round local farms and obtaining permission to take local native plants from their waterspaces. Yesterday, I peddled over to Wigsthorpe and got permission from Mr Racey to take Greater Pondweed (*Potamogeton natans*, much prettier than it sounds) from his pond. I stumbled about in the water, loaded up my pannier, cycled back, and after lunch took it down to the lake, waded in, sploshed about in the shallows, and carefully put fourteen plants in. Now they've gone, as if I never did a blasted thing. I can't believe it. Bloody geese.

I drive into Stamford, pop into the gunshop by the bridge, and buy a bigger blank revolver, a 9mm job. I test it that evening by the observation hut. It's very loud, not as loud as the three-pounder naval cannon I once fired in the middle of Burgess Hill – the police came – but my eyes cross and my ears sing.

I sit beside the lake and watch the sun setting. High up in the dark blue sky, vapour trails become a luminous dark pink. As Polebrook church clock strikes 9.00pm, the air fills with the sound of honking and an entire air armada of Canada Geese fly in. Time for the kayak and the new pistol. I paddle out of the boathouse and pull the trigger; the gun deafens me and leaves the geese staring. More explosions. They remain dumbfounded but unmoved. The kayak's full of rainwater and my bum's wet. I paddle back to the boathouse and walk back up to the mansion in the gloaming, thinking.

MONDAY, JUNE 18TH, 1990

I drive to the ironmongers in Thrapston and purchase miles of rabbit wire, a pile of stakes and a pair of waders. Helped by Kari – on a weeks' break from Canning – and Peter Scott, I begin to build six-foot by eight-foot anti-goose plant pens, a very time-consuming, messy, muddy and wet job. Eventually, with other matters pressing, they leave me to it.

In Kari's case, 'other matters pressing' probably means Miriam wants her, although it might also mean she wants to get on with her painting. She's becoming more and more interested in producing small, very beautiful representations of flowers. She's currently working on a single flower head, a crimson pansy. It's perfect down to the tiniest detail.

Anyway, I lay out the correct length of wire for a pen, place the six freshly shaped posts into position under the wire and staple wire to posts. I roll up the whole thing, hoist it onto my shoulder and squelch into the lake, planning to unroll it again where it's needed. It's a very heavy bundle, like carrying six sections of flagpole cushioned by bouncy metal. I ease it downwards and the fence-posts immediately splunk into the mud like a quiverfull of giant arrows from a Roman artillery piece. I wade further into the mire and try to lift the bundle bodily once more but it's developed a life of its own, uncoiling in parts and tipping drunkenly over at others. What moments before was shiny wire and clean posts is now a slimy web determined to topple me backwards into the black custard. Then the wind gets up and the lake turns into an angry little sea, slopping waves into my waders as I stagger about in a slow waltz amid towering coils of chicken wire, howling and sighing in the freshening gale. The heavens open, the lake begins to hiss and I might as well be standing under a cold shower. When I finally get things into place, the posts are as far from straight as a group of elderly people listening to a joke at a cocktail party.

Nevertheless it's quite exciting to be able to move about in the lake in waders and to stand in the water inside the boathouse. It would be much easier with four legs. Now I see how easy it is for the deer to move about in the lake. Broken Wing, the tern, seems very surprised that I've got a new way of operating and squawks disapprovingly. I head back, very wet, to a hot bath and supper.

Over the next few days, we make three pens and set up paperwork ready to record the development of the plants inside. Coots get in occasionally, but it stops the Canada Geese. They immediately start to devastate all the other non-protected vegetation.

Our first pen plantings are Marsh Marigold (*Caltha palustris*), Greater Pondweed (*Potamogeton natans*) and Reed Mace (*Typha latifolia*) – the proper name for Moses-style bullrushes. Norman Moore comes to inspect what we've done. He's very pleased, but frowns at the sight of the bullrushes. 'I'm not sure that's wise,' he says. Which, I suspect, is a polite way of saying I've boobed. I find out later it's one of the most invasive species in the country.

In the observation hut, he notices the revolver and tells us of a time when he was in Africa, studying raptors. He was walking back one evening with his troop of African helpers, none of whom could speak English. He looked up and saw the silhouettes of thousands of dragonflies passing above him. Unable to think of any other way to identify a species involved in what was clearly a migration, he loaded his shotgun and blasted away into the darkness. It was, he says, very difficult to explain his actions to his companions.

I drive into Peterborough and buy another anti-goose weapon, a catapult. Back beside the observation hut, I set up an old tin on a log and walk backwards for fifteen paces. The first shot hits the tin dead centre. The second shot smashes my left thumb.

Chapter 14

Well, it's five weeks today, five weeks of freedom. I'm sitting down by the lake in the sunshine, watching the last silvery wisps of morning lake-steam drift away. The forecast 'gives for' rain, as Peter Scott the gardener puts it, and so this moment with its brightness and birdsong feels very poignant, as did last night's sunset and mighty cumulus.

How do I feel about my sabbatical? I love it. I love the freedom. Yes, of course there are constraints, but most – apart from the weather – are of my own making. Do I miss not being Mr Important Quick-thinking Decision-maker? Not a bit. Really, not a bit. And it would be great to get the kids up here.

One of the ideas for driving away the Canada Geese is to import a pair of black swans. They have a reputation for being aggressive and territorial. I ask Miriam who, of course, knows someone who has a pair, and so this evening I meet Tony Cook and his wife Ann, both very lively and amusing. Tony used to run the Wildfowl and Wetland Trust's site at Peakirk. We have a drink at the Chequered Skipper then walk round the lake. Tony listens carefully to my proposal and gently demolishes it: the lake's too big; Black Tasmanian Trumpeter Swans would only territorialize a small part of it, he says. The Canadas would continue to occupy the rest.

We go in to see Miriam. She obviously likes Tony and Ann. They talk fleas. Miriam recounts how she'd been involved in

71

sending rabbit fleas to Australia: how she'd organized special Spanish fleas ('complete with rabbits') to be sent all the way, how they'd been customs-cleared, with great difficulty, through India and had finally arrived in Australia. However, it being a Saturday, there was no one in authority on duty at customs, and so the rabbits were promptly sprayed with DDT by a helpful assistant.

Tony's real speciality is birds, and Miriam gets out the enormous and fabulous *Birds of the British Isles and Their Eggs*. Earlier in the day, I found Miriam slumped in a chair, absolutely shattered. Now I watch her at war with her own exhaustion.

MONDAY, JUNE 25TH, 1990

I'm having difficulty writing. My thumb wound has healed but it's still badly bruised. I've just chased off five geese from the north bank; shit everywhere, but I won't bother with the catapult again, thank you.

The weather is now against me. Too many dull rainy days, too many fruitless emergence checks. Too often I've been becalmed in the middle of transect walks as the sun went in, too often finished up glumly watching reflections of terns and gulls winding up and down the Nene. I've only managed thirty-four transects in three weeks. But I've used the time to clear a proper path right round the lake and to build two more plant pens, this time for Yellow Iris (*Iris pseudacorus*) and Fringed Waterlily (*Nymphoides peltata*).

On the only sunny morning I try a short-cut through the thick blackthorn and barbed wire hedge bordering Miriam's massive wildflower meadow. I drop to my knees but only manage to get my head through before I become completely trapped, totally immobile. As I gingerly attempt to extricate myself, I hear the sound of a Volvo coming across the field and Miriam herself appears, showing two nervous po-faced wildflower-enthusiast ladies around. The three of them peer at me and Miriam winds down the window. 'What are you doing?' she says. Before I can answer, she drives off.

I really need good weather now, and yet I could do with an hour or two away from things, too. So I stroll to Polebrook church in the rain and find that its bells were made in the 16th and 17th centuries. No wonder they sound so sweet: four bells whose chimes were heard by men who spoke of their Queen Elizabeth and their King James, and who worked the elegant corduroy curves of the ridge and furrow down which I walk every day.

Today, in the finally returned, still-broken sunshine, there's a quality of green reflected in the lake that's so pure I've tried to photograph it. It's the darkest Brunswick, with deep chocolate tones, and so still that the thrush's song seems to skim along the surface as if the lake is painted metal. The two terns meet above this radiant stillness, then fly off.

A ball of turquoise hurtles along the water's edge. A kingfisher. I watch it perch, look jauntily about, then dive. I move closer and it disappears.

TUESDAY, JUNE 26TH, 1990

Kari has swapped her Canning workdays round this week, so she's still here. She's a million times better at exuvia-hunting than me, has found four damselfly exuviae – head downwards, she points out – on Watermint (*Mentha aquatica*) plants. Perhaps this really is a new discovery.

I've had two Blue-tailed Damselfly larvae in a small fish-tank in the observation hut for some time and today Kari notices one of them has begun to climb up the reed stem I've taped to the side of the tank. She calls me back from attempts to photograph an emergence sequence and I make a note that the larva starts its journey upwards at 9.15am. At 9.50am its splits in larval skin, hauls itself out and begins to expand its wings and its abdomen, and at 10.55am it flies off. So roughly an hour and a half from appearing above the water to take-off. To my surprise the second larva begins its ascent, climbs up the stem, turns round and emerges upside down. I manage to take photographs to prove it. Later, I talk to Miriam about it. 'Well, maybe you've seen something others haven't,' she says. 'You'd be surprised how little people know about insects.'

The kingfisher is darting hallucinogenically about just as an American four-engined Hercules drones over.

Peter Scott and I spend much of the morning sawing up fallen willows on the east bank. Rod, a local man, turns up and tells me there are roach, rudd, bream and eels in the lake. He says the whole thing disappeared in the great drought of 1976, and in 1985 it burst its banks and completely flooded Polebrook. This lake has an interesting life.

Kari and I sit and gaze at several of our new arrivals, Red-eyed Damselflies (*Erythromma najas*). They really do have bright red eyes. They have come at the same time as the recently planted Fringed Waterlilies have flowered in their pen. Might there be a connection between the insect and the plant? I talk to Norman Moore; he doesn't think so. Which, I suspect, is a polite way of saying no.

We're amazed to watch an Emerald Damselfly (*Lestes sponsa*) emerge and make its teneral flight at 4.45pm. It strikes us as very late in the day. We wonder what it knows that we don't.

I drive down to London for a meeting. There and back, it's two hundred miles. The very knowledge that I'm returning to Ashton makes it almost effortless.

WEDNESDAY, JUNE 27TH, 1990

Back from London at 1.00am, and up at 5.30am to go down to the lake to record weather conditions and search for exuviae. Geese all over the lake. I shoot at them. The noise is terribly loud in the dawn. Gunsmoke drifts eastwards. Otherwise nothing moves. I collapse back into bed, up again at 10.30am and down to lake for a successful transect walk and, a real surprise, here's a female Banded Demoiselle. Kari finds a teneral Black-tailed Skimmer (*Orthetrum cancellatum*). We now have ten recorded species, twice the number recorded last year. Our work is bearing fruit.

A young man called Peter Mayhew rings. He's nineteen and mad about natural history. He wanted work experience in Miriam's garden and she has shunted him onto me. He sounds keen.

FRIDAY, JUNE 29TH, 1990

Up at 5.50am. It's another of those can't-sleep-it's-so-beautiful mornings. I'm sitting in the sun outside the observation hut.

I've just killed my first dragonfly and I feel terrible. It was a female Black-tailed Skimmer, exactly the same as the dragonfly that first landed on my shirt back in 1985. Two days ago she emerged, and during the process the wind kept pushing her starboard forewing against rushes, with the result that by the time I found her the wing had become deformed and she was unable to take off. I've seen dragonflies in flight with half a wing missing so, after a long consultation with Kari, I decided to try surgery and snipped off the damaged part of the wing. It was the first dragonfly I've ever touched. She was very delicate yet surprisingly strong. The operation was brutal and in the end ineffective. She never flew. Several times her head bobbed as flies passed but otherwise the poor thing didn't move at all. It does point to the fact that dragonflies can go without food for long periods, in this case forty-five hours after emergence. But, rather than let her starve slowly, I killed her.

We spend much of the day setting up an exhibition in the observation hut, ready for an influx of eminent naturalists on Saturday. Thunder looms and finally breaks just as we finish.

SATURDAY, JUNE 30TH, 1990

It's been a hectic day. Up at 5.30am and down to the lake to do a weather check and an exuvia hunt. Back up to the mansion in time to iron shirt, clean the Bentley and make sandwiches. Last-minute jokes with Sid before driving off to Woodwalton Fen with Miriam. We're far too early, so we sit in the big upright beech wood armchairs in Charles Rothschild's bungalow and wait for the guests. The interlude reminds Miriam of sitting in a bar in Wales, waiting for her husband during the war; another member of his unit – the notoriously ferocious '10 Commando' – walked in, went up to the bar, took out his revolver and shot himself.

Ron Harold, Woodwalton's manager, appears and Miriam changes the subject to ask whether any work has been done on the fluid excretion carried out by dragonflies during emergence. What does it consist of? Is it poisonous? And she recounts the life-cycle of a trematode worm that lays eggs under the tongue of a frog, the eggs pass through the frog into the water, they hatch and penetrate snails, they grow, leave the snails and get eaten by water fleas, who in turn get eaten by dragonflies, who – either as larvae or adults – get eaten by frogs, and the cycle is complete. A simple life, then.

The guests arrive and despite the changeable weather we have an excellent morning and then all drive back to Ashton for lunch. Everyone troops down to the lake, I drag them round, answering questions about dragonflies. Then John Gurdon asks, 'What's that plant, Ruary?' and I – much to my own surprise and delight at knowing the answer and being able to help such a genius – reply, 'It's St John's Wort, John.' Our exhibition is a success. We totter to bed exhausted.

SUNDAY, JULY 1ST, 1990

I arrange to meet young Peter Mayhew at the lake and explain what we're trying to do. Bright-eyed and ginger-haired, he looks all round, then says, 'This looks very promising, very promising indeed.' Evidently his grandfather got him crazy about biology and he's now keen to learn about dragonflies. I take him on a transect walk. He says he misses his former home in Amersham and is comforted by his love of Monty Python, some of whose sketches he now repeats by heart, playing all the roles, from start to finish. But I reckon he's a hard worker and he's already show-ing a real interest.

Chapter 15

TUESDAY, JULY 10TH, 1990

Down to London Zoo and a very warm welcome. Taken through to the big refrigerators in which, thanks to Tessa and Jean, are the bags of lion dung ready and waiting for me. I push a piled-high handcart through crowds of sunny zoo-goers.

'It's frozen lion dung,' I tell a granny with three kids clustered round her.

'Of course it is, dear,' she says.

I load it into the Bentley's boot, onto the deep plush carpet in the back, even onto the soft leather of the back seats. No Bentley will ever have carried such a load before, surely, and I wonder how the police will react if I have an accident en route to Ashton. I spend some time dreaming up possible constabular comments.

Safely back at the mansion, I unload the dung into the garage, get washed and, already late, hurry in to lunch with Miriam. Then other events supervene and the dung remains in the garage.

It's a hot week, good news after the miserable previous one. I forget all about the dung and seize the chance that the fine weather brings to get stuck into transect walks, weather checks and exuvia hunts. On Friday the staff at the mansion complain about the smell in the garage. I hastily stash an emergency supply in a deep-freeze and barrow the rest down to the lake – three hot sweaty trips – and distribute it in small heaps along the 40m-stretch of open bank.

SUNDAY, JULY 15TH, 1990

How many more times will I stumble out of bed soon after five and head down to the lake, planning to slide back under the sheets after recording weather details and counting exuviae, only to be seduced by stillness, sunshine and birdsong? The mist is here and though it's hardly the season of mellow fruitfulness yet, there's been a change. Wildflowers are in full bloom: Ragwort and Meadowsweet shine everywhere, and Honesty, tall and white, stands in the woodland. It feels as if we've crossed a watershed into the second half of the year.

The water plants are doing well, too. The Greater Pondweed is thriving, as are the Marsh Marigolds and the Fringed Waterlilies. Loosestrife, Hemp Agrimony and Broad-leaved Willowherb are reflecting different shades of purple on the lake, and the Great Water Dock looks like dragon's teeth in the mist.

Dragonflies particularly like to set up territories over margins of water spaces, so we have cleared a channel through the now-abundant reed along the north bank and christened it Chaser Channel. It's a lovely place to stand and watch dragonflies zooming up and down, and it's now a carpet of twinkling blue Water Forget-me-not (*Myosotis scorpiodes*).

Peter Mayhew is now helping me with planting and, after only a little training, he's already doing transect walks and meteorology checks. Over lunch, Kari reduces him to giggling helplessness by reading him verse by EJ Thribb, *Private Eye*'s 17½-year-old poet.

Later, Peter gallops breathless towards us with a small, newly emerged dragonfly clamped between his fingers. It's a male Ruddy Darter. Though it's still a pale brown, we know that it will shortly turn the brightest scarlet. We're also surprised to find one so early in the year; they normally appear in August.

With Peter's help, we're now up-to-date on our several transect walks and plotting our weather records on a graph. We're also keeping careful notes of exuviae and adult dragonfly activity. Identifying tiny damselfly exuviae is a slow hand-lens task. Kari and Peter do almost all of it. I'm no good, I get impatient, so I slope off, do transect walks and catch up with outstanding paperwork and phone calls.

At about two in the morning, Miriam presumably decides on a solitary midnight feast and sets quails' eggs on to boil. She goes back to her microscope work and forgets all about them. They boil dry and the fire alarm goes off. It's directly connected to Oundle Fire Station. This has happened before but no amount of angry telephoning from Miriam will stop them coming out. ('We have to make sure, Mrs Lane.') Everyone local knows her as Mrs Lane. She used to be married to George Lane, with whom she still gets on extremely well. The fire engine arrives minus its aerials, torn off by the overhanging trees on the 'drive'. Miriam refuses to let the firemen in. The big red machine ticks over noisily and the yellow-coated men stand about in the flickering orange and blue lights. Finally a ground floor window next to the back door opens and a bare arm appears, slim and pale, holding a bottle of scotch. The firemen reverse laboriously and drive off into the darkness.

The lion dung seems to be working. No sign of deer anywhere near the lake.

WEDNESDAY, JULY 18TH, 1990

A day's work at the Sanctuary, then I drive into Peterborough to collect Kari, returning from work in London. We drive to the Haycock at Wansford, an idyllic riverside hotel, a study in 18th century Barnack stone. We sit in the garden in the evening sunshine and, over a glass of white wine, Kari says she has some Canning School news. I almost fall off my chair when she tells me that Donald, the senior partner who founded the outfit back in 1965, is going. Kari and I both feel that Canning as we know it will completely change now. We agree that we've learned a tremendous amount from the outfit: our contact with people from all over the world, our time with an astonishing spectrum of colleagues, our chance to visit places we'd never have otherwise been.

We've learned about ourselves at Canning, how both of us do any job we're given as best we can, how we work with others, cope with severe pressure and handle unexpected situations. But enough is enough, and Ashton is offering us another dimension now, a chance to do something really interesting: in my case promoting dragonflies; in hers dragonflies too, yes, but painting also, painting as a career. Here at Ashton, it feels as if there are fewer limits, more scope for potentially … potentially … what? Who knows? There must be some way we can escape from Canning. Nica would have been out of there in seconds. We raise our glasses to escape.

FRIDAY, JULY 20TH, 1990

Another boiling day. A week or two ago, Kari watched a dragonfly laying her eggs. She collected the white pinhead-sized eggs and put them in a tank. She intends to rear them through and today we watch them turn into little dragonfly larvae and photograph the process. I'd never even have thought of this.

When we arrive at the lake we're amazed at the number of dragonflies already in action. Somehow a Common Darter has got itself into the observation hut. I net it and release it; it shoots up into the blue sky. I photograph a Brown Hawker (*Aeshna grandis*) laying her eggs on a soggy log close to the south bank. A clutch of flickering Large White Butterflies crowd round a boot mark in the drying mud at the lakeside. We make a list of butterflies we've seen near the lake: seventeen species.

We both head out into the lake in kayaks, Kari to check on Canada Goose activity on the little island, me to see what I can find. I spot a dragonfly larva hooked to an iris stem, just breaking through its exuvial case. A slit has appeared in the dark brown thorax, and the pale green head of the future adult is just showing beneath. By a miracle I have my camera with me and I start shooting what I hope will be a perfect emergence sequence. Over the next half hour, the dragonfly hauls its head and wings out of its case and tips backward ready for the final thrust that will bring it free. I'm getting some excellent shots when Kari calls out across the water.

'Ruary! Quick! I'm stuck! I'm capsizing!'

I unglue my eyes from the viewfinder for a moment and establish that she's tipped sideways, clinging onto the stones at the edge of the island. She's not going to drown. Good manners desert me and I tell her to look after herself. Which she does, although not entirely happily. But I can't really concentrate fully on the dragonfly emergence any more. Emergence, emergency, too much.

Peter Scott comes down to do more work on the tiny panes of glass, and the three of us sit having a drink in the semi-darkness. I've located two old-fashioned camp beds, so, when Peter leaves, Kari and I decide to spend the night in the observation hut. As darkness falls, we light a candle and I look around the hut, with its tables, chairs and scientific paraphernalia. The observation hut is alive again. We have a candle-lit snack and settle down for the night. A stag starts to roar right outside but eventually we fall asleep, fully expecting to be up at 5.00am or thereabouts. I wake to the sun streaming in through the tiny panes and automatically check my watch: it's just after 10.30am …

SUNDAY, JULY 22ND, 1990

Up very early and down to lake for all the usual checks. Then off down to Hurst Green in Surrey to collect daughter Catharine, twelve, and son Richard, ten. Wonderful. We're going to spend a whole fortnight together. They live with their mother and stepfather, and this will be their first visit to Ashton. We're back in time for a quick late lunch and I take them down to the lake.

As if to welcome them, a new dragonfly appears, a Migrant Hawker (*Aesha mixta*), jinking and darting. More dragonflies do a display above the children's heads. We go back up to the mansion for tea, and Catharine and Richard meet Miriam for the first time. She offers to teach Catharine to drive. Catharine responds politely, looking hard at Miriam and clearly wondering whether she's the right sort of teacher. We go swimming – there's a pool in the walled garden – then drive down to the pub. It's a good start.

MONDAY, JULY 23RD, 1990

I drive Kari to Peterborough station. She's not looking forward to going back to work, and I feel a bit guilty.

The days develop a routine of the usual dragonfly work with Peter Mayhew – on Tuesday, it's five Blue-tailed exuviae head-down, and nine head-up; on Wednesday, it's five head-down and one head-up – plus kayaking, swimming, riding for the children, and ferrying Kari to and from the station. Catharine and Richard are beginning to identify dragonflies and join in some of the work.

On the way down the 'drive', we pause to watch a massive combine harvester at work. Sid Jackson pokes his head out of the cab and beckons Richard over. Richard clambers up, climbs into the driving seat and, under Sid's instruction, sets off up the field. Richard sits quite still, arms relaxed on the levers, making the smallest of adjustments from time to time, totally concentrated on keeping the monster exactly on line.

TUESDAY, JULY 31ST, 1990

A lovely morning. Less than two months of my sabbatical to go now. I take Kari to the station early, but it's too good to go back to bed and give in to a horrible cold that's suddenly struck me.

Down to the lake hand in hand with Catharine and Richard in the sunshine. Catharine sketching the west bank, Richard mending the battered fence, me sneezing and sweating on the bench. Only one Canada now; has been for three days. There are Peacock butterflies on the teazles. A Common Darter perches on same reed stem as a Black-tailed Skimmer. The Skimmers have almost finished their aerial lives now and the Darters are just beginning. Both species use the same perching points, but it's unusual to find them both together like this. I forget all about illness and get the shot. The Broad-bodied Chasers have completely gone, but there's still bags of action from the Blue-tailed Damselflies; and Southern Hawkers (*Aeshna cyanea*) are whizzing about wonderfully.

I'm very wobbly. I manage an exuvia hunt and find one head-up and one head-down. I have to rest in the hammock. What will I do if I'm ill? I stagger back to the mansion, pulse racing, sweating profusely, and Kari – who's spending as much time as possible up here at the moment – has to come back from the station by cab.

WEDNESDAY, AUGUST 1ST, 1990

Feeling rough but operational, I take Kari to Peterborough station, then walk down to the lake alone. Miriam has given me a photograph of the lake taken in 1912 and I take it down with me to compare. The huge willows that now dominate the east bank weren't even planted back then. It's extraordinary to think that those massive trees are younger than Miriam. I have finally grasped that a willow's life can be as little as fifty years. I thought Miriam was mistaken when she said that a week or two ago. And, in 1912, the view across the lake and up to the mansion was superb. Like a giant Sussex ironmaster's house, the still-raw building looked imperiously down the bare slope. What jibes it must have attracted from the local gentry. Yet now, sunk deep into encroaching vegetation, reduced in height, its middle storey removed, it stands dethoracitated, humbled. Or as humbled a grand mansion is ever likely to be.

Last night, the Pakistani taxi driver who brought Kari back from Peterborough station, bumping his way up the 'drive' in the darkness and coming to a stand amid the thickness of the laurels at the top, said tremulously: 'It's like a jungle here. At home we would be afraid.'

The children come down and help me with the work. Richard finds his first two exuviae, a damselfly and a dragonfly. Later we drive to Magdalene College, Cambridge, and I deliver a lecture on dragonflies. Even Catharine and Richard enjoy it.

Chapter 16

THURSDAY, AUGUST 2ND, 1990

I'm starting seriously to snivel, sneeze and stagger, but I still manage to get down to the lake to check for new exuviae. To my horror I find several deer in the water. The dung must be losing its pungency. Time to raid our emergency supply, stashed in a deep-freeze down in the dusty labyrinthine cellars under the mansion.

Richard and I go off to do two transect walks, nip into Oundle for shopping and come back for a quick swim, which perks me up enough to slog through Transect 4 at the far end of the estate.

Adrian Colston, the Director of the Northamptonshire Wildlife Trust, arrives and I take him down to the lake. I've met him before up at the mansion, as Miriam is President of the Trust, so she has Adrian along for tea fairly frequently. She always calls him Coulson. Adrian is young with angelically curly blond hair and a positive, forceful manner. As we walk round together and I blather away, he appreciates what we're doing and we get on well. I have a feeling this man will be important.

Battling with a wheezy chest and general ague, I go back up to the house for phone calls and paperwork while Catharine and Richard return to the lake to distribute fresh – if that's the right word – lion dung along the open bank, and to carry out a further exuvia hunt. I go to bed. There's a fashionable phrase at the moment, at least among women: man-flu. Is this it?

FRIDAY, AUGUST 3RD, 1990

I catch the news that the United Nations have condemned yesterday's Iraqi invasion of Kuwait, and I wonder what's next. The weather is really picking up now and today it's 41°C (106°F) by the boathouse. We invite Kari's great-niece Nica and her mother Barbara to tea in the observation hut, but have scarcely begun before we have to abandon the area due to a jam-tempted wasp invasion.

Kari, Catharine, Richard and I have a late swim in semi-darkness, and decide to spend the night down in the observation hut. Tucked up inside the hut, it's really very cosy, now it's been re-glazed. Just as before, we sleep until late. Maybe it has something to do with the sun filtering through the ever-waving willow leaves that give a rippling, watery, sleepy-making, comforting effect.

SATURDAY, AUGUST 4TH, 1990

I telephone hoping to extend the children's stay but find they're needed back in Surrey. So I hide my disappointment and we slot in a final couple of transect walks and a swim while Kari prepares us a delicious lunch, then we set off on the 121 miles to Hurst Green. It's an uneventful journey, made shorter by listening to Alan Bennett reading 'The Wind in the Willows'. Richard sleeps most of the way, but I catch him giving a combine harvester a hard look; he'll be seeing them differently now he's driven one.

I think it's been a good fortnight for them. They've got to know Ashton and Miriam. They've been swimming daily and learned to use kayaks. Richard has driven that combine harvester once and the Fergie several times. Catharine has been riding. And they've helped me a lot and shown a real interest in natural history. Some lovely moments remain: Richard, insect book in hand, puzzling out a species of bee; and finding his first exuvia; and sowing seed; Catharine drawing the lake; their interest in ladybirds; their different ways of canoeing.

I finally get back to Northamptonshire, with a huge red setting sun reflecting along the Bentley's bonnet, the black paintwork accentuating the purple aura in the sky. Kari has prepared yet another meal, and so to bed, feeling the quietness after the children. It's been so good to have them.

SUNDAY, AUGUST 5TH, 1990

It's 9.30am, exactly twenty-four hours since we all awoke here in the observation hut. Today is cloudier and windier than yesterday but otherwise things outside are much the same. It feels very different inside. I miss my kids.

I plant the Yellow Waterlily (*Nuphar lutea*) that Richard and I dragged out of the millrace down on the Nene last Thursday. We both could see exactly why they're nicknamed 'brandy bottles': their pods have a beautiful curved greenish-glaze flask shape.

Kari and I spend the morning building a landing stage in the lake to make it easier to get in and out of the kayaks. I'm filthy already but Kari gets sodden and mud-splattered too. We go up to the flat, have a bath, and go round to the main house. It's Miriam's birthday, and, although she says she hates being reminded of it and there mustn't be any sort of celebration, there is of course a big family lunch and several of Miriam's friends are here. When Miriam strides in, no one says anything, but her daughter Charlotte and one or two others are wearing T-shirts with "Happy Birthday, Mum" on them. Miriam pretends not to see. There's a lot of twinkly eye-contact and discreet grinning.

After lunch I haul everyone down to the lake in the sunshine and they clearly enjoy being taken round and shown all the little successes in getting dragonflies to set up home here. Now the dragonflies are here, maybe it's time to think of getting more humans – other than friends and family – here. Back to the house for tea and – very soon – Château la Cardonnne, but Kari wisely takes a cold-ridden Ruary off to bed.

MONDAY, AUGUST 6TH, 1990

Feeling very heavy this morning after a night of coughing. I take Kari and two of Miriam's friends to Peterborough station, then go down to the lake with a new young gardener. We have put in another plant pen and I'm in the process of praising the beauty of and describing the environmentally-healthy significance of Flowering Rush (*Juncus umbellatus*) to him – well, he's a gardener – when an American F111 from Lakenheath appears in the sky above and puts on an amazing long-drawn-out show of acrobatics. Is this a USAF statement about Kuwait? I'm very sensitive about aircraft movements now. When I started this sabbatical I got completely fed up with jet fighters blasting over, scarcely higher than my head, completely destroying the tranquility of the lake. So I decided to make a virtue of it – fighters have wings, after all – and bought a book on modern military aircraft recognition. Now, of course, I'm hooked.

The young gardener is utterly uninterested in the antics of the F111, but it's impossible for me to concentrate on plants, and when the tumbling and roaring aircraft is joined by two A10 Tank-busters, I give up, gawp upwards, and the young man drifts away.

I set off for Transect 4, the one at the far end of the estate. It centres on a soggy area – a former pond – not far from Charlotte's house in the middle of the woods. Charlotte hasn't yet gone back to London and greets me as I arrive. The Migrant Hawkers put on their own aerial display for her, swooping and looping, jinking sideways after mosquitoes and hurtling upwards into the sky. Far more spectacular than the USAF.

TUESDAY, AUGUST 7TH, 1990

Feeling on form again, I'm sitting on the style, the one I've made, beside the observation hut. The sun has gone in and the wind has picked up a little, making it impossible for me to continue the transect walk. For proper dragonfly recording, you need to be able to see your shadow and for the wind to be little more than a very gentle breeze, just as Steve Brooks told me. When I got down here earlier after ringing son Richard – his birthday – it was wonderfully sunny and calm. I stood for a long time, watching the reflection of fifteen poplar trees in the water.

I'm used to the pattern of local military aircraft activity now and am very aware of any new types to identify. Today is strangely different. No RAF Tornadoes and no sign of any Tucanos, those lovely little propeller-driven trainers that growl over like up-to-date Spitfires. But a large tightly-knit formation of Harrier Jump Jets sweeps majestically across the sky and a solitary high altitude red and white reconnaissance Canberra appears. Whatever the radio is calmly telling me, something's up.

I decide to cycle to Fotheringhay for a long lunch break. Why not? I'm my own boss and it's a gorgeous day. There's a beautiful church beside the river there, and the forlorn remains of the castle where Mary Queen of Scots was executed. There's also a good pub, the Falcon. Afterwards, I pedal back up the hill to the ridge overlooking the Nene, cycle along the straw-coloured gravel road, then plonk the bike in a hedge, open my flask of tea, and gaze out across the valley. It looks like a magnificent brown and green chess-board. The brown makes me think of big square chocolate biscuits.

I go back down to the lake, watch dragonflies and damselflies dart among the reeds, and doze in the hammock until Miriam and her friend Elena Cardenas arrive in the white, blackthorn-scratched Volvo. They're full of praise. A note tells me that I need to remember Miriam's tale about Mrs Thatcher and the moth-trap. I no longer do.

THURSDAY, AUGUST 9TH, 1990

Having been to London yesterday, I intend to sleep in late, but the sun drags me out of bed at 6.50am. I putter down to the lake on the Fergy. The Fergy and its attendant trailer are not just a pleasant way of getting about; they're essential for transporting all the tools we need from the garden near the mansion down to the lake. Not yet being able to afford proper equipment, we're kindly allowed to borrow kit from the garden when it's not in use. We have access to a rugged Hayter, for example, quite a struggle for one man to lift off the back of a trailer, but which enables us to keep our new-hacked paths open and to mow even the most overgrown areas. The Canada Geese are back in force. I succeed in driving eighteen away by paddling about and blasting away with the revolver.

There are dragonflies everywhere but the lake itself is giving trouble. It's the heat. A horrid green algae is beginning to appear and spread alarmingly. Whilst out in the kayak, I see it's 19.5°C

(67.1°F), just before the thermometer-string slips out of my hands into the murky depths, never to be seen again. I'm desperate to think of some way of getting oxygen into the water to combat the algae.

I sit in the observation hut and have a think. Then I have a brainwave, go and see Peter Scott and talk him into letting me borrow his big leaf-blower. Will it blast air into the water? I lug it down to the lake and after a lot of experimentation with duck-tape, bricks and plastic tubing, during which I spray myself wet through several times, it does. I wait to see whether it has any effect.

Back to the mansion for a teabreak and I get the news that my daughter Anna has just been delivered of a baby girl, Sally Louise. Which means I'm a forty-three year old grandad. Miriam is about to have her second grandchild. She's forty years older than me. I make plans to go down to Sussex and, more good news, I can collect the Catharine and Richard and bring them back to Ashton again.

Chapter 17

FRIDAY, AUGUST 10TH, 1990

I set off on the long drive south to Cuckfield Hospital in Sussex. Daughter Anna is alone and we have a lovely chat, then new-born Sally Louise is brought in, I take her in my arms, she turns her face to me, and I see that Sally's eyes are not merely like my father's, they really are my father's. I'm looking at my Daddy inside my grandchild. He only died last year and I desperately, desperately want to talk to him. Stunned, I say nothing. I'm in a ward full of mothers and babies, overflowing with wonderful new love. It's definitely neither the time nor the place to blurt out that I'm having a psychic experience.

Only Kari knows that shortly before my father died of oral cancer, at a time when he was having serious difficulty speaking and was in any case forbidden to contact me by my stepmother, he waited until she went out on some errand and then rang me. I was away shopping and Kari simply could not grasp exactly what he was trying to say, despite him trying three times. When we'd last spoken he'd expressed doubt about my obsession with dragonflies. Kari was sure that whatever that last message was, he was saying he still loved and believed in me. Now, torn between shock and the love I feel for my first grandchild, I stand holding her beside my daughter's bed.

I drive to Oxted, aware that my hands on the wheel are still shaking, and collect Catharine and Richard. We set off back to Ashton an hour later than hoped, get stuck in ferocious Friday evening traffic, nurse the old car as its water temperature rises steadily into the red zone, and arrive all utterly shattered.

SATURDAY, AUGUST 11TH, 1990

I wake after a long sleep, feeling much better. Down to the lake with Catharine driving the Fergy and Richard on the trailer. We check that the bubbler is operating, and work on clearing a path on the east bank. Then, with Richard at the wheel this time, we fergy back up and go off to the Chequered Skipper for lunch with my brother Ramsay and sister-in-law Pauline. Ramsay's four years older than me; there are just the two of us and we've been through some very tough times together, mother's early death, father's alcoholism, sale of family home, putting down of beloved pets, and so on. He thinks this whole dragonfly business is mad but he's very supportive. Down to the lake to show them our work, then off to the Mill Tea Room. It's situated in the former miller's house beside Ashton Mill. Though Miriam's Fish Museum in the main mill building is defunct, the tea room beside it is still operational. We sit in the garden talking, Ramsay and I looking at the placid millpond, recounting and laughing at some of the ghastlier events that overtook us; and I get a strange feeling about this place again, just as I did when I entered the Mill itself. What's going on? It feels the same as when I first went down to the lake, but I can't see why I should feel it here.

Back up at the mansion I hear the honking of Canada Geese coming from the lake; I dash down, count eighty-five of them, leap into the canoe and drive off a splashing, cackling cacophony.

SUNDAY, AUGUST 12TH, 1990

I try to have about fifteen minutes to myself in the mornings, if I can, and if I can be bothered. I'm sitting quietly on a little seat in the corner of the west and south banks. I hadn't noticed the seat's existence until I found a young Polebrook couple sitting on it one hot afternoon recently. I saw them seconds before they saw me, and in that moment, I saw how conscious they were of their near-ness to each other. They hurried away.

From the seat I look across the lake past the two little islands to a scene of receding willows. Three species of willow stand layered at different distances, as if they've been placed to lead my eye further and further away until my gaze comes to rest in the shady depths of a glade over near the gate to Stanborough Hill.

I lose count of the number of shades of green that my eyes take in en route from here to the glade. The crack willows on the islands are almost brown, and the tall bank willows behind them have their greenness heightened by the line of almost blue *Salix alba* beyond. The morning sun has just come out, backlighting the whole scene, deepening the distances and flecking the greens with gold.

The kingfisher's giving his imperious bos'un's-whistle, echoing around the lake, heralding the start of another long summer day, one of the kind when, as a boy, summer holidays seemed sun-filled and infinite. Those days are still here. It's just that I'm not; and even when I'm here like this, it's not the same. I now have the doubtful advantage of knowing that all this green will go, these billions of leaves will fall, the frost will come, and I'll be back at my dull desk in London.

Kari and the children come down and we do three hours' hard work sowing Burnt Close Wildflower seed mixture on a little meadow I've cleared beside the observation hut. Then we declare a holiday and go to watch an air show at Alconbury. A perfect day for flying: the Battle of Britain Memorial Flight drones over in a Merlin-engined symphony. The French Patrouille de France attempt – unsuccessfully – to outdo the Red Arrows' amazing red-white-blue vapour trails. We watch impressive acrobatics by Tornados, Jaguars, Falcons, Phantoms and F111s. The commander of all the ugly A10 Tank-buster squadrons on the base climbs into his personal aircraft, does some clever tricks, and makes a rather frightening point of staying within the limits of the airfield throughout his display.

Back in time for a glass of wine with Kari by the lake and then up to join the kids who've been in the swimming pool ever since we returned. I jump in fully clothed.

MONDAY, AUGUST 13TH, 1990

A breathless, clear day. As I arrive, two herons flap slowly, reluctantly away. The surface of the lake has a greasy look this morning but the martins are still spiralling round. The Polebrook church clock strikes eight and I hear the rest of the world begin to stir itself for another week. I watch the kingfisher through my binoculars, then carry out the usual weather-recording and exuvia-hunting chores, and am brought to a sudden standstill by a glowing red jewel of a dragonfly, a hovering Ruddy Darter. I dare say that when the great lady of early dragonfly work, Cynthia Longfield, made that English name official, it didn't have the same meaning as now; at least I hope not. As I think I've said before, I definitely prefer *Sympetrum sanguineum,* but I admit that whenever I see one, before I can stop myself, I've called out 'Ruddy!' to whoever happens to be around.

TUESDAY, AUGUST 14TH, 1990

I take Kari to the station and by the time I'm back the children have gone off exploring, so I go and find Miriam to discuss opening the lake to the public. I've learned that there are already two private dragonfly reserves in England – Norman's is one – but we talk about a public dragonfly reserve. There's one in Japan run by a Mr Sugimura. Kari spotted an article on him in *Time* magazine and we've already been in touch with him. I think the lake should be a public place, an educational resource, a way of highlighting the plight of dragonflies. Miriam's very positive. She talks of involving the National Trust. I walk down to the lake with my head full of dreams of a car park, a cafeteria and lots of visitors.

Back to cook a fry-up lunch for the children, then to the lake once again at about 4.00pm in time to see a Black-tailed Skimmer perched on a reed stem. It's a male and he's powder-blue with black at the bottom of his abdomen. The female, not on parade today, is brown with a black ladder-pattern along her abdomen, nothing like the male, indeed could be mistaken for an entirely different species. A Brown Hawker darts over the lake, its copper-coloured wings glinting in the evening sunshine. I catch the first whiff of warm blackberries and just a hint of autumn.

Catharine, Richard and I drive over to Little Gidding Church. Catharine and I sit together in its absolute calm and I read her T.S.Eliot's 'Little Gidding'. Richard joins us and looks unimpressed. I drive to Peterborough to collect Kari for the last time. Now she's on holiday and will stay here. Maybe I'll sleep in a little tomorrow.

THURSDAY, AUGUST 16TH, 1990

I wake just before 6.00am. It's cloudy and still almost dark, but by 6.30am the blue sky and the sun are calling me. For the first time, I roll over and turn my back on the morning.

Later, I wheel out Moonshadow and cycle down to the lake, arriving only a minute or two after my 8.30am target. It's the coldest morning for some time. Everywhere is heaving, rustling and sighing in the gusting wind.

Sitting on the Ashton blue bench on the north bank, out of the corner of my eye, to the left, there's a small movement. A weasel? A stoat? I turn my head slowly and watch. It's a stoat, black-tipped tail, performing a series of leaping and sliding movements very close to a hunched, hypnotized, myxomatose rabbit. The stoat glides alongside the rabbit, slipping his jaws through her fur then slithering away for more jumping and rolling before gliding up to her once more. He goes through the routine again and again. I'm watching a death-dance. I dread to think what the rabbit must feel, although to be realistic, a neck-bite from a stoat might be the easiest and simplest way out for her.

I find myself shouting angrily, striding towards the stoat, automatically imposing my human sense of justice, breaking his ecstatic murder-trance and sending him rocketing into the undergrowth. The rabbit scarcely moves and pathetically tries to nibble a few shoots. Standing in front of it, I run through the kill-or-not-kill option that I faced every time I confronted a 'mixie' rabbit when I was seven at prep school in Scotland, and the masters sent us all out on so-called mercy missions. The first time I stick-hit one, I was revolted; looking at the blood in the sunshine, it felt like murder. I remember being torn between my revulsion and my worries about how my schoolmates and teachers would feel. Would I be branded a 'weed'? Desperate, I found what I see now as a slimy compromise: I became the best 'mixie' scout. I moved further and faster than the main pack of boys, finding myxomatose rabbits and directing the killers towards them without doing the work myself.

I can't help admiring the stoat's death dance, its horrid purposeful beauty. Given real craving hunger, I know I'd pick up a rod, a gun or a knife and forget my squeamishness, though there'd be no sport or fun in it. Am I a tamed killer, like a pet cat, my instincts dulled by easily-accessible food? The rabbit saves me the decision: half-blind, it lollops away and disappears deep into the undergrowth.

I haven't had to face many blood-in-the-sunshine moments, and like many westerners I've been protected from many of the realities of death and dying, other than – aged fifteen – losing my mother, that is. Impossible to forget that moment by her bedside: above the folded white sheet her eyes were closed, but her face wasn't at peace. She looked very serious, as if she was away in a distant struggle. For the first time in my life, she ignored me. I stood close to her, very lonely and a bit afraid. Only then did I realize how much she'd loved me, how I'd taken her love to be never-ending, and how, unconsciously, I gauged everyone through the lens of that love.

Anyway, there have been several other animal-killing moments. I liked the idea of fishing until, standing by the River Welland, I had to take the hook out of the mouth of my first fish; it finished the whole romantic idea for me. Then, borrowed shotgun in hand, having to break the neck of a mutilated pheasant in a kale field in Lincolnshire stopped me enjoying that particular sort of shooting. Skinning a rabbit in my brother's kitchen put me off rabbit stew forever. As a teenager, watching someone being blooded at the end of an otter hunt made me realize I didn't want to be a party to it any more, regardless of my real reason for attending, namely the extremely attractive girls who tagged along.

I cycle back up to the mansion, and Catharine and I do the long transect walk by the Nene then prepare tea for Miriam in our flat. We're a bit nervous about getting it right. But Miriam comes thumping up the stairs and enjoys our efforts. We have a long conversation about the difference between memory and recall. She talks to Catharine, aged twelve, exactly as an equal.

I go down to the lake to carry out an emergence check and stand in awe of its beauty in the changing light. Tomorrow I'm saying goodbye to the children again.

Chapter 18

FRIDAY, AUGUST 17TH, 1990

We get up at 4.00am, I take the children back to Surrey and, three hundred miles later, I'm back to meet my very best friend Mike, his wife Sue and their little daughter Alex. Mike's driving a grey Ford Mustang. We've shared our love of cars ever since we met aged nine at a prep school in Norfolk, to which I'd thankfully been transferred after two years of schoolmaster sadism in Scotland. Had we but known it, our respective families were already slowly and grimly disintegrating, and, though of course we've enjoyed each other's successes, since boyhood we've consistently cheered each other up as one or other of us was hit in the face by yet another custard pie. How many times have we looked at each other and said, 'Weird, in' it?'

We go in to tea with Miriam. She and Mike immediately fall into conversation. I've begun to measure people as to how they react to Miriam. Mike does brilliantly.

He's brought champagne. He's now a pilot for Rolls-Royce and jets around the world staying in top-class hotels. Unless you asked, you wouldn't know that he's been a shed-builder, an RAF Flight Lieutenant and a fully qualified NHS dentist. The four of us eat dinner in candlelight and, over the laughter, I hear the Canadas coming in to the lake in the gloaming. I leave the party, bounce down to the lake in the darkness on Moonshadow and find the lake looking like a market-day car park with geese instead of cars. Careful not to trip or fall into the mud, revolver in hand, I charge.

A great orange flash and bang. Another. And the sky instantly full of flapping, honking geese. The lake empty except for the ripples of their take-off and a few floating feathers. Waiting in the gathering darkness, I listen to their fading calls, bats puttering about, and the startled hoot of an owl. Then, with the heavy pistol bumping against my chest, feeling like a Maquisard, I cycle back up the hill and take my place at the table once more. The others are so busy talking they assume I've just been to the loo.

SATURDAY, AUGUST 18TH, 1990

Kari and I come down in the damp still air to a lake that feels cold and autumnal. A robin sings very near us, and is answered by another. We've been very cheered by a lovely letter from Professor Philip Corbet, the doyen of dragonfly science. He's tremendously encouraging about setting up a publicly accessible dragonfly place. We sit on the bench dreaming of how we'll organize everything.

As the day warms and the sun comes out we watch a Southern Hawker patrol among the reeds. Two Brown Hawkers appear and fight for territory, clashing, biting, smashing each other with their wings. Common Darters are fighting, too. When a female appears, one of them zooms up, grasps her round the neck with his abdominal claspers, forms a heart-shaped pair and hurtles off into the woodland.

I spend time, Cyril Hammond's book in hand, staring at a powder blue neon-bright damselfly. I check the blue stripes on the top of its black thorax: they're thin. I look at the upper segments of the abdomen and see what looks like a cross-section of a whisky tumbler, black on blue. I examine the lower end of the abdomen and there's a black mark, like a right-angled C on its side. It's a male Azure Damselfly (*Coenagrion puella*). I glance at my watch; it's taken me twenty-five minutes to work it out, but it could have been two other similar species. My back aches and my knees are soaking wet. I realize that I've now definitely gone mad. Is this to be my life? Crawling about, squinnying at tiny insects, trying to spot the size of their stripes? Mad or not, the sun is shining, the birds are singing; it could be worse.

I stand up and grin at a squadron of Blue-tailed Damselflies zipping about. They're easy to identify: they have bright blue blobs on the end of their abdomens, and the sides of their thoraxes are usually Ashton blue, but as I think I've noted before, the red or green or brown or even purple female variants make really exciting photographs.

WEDNESDAY, AUGUST 22ND, 1990

About a month to go now. To bed last night determined to get back into action today. Yesterday, someone's car broke down, I offered to help, and almost the whole day went by before everything was sorted. Nearly a whole day wasted. It makes me realize how much I value this time. I arrive at the lake at 7.15am. What a welcome: an idyllic blue calm. The heron still can't get used to us. It gives a very irritated bark when it flies off.

I notice that flies are already buzzing. They do seem to increase in August but perhaps that's good news as all the dragonflies and even the Blue-tailed Damselflies eat them. I sit quietly on an empty fertilizer bag, and am rewarded with the sight of a water rat busying across the mud.

By 9.30am Brown Hawkers and Migrant Hawkers are on the wing and I'm down on my knees again watching another blue damselfly. It has thick blue stripes on the top of its thorax and what looks like a black ball on a stick at the top of its abdomen. So it's a male Common Blue Damselfly (*Enallagma cyathigerum*) and that means we have two species of what are generally lumped together as 'blues' and that they're both still here quite late in the season.

It's very noticeable that the planes have their seasons too. Patterns well established at the start of the Gulf War have now changed. No more gently approaching USAF high altitude reconnaissance TR1 spy planes – better known as Gary Powers U2s – returning to Alconbury, their engine note rising and falling, their long slim wings catching the early morning light. No more midday brutish A10 Tank-busters cruising past, wingtip to wingtip. Today, at 1.00pm, RAF Harriers fly east in groups of twelve, in a series of enormous, ominous roars.

THURSDAY, AUGUST 23RD, 1990

I arrive shortly after 7.00am to an extraordinary Sunday-like silence, long after trucks normally begin to send their dull roar from the Oundle bypass and London-bound planes start to groan across the sky. Are people being careful with fuel? As if to emphasize the unusual stillness, a little sika deer wanders out of the undergrowth, stares, and then disappears again.

Today is one of those days that become so hot and still it's as if the world has been flattened by the blinding sunlight. At 3.00pm my thermometer in the boathouse says it's 25.5°C (78°F) in the shade, but I'm doing transect walks and taking photographs so I'm keen to know what the temperature is in the sunshine. I pick up my replacement weighted water thermometer and put it on top the wall in the sun. I come back after successfully getting a shot of a Migrant Hawker and see the thermometer is reading well over 49°C (120°F). I stare, afraid, at the sky and then realize that the lead wrapping round the thermo is hot enough to fry an egg. In fact the temperature turns out to be a mere 35°C (95°F).

I tidy up the boathouse landing stage and make a lakeside table of logs and planks for us to work on.

SATURDAY, AUGUST 25TH, 1990

It's time for the accounts. Bloody paperwork. I choose to work in the open air at the new table by the lake. Those endless columns of figures to be added and checked seem bearable when the solar-powered calculator really is being run by the sun. I discover that even paying bills is quite acceptable if it's accompanied by birdsong, and, with Kari in the canoe calling out she's seen a Sandpiper and that Black-tailed Skimmers and Red-eyed Damselflies are still scudding about, never has the doing of accounts been so agreeable.

SUNDAY, AUGUST 26TH, 1990

It's late afternoon and Sid the Farm Manager is fishing in the lake. I leave my canoe-borne hunt for exuviae until he reels in and goes back up the hill. I sip beer, watch pigeons taking turns to drink and see a Brown Hawker laying her eggs in the boathouse.

A kingfisher flashes through the evening sunshine. A second one appears and they loop around together. Early bed. A thunderstorm is brewing, I think. Miriam maintains that Ashton gets very bad lightning as it sits on an ironstone ridge. She has a diesel engine mounted in one of the garden sheds, and whenever there's a power-cut, which is frequently, the engine leaps into life with a sudden snarl.

THURSDAY, AUGUST 30TH, 1990

I come across the deer field a little late this morning. After the lightning and rain of last night, it's as if the sky has been washed. The cloudless blue has that ultramarine iridescence that's a feature of Scottish skies. I arrive at the lake with the day's chores chasing each other round my head, only to be brought up yet again by the green serenity. How can I come again and again to this place and somehow never be able to take it for granted? The lake is wearing its Royal Parks green today, that deep, deep colour that could almost be a brown.

The forecasters say it will cloud over. They often do, and it often doesn't, but the knowledge that it might do adds a poignancy, as before, to the sunshine. I've managed to photograph an Emerald Damselfly this morning. I worry once more about the value of these English names. The insect I see through my lens is in no sense emerald. It has a huge splash of copper and a generally blue and black colour scheme, the blue being the sort often found on dragonflies, a type of dull Cambridge blue that reflects not only the hue that reed-leaves take at certain angles, but also the pruinose lustre of sloes. Until this summer I'd never realized just how common sloes are, nor did I fully understand why Victorian writers went in for sloe-eyed maidens. Time to go and get started on Transect Walk 4.

Returning at midday, I'm confronted by a grey squirrel standing on its back legs by the water's edge, contemplating having a drink. It looks thoughtfully at the water and then at me. It gives its chest a scratch with its forepaws, then holds them together as if wringing its hands in indecision. Thirst gets the better of it.

The forecasters were right in the sense that the sky is now full of clouds; but what clouds! Mighty cumulus galleons sailing majestically in formation across the sky. It's been a day of warm breezes and working stripped to the waist.

There's a Migrant Hawker ovipositing in the boathouse today, very intent on her task. Big hawkers clearly like semi-submerged old bits of wood for egg-laying, so I spend some of the afternoon, while Kari clears excess vegetation, putting several soggy logs into the water as ovipositing platforms.

Out in the canoe I spot several 'blues', too quick for me to identify, and two Blue-taileds. So we still have some damselfly action.

The placid weather continues and Kari and I take a moonlit walk, arm in arm, crossing the little footbridge over the Nene, to the Indian Restaurant in Oundle.

Chapter 19

SATURDAY, SEPTEMBER 1ST, 1990

Whilst paying another visit to Ashton Mill, I've spotted another watercraft gathering dust in the rafters of an outbuilding. It's a beautiful blue Canadian-style canoe, lovely curved-up prows at each end, a vessel that could be extremely useful as a working platform in the lake. More sensitive now about boat ownership than during the earlier two-kayak raid, I've made enquiries, and discovered it too belongs to Rosie and have obtained permission to use it.

I borrow the estate office Transit once more, wrestle the canoe down from the rafters, load it aboard the van and set off with the back doors open. The canoe is way too long for the floor-pan of the Transit and the blessed thing sticks out much too far, flexing shockingly as I drive up the long potholed track, gritting my teeth. By some miracle the canoe is still uncracked as the van edges down through the woodland and reaches the lake. I launch the boat immediately and cruise serenely about. A sudden thought: maybe I can use this thing to build some sort of barrier or boom across the water to join up the two sections of the deer fence and keep the deer out, without the aid of lion dung.

SUNDAY, SEPTEMBER 2ND, 1990

Up early, down to the lake with the Fergy and a morning's work restoring shape to the overgrown island close to the east bank. Its bushes have become trees that over the years have tumbled and knotted into the mud, virtually rejoining it to the bank. It's a filthy, smelly task. Sweaty and exhausted, but proud of the result, I set out little log seats for future visitors to admire the newly opened view.

Tea with the family at the mansion, carefully dodging the egg sandwiches, then Kari and I take a bottle of Rully down to the lake, sit on the new seats and celebrate. We watch a massive golden-pink panoply of a sunset, see a Migrant Hawker still hunting in the dusk – crepuscularly foraging, as Philip Corbet would say – and drive the Fergy back up in the moonlight. No sign of the Canada Geese. Good.

MONDAY, SEPTEMBER 3RD, 1990

I head down to the lake for usual weather and emergence checks, then out in the big blue canoe to sit cross-legged, drinking tea, thinking about a water barrier.

To the Chequered Skipper for lunch with Kari and my two Canning work-friends, Nigel and Luz. The pub used to be called the Three Horseshoes, but Miriam renamed it to remind people of a fast-disappearing butterfly. I'd rather assumed the title was something nautical until that was explained to me.

Anyway, Nigel and I tend to get over-excited in each other's company and, gently egged on by Kari and Luz, today is no exception. Behind Nigel's handsome rumbustiously cynical exterior lies a deeply sensitive man. We laugh, drink a great deal of lager and, when the pub closes for the afternoon, go upstairs with Stan the landlord to see his aquaria. We totter out, go down to the lake and, despite warnings from the girls, take to the water in the canoe. Giggling hysterically, we inevitably capsize into the stinking ooze and have to go back to the mansion for baths.

Miriam sends a message that she wants to see me to discuss the collection of reed from Woodwalton Fen. We plan to plant reed in the lake; it attracts dragonflies and Woodwalton has an over-abundance of it. Miriam instantly notices I've been drinking, but confines herself to, 'You're looking tired, dear.' I flee as soon as I can.

TUESDAY, SEPTEMBER 4TH, 1990

The sun is almost setting and I'm sitting in sweater and scarf on the little stile I've made outside the observation hut, having had tea with Miriam and having cleared Canada Geese from the lake once more. I spot a dragonfly and raise my binoculars. What's gone wrong with my eyes? Everything's blurred. Yesterday's drinking spree? I lower the binoculars and swivel my head from left to right: eyesight quite normal. I shake the binoculars and there's a sloshing sound. They're full of water, a casualty from yesterday's boating incident.

Black-tailed Skimmers and Brown Hawkers are still flying; and a mystery hawker dragonfly I'm not sure about. I'm developing my plan for building a barrier across the water. I've found a large number of long heavy logs in the woodland close to the lake. I'm planning to drag them one at a time to the bank, then float them into the lake, rope them together and make a boom.

THURSDAY, SEPTEMBER 6TH, 1990

Sitting on a new log-seat in the north-east corner, it's fairly calm, but the splendid blue sky is full of the wind's roar. Poplars are bending, leaves sparkling in the sun, and the clouds have arranged themselves to look as if a massive locomotive has just puffed across the sky. An RAF Tucano comes spanking over, quick as thought, so low and so smart that I want to give its black paintwork an extra polish.

Today, I've seen Common Darters, Migrant Hawkers, and that tantalizing mystery hawker again. Could it be a Common Hawker (*Aeshna juncea*)? They've been recorded very occasionally at Woodwalton. Common Hawkers prefer acidic water and, during his time with the Nature Conservancy Council, Norman Moore dug peat ponds at Woodwalton Fen and sure enough, Common Hawkers appeared. Their nearest known habitat was forty-six miles away in Norfolk. So it's possible.

There's a link with Woodwalton today, as four tons of Woodwalton reed has been dumped by an unhelpful truck driver on the wrong side of the lake fence, so farmhands Bill and Kenny and Fred Jackson – a new face, Sid's older brother – hear of my predicament and kindly come down to help. Though they're much too polite to say so, their discreet glances at one another reveal that they still think the whole thing is daft. Together we heave the backbreaking reed clumps over the fence and bury them in the mud by the east bank. There's lots of banter, and even more when, job done, I invite them into the observation hut for a couple of beers. After they depart I go back out in the canoe and begin work on the boom, floating the large logs out, but the wind keeps pushing the boat wherever it wants and the logs drift away in different directions.

I go into the observation hut for a rest and turn on the radio I brought down this morning. I find I'm listening to an extremely serious House of Commons debate, how to respond to Iraq's occupation of Kuwait. Julian Amory sounds just like Churchill. Is this the last summer before full-on war, another 1939? Down here, as the sun filters through the wind-dancing trees, it's hard to understand the dudgeon of the voices in distant Westminster.

A Dakota passes overhead, its twin Pratt & Whitneys burbling comfortably, like two big Cadillacs rumbling through the air.

FRIDAY, SEPTEMBER 7TH, 1990

6.00pm. I'm sitting on the bench on the north bank admiring my completed boom. It looks as if it only took a couple of minutes to rig up. No one would know how hard a day it's been. Shunted about by the shifting wind, the canoe has consistently refused to obey my paddle strokes. Time and again the blessed thing washed itself onto the bank with the boom underneath it, and, nudged by endless wavelets, the logs simply would not shift along the rope into their proper positions. Each log seemed to have a mind of its own, and the rope developed sudden underwater knots that have left my hands raw and my body shaking from having to keep the canoe from capsizing as I fumbled about in the chilly ooze. No amount of bad language seemed to solve anything. Nevertheless the boom now lies in an orderly line across the lake, and I feel a great sense of satisfaction. Let's see what the deer think of it.

I become entranced by the acrobatics of four Migrant Hawkers and a Brown Hawker, and it's only now that I realize I haven't even thought about lunch or tea.

SATURDAY, SEPTEMBER 8TH, 1990

What a change from yesterday. It's almost perfectly still. Had I known how calm it would be today I'd certainly have waited to work on the boom. Three robins are singing from different spots here on the north bank. Their songs sound out clear, and the echoes return from the trees beyond as if the lake is a huge pane of glass. The boom is lying calmly in line. No endlessly lapping wavelets or tugging rope. There's a wintry feel today. My hands are cold enough for gloves.

Seated in the canoe, I drift in the reed-fringed inlet we call Warbler Bay, using the paddle as a writing desk. I've been tracking the unidentified dragonfly and now I know it's only a Migrant Hawker; or at least this one is. I'd been hoping for a Common Hawker of course, very easily differentiated by the yellow front edges to its wings. I'm surrounded by gently waving reeds, mud and sun. Two pairs of Common Darters are ovipositing, heedless of the boat.

Miriam invites Kari and me for pre-lunch drinks with various grandees. We end up having lunch with them and then taking several of them down to the lake. Later, buoyed by success, I drive into Oundle to get a bottle of reduced-price champagne, and Kari and I go back down to the observation hut alone and sit in the silence. The bubbles ring like little bells in our glasses.

SUNDAY, SEPTEMBER 9TH, 1990

Two successful transect walks with Kari down at the lake. We catch sight of a large hawker up on the Top Pond and neither of us have time to identify it before it vanishes. So the mystery dragonfly remains.

Up to the mansion for a big family lunch before taking Kari to the station to go back to work. It won't be too long now before I follow her. Part of my heart is sad to see Kari leave, part sinks further at the thought of soon being back at my desk, and part rejoices that I'm still free. I get back to Ashton and take Miriam's grandchildren down to the lake, sitting on hay bales I've mounted in the trailer. Older children go out in the kayaks. As the sun sets, we have a barbeque, and everyone seems to enjoy the adventure.

MONDAY, SEPTEMBER 10TH, 1990

I work my way through a small mountain of data, laboriously type it all up, then head off down to the lake to attack a large willow that has slumped over into the water. It's been a week or two since I last indulged in this sort of work and I find I've already forgotten how back-breaking being a human winch is. My waders sink deeper and deeper into the ooze as I heave, the branches seem glued to the mud and salty sweat momentarily blinds me.

Later, armed with a sandwich, I cycle off for the transect walk by the River Nene. Walk dutifully completed, I select a lovely view looking downriver for my little picnic and settle down. Then an enormous Massey-Ferguson 365 grinds into the field behind me, lowers its plough and settles into a steady ear-splitting roar. I refuse to turn my head again, gaze at stunning serenity and wish I had earplugs.

Chapter 20

TUESDAY, SEPTEMBER 11TH, 1990

Dragonfly work is constantly interrupted by intriguing aircraft today. Apart from the usual low-flying Tornados and Tucanos, I watch four old Canberras in tight formation and several squadrons of ageing Buccaneers. Is this war? Ancient planes? Oh dear.

I'm contacted by Trevor Lawson, writing for the *Daily Telegraph*, asking for information about the Dragonfly Sanctuary. I worry about boring the poor man to death, but he assures me he's a keen environmentalist and we have a very long conversation.

I collect Kari from the station and we drive to the Haycock at Wansford to plan for Saturday, Dragonfly Day. Discreet persuasion has worked. For years, Miriam has had a summer party, almost always with an entomological or scientific theme, to which the great and the good from both these worlds are invited. This year, she has declared it Dragonfly Day and asked the British Dragonfly Society to come along, too. The lake and the observation hut must look their best. Kari organizes Peter Mayhew and Marcella, daughter of one of the estate tenants, come to help us prepare for Saturday. We fold leaflets and laugh.

SATURDAY, SEPTEMBER 15TH, 1990

I wake worried about the day; there are still so many details to take care of. It's not butterflies in my tummy, it's dragonflies.

Norman Moore arrives early and we go down to the lake for a preview. He's pleased with what he sees. Reassured, I accompany him back to the house and we greet members of the BDS for a very grand lunch. Miriam has organized *glühwein*; several visitors clearly have not tasted this before and do not realize its potency. After lunch, Jill Silsby, the stately BDS Secretary, makes a nice speech and congratulates us. There's a great deal of clapping, and then we all troop down to the lake for a tour round. Back to the mansion for a big tea, during which I learn that there's an extremely good article about our efforts in today's *Daily Telegraph*. Thank you, Trevor Lawson.

Later, guests departed, I leave what has morphed into a family dinner. Full of claret, I walk alone down to the lake and in rather too flowing a scrawl, write:

> *There's a red biplane above me*
> *Enjoying the bright blue sky*
> *Twisting and diving like fury*
> *Flying as high as high.*
> *I've got the ground below him*
> *As he's got the sky above,*
> *But I've got the glint of the sun on the grass*
> *And the curving views I love.*

I've written poetry ever since I was fifteen, even had stuff published, not that this is poetry; it's just happiness.

MONDAY, SEPTEMBER 17TH, 1990

Is my final sabbatical week here already? The weather corresponds to my dark grey mood. After a turgid morning worrying about overdue bills and a mounting overdraft, phoning and placating bureaucrats at the bank, officials at the electricity company and car-licensing Welshmen in Swansea, and, I'm now in the middle of emergence data analysis. Do we have any correlation between our main weather observations and dragonfly emergence? Trying to plot all the graphs onto a single all-encompassing sheet is painstaking, eye-straining, and very exciting. Initially, things look promising. But I remember Miriam's words about scientific data: 'God always sends the good results first.'

Nope. She was right. Here I am, in the observation hut, much later, tired and blurry, having missed a golden evening outside, and the collated data hasn't really proved anything. There's a pattern of greater emergences when the days are longer but that's pretty obvious. It's a strange anticlimactic sort of feeling. I understand how important the data is in itself, but it's sad I'm not able to show anything really useful. Tonight, like this morning, is now dim and mournful. I'm very depressed. Earlier in the year I'd have gone off for a drink at the Chequered Skipper, but the prospect of conversation is too much.

Tomorrow, I'll see if the temperature data shows anything.

TUESDAY, SEPTEMBER 18TH, 1990

The moment I wake, I notice the trees have changed to autumn colours. After working all morning on the temperature data, no luck; it just corresponds to air temperature, again pretty obvious. So. Day length and air temperature. That's it.

Lunchtime: I think I do need a pub after all. I decide to have a last visit to the one at Fotheringhay. What tips the scales is leaving the observation hut briefly and noticing that the rain has cleared away, leaving the thistles and burdock looking clean and bright. The view from the ridgeway will be terrific.

It's a glorious cycle-ride, and, though it's not very long before afternoon closing-time, I can't help stopping along one of the woodland paths. There are dragonflies, almost all Darters but a few Migrant Hawkers too, about one every foot. As I cycle onwards I get that wonderful, slightly acidic smell of damp beech leaves so reminiscent of Perthshire. I still have a few days left; I shout for joy at my freedom and gaze down at the green and brown Nene valley spread out map-like below.

When I arrive at the pub I'm wearing my binoculars and my monocular. 'What are you spotting? Birds?' asks a local. 'No,' I say, 'dragonflies.' Suddenly everybody has something to contribute.

Have I been to Ashton? Of course, they say, that's the place for dragonflies. Do I know about the Dragonfly Sanctuary? And so on. I'm very surprised. I didn't imagine the *Telegraph* article would have been read by so many people. Apparently the local paper has run an article too.

The upshot is that the beer sparkles and the conversation does too, insofar as it can on the subject of dragonflies. The pub closes, and on the way home I buy tomatoes and a pork pie in Warmington as a gesture towards lunch, ride back along the dragonfly path, and after munching my pie, lie back in the grass and doze off. When I wake up at 5.15pm, dragonflies are darting about over my head.

WEDNESDAY, SEPTEMBER 19TH, 1990

Today really is an autumn day. The rain overnight has brought life back to the grass. The lake is rising again and all the leaves are silver in the pale sunlight. My body may be hungover from all that Abbott Ale but, worse, my heart is terrified about next week. I must strive for a lasting escape. I can't go on loathing wasted acres of my life. I know I can get on fine with all sorts of people, and I know I can do something more acceptable to my conscience than helping people do business better, but my secret dream of effortlessly finding some simple way forward has not materialized. I think of René Buser and his words to me in the Kensington Palace Hotel: 'Canning will be, how to say, a step-stone?' Something will happen. Maybe.

I have tea with Miriam then go and collect Kari from the station. On Sunday we'll go back to London together.

FRIDAY, SEPTEMBER 21ST, 1990

I've just been sitting on the bench in the cold wind. The lake looks as if it's trying to get rid of me. Choppy little wavelets and a steel grey sheen. Almost-black clouds are speeding across an operatic sky. There's little to be done now save humdrum packing. I think we must perform a final ceremony this evening.

When my father died in Perthshire last year, among other

things Kari and I toasted him with champagne and flung the empty bottle into the Lyon, the river he and my mother loved. This evening Kari and I will throw a bottle into the lake. If it's sunny – the weatherman says it might be – maybe a few late Migrant Hawkers will attend.

I didn't expect to find myself grieving for the loss of a way of life. As someone from the BDS said to me last Saturday, 'Whatever happens to you now, you can't really go back to where you were before.'

SUNDAY, SEPTEMBER 23RD, 1990

7.00am. As I come down the deer field the Polebrook church clock strikes, like a valediction in the cold still air. The sky in the east is a classic shepherd's warning red. Up high, parts are rippled white against the patches of blue. Moving below the great cirrus panorama of gold bars and silver anvils are smaller clouds of pale pink smoke. A few rooks wheel for a moment, then head west.

It's my birthday but I feel like a condemned man. As I reach the lake, the pigeons rise one by one. It's impossible for a human to arrive at the lake unannounced; pigeons always lift a warning. I see coots scuttling from the Top Pond, and freeze as I catch sight of the heron, ghost white, standing near the island in the lake. It looks as if it's standing on the water. It flaps away slowly with its usual single irritated squawk.

At dawn now, the birds are quieter than in May and June, and here at the lake, whilst there are still wrens and robins singing, they're working against quiet snickering and whooping of starlings. A hare has just glanced through the open door into the observation hut then loped easily off across the corduroy curves of the ridge-and-furrough.

Today after lunch I will don the mask once more, the mask of commercial man of action. Well, now I know that for me it is a mask. I leave the observation hut, sit down on the bench close to the scented briar and look across the lake. The myriad of greens is now well mixed with reds, yellows and browns. I gaze up into the one remaining patch of blue.

I am faced with hard work and little money from now until next April at least. Has it really been worth it?

I've hit my targets. We have a Dragonfly Sanctuary. We have substantial data on dragonflies at Ashton. We've made some solid contributions to the body of knowledge on dragonflies. We'll write a scientific paper on inverted emergence in Blue-tailed Damselflies.

I've learned a great deal about myself and how I work. I don't need a boss or a timetable to make me work hard. I feel that for the first time in my life I've begun to make a small but tangible contribution to … to what? Something other than business, certainly. Conservation? That's a big word. To something, anyway, something out of the ordinary, something that might in future put other people into a different frame of mind. I've been in close contact with beings that have been on Earth for about 350 million years. Now it's time to go back to what most people consider as real work, but what for me now seems less important. That's a very big change.

I've been poisoned, and it's dragonflies that have poisoned me. They're flowing in my blood.

Part Three

Flying Free

1990 - 1993

Chapter 21

By the time we arrived from London in the wintry dimness of yesterday afternoon, it was too late to go down to the lake. This morning, it's a still, sunlit start. We head downhill and sense a welcome. But soon it clouds over and turns chill, as if to remind us that the magic time is finished, and we return to the mansion where Miriam shows us albums of the house in 1914. I thank her for my birthday present; she's taken the trouble to go through Blythe's *History of Haiku, Vol II,* and dig out nine Japanese dragonfly ones for me. My three favourites are:

> *The dragonflies*
> *All flying in the same direction*
> *In the rays of the setting sun*
>   RANGAI 1758–1831

> *Indian summer;*
> *How rarely the dragonflies come –*
> *Their shadow on the window pane*
>   SHIKI 1867–1902

> *Alighting on my shoulder,*
> *It seems to long for human society,*
> *This red dragonfly*
>   KOYO 1867–1903

Unable to keep away, I go down to the lake again intending to do some sawing, and find dragonflies are out in force in the fitful sunshine: large numbers of Common Darters, many ovipositing, sometimes three pairs at a time; and at least three Migrant Hawkers are still in action. By luck I've brought my camera and I get several good shots.

The kingfisher's back. I hear it first, its bosun's whistle, then, over where diamonds sparkle on the surface in the north-east corner, I see a movement, a flash of spray in the sunlight, and a glimpse of orange as it returns to its perch.

I keep making moves to go but the sun on my skin pushes me to stay. Finally it clouds over again, and as the sun disappears, so do the dragonflies. And so, I guess, will I. Work back in London is back to its usual frenetic pace and it's too far to bring the children just for a weekend, all the way from Surrey. I take a last look at the lake that has brought me so much, then turn away.

FRIDAY, NOVEMBER 16TH, 1990

Eight weeks back at Canning have taken the smile from my face and the spring out of my step. I've become immersed in all the frenetic banalities, to the point where I've started to think they're important again. A final week of intensive one-to-one training with a semi-autistic German urea trader has brought me to my knees. I've been waking to the sound of early-morning delivery vehicles machine-gunning down Holland Park Avenue and finding my body aquiver.

I keep the smile on my face as I bid the German client goodbye, then cycle through busy Friday evening traffic to Euston station. Kari wants to stay in London to get two miniatures finished so I don't feel too bad. I've booked a berth on the night sleeper to Pitlochry and I'm not due back at work until next Wednesday lunchtime. Off to my cottage in Perthshire, I'm lightly loaded and feel strangely, almost suspiciously free. I keep wondering if I've left things behind.

Once in Pitlochry I find myself alone on the platform as the train eases cautiously out of the station and up the icy gradient northwards, finally becoming just a single flashing red light, fading round the curve. I breathe in, and jump for joy. John Masters described the air in parts of India and California as being like champagne. At 7.00am on this dark November morning, it's like that here. Again I get that feeling of uneasy freedom. What have I forgotten? Why do I need so little? I think of the Sufi remark that, when you feel like this, you've probably only forgotten yourself.

The twisty, hilly back road from Pitlochry to Logierait is all mine in the dawn. Lorries thunder along the A9 on the other side of the valley but I cycle – often with great effort – in peace. At Strathtay Post Office, I find the shop already doing a brisk trade in morning papers. Retired folk walk in from the village; younger, busier ones come and go in vans. Meanwhile I pack, unpack, and try to repack my groceries. A smiling lady asks me if I've bought too much. I'm secretly worried as I grin at her and say I think I've judged it to a nicety. Eventually it's all either in the front pannier or on my back, and I'm off again.

By now Strathtay is bathed in brilliant sunshine; the river, the woods, the hills, the grand mansions, everything in the sharpest, calendar-picture focus. I resist the temptation to stop to see friends on the way. I'm just another cyclist slipping quietly past. I turn into my glen, see the three mountains behind capped with snow, and find my home quietly waiting for me.

TUESDAY, NOVEMBER 20TH, 1990

I'm sitting outside my cottage in the sunshine, mentally girding myself for tonight's great trip through the darkness. It's always the same here in Scotland. I never want to go back to London and the whole of the last day is spent secretly mourning. But today, lots of gardening, a hearty lunch, and this sunlit moment, have partially numbed the pain. I'll be back in misery soon enough, so I might as well enjoy the heart-stopping mountain panorama of sloping yellow bars and black shadows. The shadow from the standing stone in front of me, like a huge sundial, tells me that it won't be long on this winter day, so near the solstice, before the sun slips behind the Culdaremore hills to the west.

It's been a beautiful break. Saturday, the ride here, tea with Georgie and Donald MacGregor (Donald's the local joiner), a settling-in sort of afternoon with a visit to our favourite pool on the River Lyon, a hike up Ben Dearg (pronounced 'Jerrich') and a view of a pale gold raincloud lying over the waters of Loch Tay. Saturday evening's supper with Barbara and Jimmie Stewart's family, Sunday's trip up the glen to chat to Vernon, the Postmaster at Bridge of Balgie. Monday's ride into stop-every-minute-to-talk to-someone-else Aberfeldy to buy an electric blanket; I've never slept alone here before so never previously felt the need for one. And walking in the woodland behind the cottage, thinking hard.

It's time now to get back on my bike and pedal twenty-two miles through the darkness to Pitlochry station. I'm leaving with one thing firmly fixed in my head: I've got to find a way to make enough money to look after my kids and yet to spend more time among dragonflies.

THURSDAY, DECEMBER 24TH, 1990

Christmas Eve. It's late afternoon and I'm in the observation hut. I'm writing up a summary of all we've done here at the lake during the year and what needs doing next year before we open to the public. Once it's complete, I'll drive back to London. Have we done something courageous? I suppose we have. Alan Bennett once described cheek as being 'in the other ranks of courage'. Perhaps our efforts are at the back of the same squad, too.

I push aside a note that says, "Miriam: Professor EB Ford saw a dragonfly seize a moth, a Scarlet Tiger, only to look down and release it. The moth was quite unharmed. It's a very smelly insect." I wonder if dragonflies have chemoreceptors? On their antennae, perhaps? I'm not sure any work has been done on that. There's still so much we don't know.

It's almost too dark to see.

Chapter 22

SUNDAY, JANUARY 12TH, 1991

Our first visit to Ashton this year. I go down to the lake by myself and sit quietly amid distant noise: shotguns and bells, banging and ringing in the sunshine. Closer, I hear rooks, chaffinches. A woodpecker raps above my head. Suddenly, unmistakably, comes the brief trumpeting of an elephant. I cock my head and listen carefully. It doesn't happen again. Am I going nuts? I think carefully about the direction of the noise, replaying it in my head: somewhere on the far side of Polebrook. I set off, if only to be sure of my sanity. Camped for the winter in a field on the other side of the village, I find a circus, and through the bushes I glimpse my elephant.

There's little to do except repair the damaged iris plant-pen, hit by a fallen willow, and mend some of the holes in the thatch walls of the observation hut. The thatched roof of the boathouse is now in terrible condition and several of the roof timbers are exposed. They'll rot if not protected.

The lake is much fuller, at least two feet higher. I'm concerned that it'll burst its banks again as it did years ago. Kari comes down with her sieve and guddles for larvae; unsuccessfully.

FRIDAY, JANUARY 25TH, 1991

I sit with fellow Canning School departmental heads in a sun-filled training room overlooking Olympia station. We have no participants whatever. The recession has been bad enough but, now that Britain is at war with Iraq, no major foreign company is prepared to permit their employees to fly here. We've suddenly been inundated with cancellations and have no business. At all. We hadn't realized, until this week, that our income depends entirely on safe aviation. What a pity the Channel Tunnel isn't finished yet.

We sit and ponder how else we can make money during this conflict, coming as it does in the middle of a serious recession. I share our collective fear; we all have families, houses, financial commitments. Yet I have a curious sense of detachment, almost a wish that we'll be forced to close down. Or become smaller. Perhaps I might be able to work part-time. Dragonflies beckon.

SUNDAY, MARCH 17TH, 1991

Our business is back to normal; people are flying again, as cheer-fully – or cheerlessly – as they did before Saddam Hussein was ever heard of. But I'm under a horrid black cloud. A couple of weeks ago, during a routine health check-up, they found some-thing, and now they want to do a testicular biopsy. I already knew what the grim word 'biopsy' meant, and I've been through the possible outcomes with the specialist. Apparently I may, just may, have to face the worst. 'Hope for the best, prepare for the worst.' But how to prepare for the worst? 'Keep calm and carry on.' These platitudes suddenly develop real meaning. I catch myself saying 'concentrates the mind' quite a bit. Because it does. There's not much Kari can do, but she hugs me whenever she sees I need it, which is more often than I realize.

At the Sanctuary, there are toads everywhere, mostly in pairs. It's raining hard and the lake is still horribly high with more water pouring in from the Top Pond above. The west bank, the origi-nal dam that created the lake, is in serious danger of giving way and emptying the whole thing into the village of Polebrook below. Why isn't there an overflow to take excess water away, just as in a bathtub? Even if there's nothing now, surely there must have been some sort of arrangement when the lake was constructed? Though of course there have been changes since then, I can see no sign of any overflow anywhere on the west bank.

I check the south bank. The layout of the rough-cut stones along the water's edge changes at one point, with two neatly carved end-pieces about six feet apart and a stoneless soil-filled space between. I've wondered about this gap in the stonework before. It's difficult to see what the intention was, as there's a substantial earth mound built up over and behind it. With the rain hissing on the water beside me, and the lake level still rising, I consider whether this is the original overflow, now buried. I think back to what I've been told and remember that in the Seventies when the lake was dredged, the dragline operator simply dumped the spoil on the south bank. I set to work, digging between the end-pieces. I hit stone; and again; and again, and gradually unearth a set of beautiful, gently-sloping flagstones, a perfect overflow. Through rain and sweat-blurred glasses I gaze at the mound behind; it's going to be a massive job to dig through it and set the overflow working again. But I might as well start now. Keep calm, carry on. Next week I go into hospital.

Noga Arikha, delicate super-intelligent gifted academic daughter of well-known artist Avigdor, comes down from the mansion to help. She stands shovelling mud, grinning, as rain pours onto her thin arms.

SUNDAY, APRIL 7TH, 1991

I'm down at the lake again. A year ago today, we built the WWF fence. I think it's fair to say we've achieved quite a bit since then, although I've hardly worked at anything since my two grisly Hammersmith Hospital operations. They've taken bits out of me, done something slightly wrong it seems, given me another operation and put me back together, but I'm still very wobbly.

It was just under a fortnight between the final operation and the result of the tests. Every morning I'd wake up, then remember. Facing the prospect that they'd say it was not good news, I'd selected the analogy of red light/green light. I decided that, were it to be a red light, I'd leave Canning immediately to spend as much time as possible with Kari and my children and working for dragonflies. When the call eventually came, and it was a green light, I put the phone down, breathed, stared out the window, then wondered why, just because I'd got good news, I was still at my desk. Of course small details like earning money came to mind, but at that moment something became very clear. Time to seek a way out. Not just the part-time escape I'd secretly hoped for back in January, or the vague determination I'd had up in Scotland.

Here at the lake, so much has changed in these last three weeks. No toads at all now, again. And the Canada Geese – plus three Greylag – are back in force. I drive them all off. One female has a nest on the bigger of the two islands. We decide on a cull. Kari climbs into a kayak and removes four of the seven eggs. She leaves three, two of which look damaged.

Last year I cleared a fallen poplar, leaving bare earth, and Kari made a little pen around the spot wondering what might appear. Where does her extraordinary instinct come from? It really must be genetic. We now have a fine show of white violets, and Kari settles down to produce a perfect little miniature painting of them. There's lots of other new growth too. Three of our plant pens are full of exciting things, some mysterious, but Marsh Marigold is in flower already and the water lilies are looking healthy.

I have today (gingerly; I'm still waddling rather than walking) finished laying steps down to the boathouse. Let's hope they bed in before the summer.

The overflow is working well. I won't congratulate myself too much until it dries up, which will hopefully be soon, as the Top Pond has stopped sending water down into the lake. I'm glad I trusted the original designers. It seems they had it perfectly organized. How they would have cursed that Seventies dragline man.

Kari mends the fence in the plant pen nearest the boathouse.

SUNDAY, APRIL 14TH, 1991

Miriam is in Rome, and Catharine and Richard with us again. So much springtime activity to point out to them: Kari spots Mandarin Ducks in the trees on the west bank. There are millions of toadpoles – I don't know if that's their proper name, but that's what we call toad tadpoles – in Warbler Bay. We now have Fringed Waterlily, Greater Pondweed and Marsh Marigold growing outside their pens, a sure sign that the Canadas are surrendering. Up in the garden by the mansion there are Oxslips, Cowslips and Pasque Flowers, and we count six grass snakes in the lily pond.

The children meet Simon Marks. He's a Marks of Marks and Spencer and he's staying with his family in the village. He's a large man with dark mad-professor hair. He's very clever and kind, and the children love the fact that, like Miriam, he talks to them as if they're adults.

SUNDAY, APRIL 21ST, 1991

The overflow is dry and the lake has stopped leaking. There's a grass snake here at the lake now. Kari and I rage at a coot that skips into one of the plant pens, munches a few shoots, climbs the wire and flies off again. We construct another pen to protect the Greater Pondweed, and thread coot-deterrent string across the tops of all the pens.

Resting in the observation hut afterwards, Kari tells me she's calculated she can afford to go properly part-time at Canning if the company allows her to. How I wish I could do the same. As we walk back up to the mansion, snow falls.

SUNDAY, MAY 5TH, 1991

Supper last night with Miriam and Noga. One of the shelties, Tango, isn't well, but Miriam still hummed happily while fetching us what she calls chocolate 'sludge'. In response to my worries about the state of the roof-timbers of the boathouse, she tells us they plan to cover its roof with polythene and pig shit. I'm delighted to hear the roof is to be protected but I'm not sure about the pig shit. I don't say so.

I weed around our butterfly-attracting buddleias, and strim round the observation hut and along the paths round the lake. Yesterday I brought down a boot scraper, a great stone block with elaborate metalwork set in it, which I'd found dumped among garden rubbish. I manhandled it off the Fergy trailer, heaved it over the style and set it outside the observation hut. It will save a great deal of sweeping up dried mud inside.

WEDNESDAY, MAY 15TH, 1991

1.30pm. I've come straight down here after a good drive up from London. The boathouse is now sheathed in polythene. The lads have done a fair job but they've left a lot of tidying up to do and have burned a big hole in the clearing, but we now have a dry boathouse. And no sign of pig shit.

I'm bombarded with aircraft. In about half an hour, a Jet Provost, a Scorpion, a Lynx, two A10s, a massive four-jet transport and three Tornadoes, one in its Gulf pink. It's lucky I now like modern planes.

The heron has come to perch in a tree opposite, and a tern is back, too, not Broken Wing but a tern nevertheless, doing the same circling, circling, circling, squawk and dive. And here's a cock mandarin, no, two.

I've just crossed my legs for the first time in eight weeks.

THURSDAY, MAY 16TH, 1991

Another trip from London. No sooner arrived than we come down to the lake and see our first damselfly of the year, a Blue-tailed. Kari finds and identifies an exuvia of the same species.

I've spotted a spare door lying against the wall in the wood-cutting shed up in the gardens. I obtain permission to uplift it, take it down the lake, fit it into the boathouse doorway, and screw on a lock. The Canadian canoe and the two kayaks are now relatively secure. A wren, nesting in the boathouse, nips untroubled in and out under the new door.

We now have at least ten species – dragonflies and damselflies – at the lake. So the dragonfly part of our aim is achieved. Now it's time to think about how to get people here. Miriam's in favour of allowing visitors in, but she's unsure how I'll manage it without letting over-curious folk wander into the family's private areas. She's rightly very sensitive about this.

Whilst walking along the western perimeter between the lake and Polebrook, in among the undergrowth in the north-west corner, I've found a set of completely rusted gates, part of Charles Rothschild's original lake fencing. Could this be the answer?

Working on the premise that, even it's not, it's always good to have a secondary entrance/exit, I clear a path from a point on the north bank between the boathouse and the observation hut through the fir trees, parallel with the lake to these western gates. It's back-breaking work, sawing broken branches, hacking through brambles, filling in old rabbit holes and levering fallen tree-trunks out of the way, but it brings a great moment when I borrow bolt-cutters, snap an ancient chain and open the gates wide. And I'm triumphant when, having driven the Citroën Dyane round through Polebrook and up the small track that leads into the field adjoining the lake, I finally – bouncing wildly, then halting and standing up occasionally to check on clearances from the open roof – thread the car, jeep-like, down Fir Avenue from gates to lake. Kari is up at the mansion working on a painting. I drag her down to the lake to see what I've done.

This is all a bit of an act of faith as no permission for visitors has yet been given, but at least it will demonstrate an obvious entry. It's now possible for future visitors to come up the track, park in the field and walk to the gates and into the Sanctuary, but it will need a great deal of diplomacy to persuade the family and the farm to agree to this idea.

Kari and I have tea with Miriam and tell her we've just seen six Père David's fawns; she says she knows about them and two of them are twins, very rare. She tells us that Ann and Tony Cook's Wildfowl and Wetland site at Peakirk is to close. There's an attempt to stop it happening. She's worried about her eyesight but pleased with the reviews of her new book. And she's interested in my plan for an entrance through Polebrook. Very good news.

I go back down to the lake and titivate Fir Avenue until 9.00pm.

SATURDAY, MAY 18TH, 1991

It's time to set a date for opening to the public. The best time to see adult dragonflies in action is typically the last two weeks in July and the first two weeks in August. I take a deep breath and propose Saturday the 27th of July. Miriam agrees.

Chris Newbold, the Nature Conservancy Council's Chief Advisor on Freshwater Spaces, comes to look at what we've been doing. We're nervous. Small, square and dapper, sipping tea in the library before heading down to the lake, he's very pessimistic. He suggests that in order to get a good variety of water plants it might be best to mud-pump the lake first. £30,000 anyone? But when he sees what we've done he changes his view, says several times how impressed he is, loves our plant pens and says we ought to make them larger. He suggests more plants for us to put in, and recommends removal of the bright red ornamental waterlily. Not native. Shame. I think I'll maybe forget that particular piece of advice. I really like that red waterlily. It's like the classic dot of red in a landscape painting.

The water in the lake has never been clear and so we talk about turbidity. He doesn't have an answer, but I think back to the River Welland. I was born a few yards from it and as a child looked out at it every morning from my bedroom window. Tidal in those days, it always looked like coffee with not enough milk. The lake's the same.

Chris suggests we might think of Canada Geese as managers of possibly invasive plants. He admits that what we have done surprises him and he didn't think it would have been possible. We're lucky, he says, and we've obviously worked hard. We go out in the canoe and Chris measures turbidity – muddy and mobile, well we knew that – and also establishes that the lake has a pH balance of 7.9. The Top Pond is 7.5. So it's alkaline water, not acidic. Quite a few dragonflies like acidic water, which is why they prefer the north and west of Britain; and which is why the Golden-ringed Dragonflies that grace our garden in Scotland will be unlikely to show up here.

Kari shows Chris a water ladybird; they pore over it while I work out what else we need to ask him. Then we go for lunch at the Chequered Skipper.

SATURDAY, JUNE 1ST, 1991

We arrive in time for me to take visitors, including John from the Peterborough Conservation Volunteers, round the lake and to plan for what work the volunteers will do on the 30th of June. This has made me think; it would be very good to have our own team of dragonfly volunteers here. John, an entomologist, picks up a beetle, very bronze, and squeezes it. Red pustules come out of its side.

Later, back up at the flat, we plan the layout of the British Dragonfly Society's stand at the forthcoming *Sunday Times* Wildlife and Conservation Exhibition at Olympia. We'll need to write simple texts, get dragonfly photographs enlarged and buy several tons of Letraset and Pritt Stick.

SUNDAY, JUNE 2ND, 1991

We go down to the lake and look carefully at the plant pens. I spot damselfly exuviae in both the Fringed Waterlily and the Greater Pondweed pens. Hawk-Eye Kari, who has been identifying new plants and making notes, sets to work in among the pens – it involves clambering over the rabbit fencing into black mud that oozes over the tops of her wellingtons – and finds twenty damselfly exuviae, of which seven are upside down. Here is clear evidence that our pens are good for dragonflies. And that inverted emergence is not exceptional.

Miriam, unwell, stays in her room and we don't see her all weekend.

FRIDAY, JUNE 28TH, 1991

It's the start of the *Sunday Times* Wildlife and Conservation Exhibition at Olympia. Kari and I, and Kari's sister Berit, over from New York, have spent three virtually sleepless nights gluing Letraset texts and large photographs onto great sheets of white foam board. Now we have to manoeuvre them over the footbridge of Olympia station, there being no parking for us minor exhibitors nearer, apparently. We're joined by Jill and Ronnie Silsby, the British Dragonfly Society's Secretary and Treasurer respectively, and by Kay Medlock and Ray Thompson, Society volunteers. I haven't met Ray before. He's a doctor and he looks formidably severe, but he's devoted to dragonflies and soon reveals a terrific sense of humour and a penchant for champagne. The stand looks great and attracts a lot of attention.

Kari gets agreement that she can go part-time, three days a week now, and I receive the final all-clear on the cancer front. I really am free of that awful black cloud now. Why am I still at Canning?

SUNDAY, JULY 14TH, 1991

As I approach the lake, two young stoats, playing tag with each other on the short grass near the boathouse, catch sight of me and shoot into the undergrowth. The air above the north bank is heaving with dragonflies. There are dozens of Red-eyed Damselflies scooting round the fringed waterlilies, more Black-tailed Skimmers above them than I can count, and three Brown Hawkers zoom up and down the water's edge, gliding briefly from time to time. There's so much movement and so many individuals whirling and turning it's impossible to see all the action at once. I think of the dog-fights in the sky over Kent in 1940.

Kari joins me, notes the continued emergence of upside-down Blue-tailed Damselflies and finds a lovely beetle with amazingly long antennae, a longicorn with a splendid name, *Agapanthea*.

I select a tall, slim pine trunk, blown down in a gale, lop off its branches, attach a pulley and rope, and erect it as a mast by the gates in the north-west corner of the reserve by the rusty gates. I cut the back out of my old red shirt and hoist it as a flag.

SATURDAY, JULY 21ST, 1991

Today is Dragonfly Day. Following last year's splendid party, Miriam has decided to repeat the operation, only this time at a better moment for seeing dragonflies. She has agreed that we can invite the British Dragonfly Society once more.

I'm up early in the sunshine and, scruffily dressed, go down to the observation hut to make sure everything is absolutely ready and to give the place a last sweep. Trailing back up, I almost run into the first elegantly dressed guests who have arrived far too early. I hide behind a wall.

Catharine and Richard are here again and it's lovely that they've mucked in with the preparations. They appear now, looking very smart, and, while Miriam plies champagne (touching none herself) and talks to the steady trickle of arriving visitors, Richard and I take a walk round the garden to try and calm down.

Kari has designed and organized a consignment of Ashton Water Dragonfly Sanctuary sweatshirts, powder blue, with a Migrant Hawker emblazoned on the front. She and Berit have spent weeks on their creation, production and delivery. They look a great deal better than the lurid yellow BDS jobs. We present one to Peter Mayhew.

We all parade down to the lake, a small army of chattering grandees and enthusiasts. My diary says I accompany someone very important called Fink but all recollection of him has sadly disappeared. The sun has gone and the temperature has dropped; it's now dull and unpromising, and we see very few dragonflies. Here's one of the chief problems with these insects: they vanish if there's no sun. It's one of the issues we're going to have to face when the public arrives; how to explain a disappearing product, surely a headache that most organizations don't have to deal with.

We go back up to lunch. It's a vast affair, everyone serving themselves and finding a space where they can. The dining room is full to bursting, both tables crammed, and people spill out into the library to sit on sofas and perch in window seats with plates on their knees. Château la Cardonne flows freely. I drink three glasses of it and sit talking with two greats of the dragonfly world, Philip Corbet and Steve Brooks.

After lunch those of us sober and energetic enough go down to the lake once more but it's still no good and we head, rather quieter, back up for tea. Guests depart and the evening morphs once more into a family gathering, including Kari's cousin, Lionel. He has a disturbing habit of looking over your left shoulder as he talks to you, but what he says holds your attention.

One of the people staying in the mansion is Gunnar Bergstrom, an expert on gas chromatography. He has the slightly grey complexion common to many Swedes. I've worked a great deal with Swedish people and don't usually find them enormously amusing but, next day as we walk in the woods together, Gunnar makes me roar. He tells me he was in charge of a weather station on the island of Oland at the time of the first moonwalks. Fascinated, he constructed a harness and attached himself to three weather balloons to mimic the effect of walking with moon-level gravity. He had a tremendous time, floating across fields, leaping over hedges and so on, but, 'I had forgotten the wind.'

A Scandinavian pause: 'And I had forgotten I was on a little island.'

SATURDAY, JULY 27TH, 1991

Today's the day. Our first day open to the public. I get up at 5.00am, leave Kari and the kids to sleep a little longer, make sandwiches, and head down to the lake in the Dyane, loaded with Dragonfly Sanctuary sweatshirts. I drive round to Ashton and Polebrook, put up big signs, then go back down to the Sanctuary and raise the red shirt-flag. Our signs tell visitors to park in the far corner of the field and walk to the red flag. We open at 10.00am and by 10.05am, three cars have already arrived. Lots of visitors and I'm kept busy all day showing people around and extolling the wonders of dragonflies, who kindly perform exactly to order. A cameraman appears but goes before I can catch him.

Miriam has asked me to read something out to visitors:

"Firstly I would like to tell you how extremely disappointed I am, because I cannot be here today to show you some of the flowering hayfields I have created during the last thirty years and at the same time launched what I call 'The Wildflower Movement' in this country. But I have had to go to a meeting at London Zoo where, where, as President of the Entomological Society, I have been asked to advise on the creation of a new insect house – or rather houses.

"I need hardly remind you that Ashton saw the birth of the Society for the Promotion of Nature Reserves, the brainchild of

Charles Rothschild who lived here from 1900 until 1923 and redesigned and rebuilt Ashton village. I feel the Dragonfly Sanctuary, which is essentially a recreated habitat reserve, is in the tradition of the SPNR and the RSNC.

"Ashton has been famous for its butterflies. I fancy there are only two other areas in the UK which can boast of forty-six species of butterfly actually caught in such a small area, about 500 acres of mixed woodland. I hope the dragonflies will do as well, too."

Apart from local people, two colleagues from Canning in London show up, and Kay Medlock and Ray Thompson come armed with champagne. Between tours round, they sit me down and force drink on me. Peter Scott comes down and says we've been on Anglia TV. Which explains the cameraman.

At the end of each tour, I ask for donations to our work – money for petrol, paint, tools etc – and plead for volunteer help. If anyone is interested could they please put their names and addresses in the Visitors' Book. Among others, a couple put their names down: she's large and quiet, he's thin, young, bearded, bespectacled, enthusiastic, with a ready laugh and a London accent. He says he's already rung Miriam and wants to help. I make a note to contact them; then, unbelievably, forget.

When everyone has gone, we tot up what's in our wooden donations box, a former two-bottle Graham's Port presentation case, now with a slit cut in the top, screwed to the wall in the observation hut. We've had over a hundred visitors. We've made £40. I discover later that son Richard has secretly contributed 65p. Tomorrow we do it all again.

SUNDAY, JULY 28TH, 1991
150 visitors.

MONDAY, JULY 29TH, 1991
On our way to the lake, Richard and I go down the set of stone steps at the far end of the so-called tennis court, open the little rabbit-wired gate and pause at the lily pond. We watch a fat, blue Broad-bodied Chaser, little lemon crescents down its

abdomen, perch on an iris stem. It leaps into the air, hurtles back and forth, then lands on the same stem, munching a mosquito, as if it had never moved. I'm surprised it's still around. We've been seeing them since May and, bearing in mind that a typical adult dragonfly's life is eight weeks, I expected them all to have gone by now.

Richard goes very still. He's spotted a red dragonfly; it's our first Common Darter of the year. So here we have a species that hangs on until November, flying at the same time as a Broad-bodied Chaser, the first dragonfly species of the Ashton season; they appear in May. Which shows that late July really is a wonderful time to be dragonfly-watching. It sets me thinking: isn't this the time of the year when birds are at their quietest? Perhaps this is a way to involve bird-watchers. Dragonflies are big enough, after all, for birders to spot with their binoculars and telescopes. I'll keep that in mind.

Opposite the lily pond, in the wall bordering the deer field, there's a much bigger gate, a masterpiece of local wrought-iron-work, all curls and swirls. As it squeaks open, we see a fox trotting across the grass with a rabbit in its mouth; it barely gives us a glance. And we watch a hornet – they're so much bigger and scarier than bees – drone noisily in the sunshine among the walnut trees.

TUESDAY, JULY 29TH, 1991

As a result of my publicity efforts, I've been contacted by the BBC. Fantastic. And today a team from the BBC's *Really Wild Show* arrive, including a presenter, Chris Packham, spiky-haired, dressed in a black shirt and immaculate black jeans. Catharine and Richard have seen him on the show and think he's good value, Catharine especially. I know nothing about him and expect fairly banal questions from someone dressed in such a non-naturalist's outfit. Chris skewers me within three seconds with a question about the prolarval stage of dragonflies. Fortunately I know the answer. It takes about ten more seconds before we recognize that, when it comes to natural history, we're both verging on the insane.

We get on fine, even though the high-speed camera that the team has brought struggles to keep pace with the whirling of the dragonflies. We finish up filming in virtual darkness. Catharine gets a ride back up to the house in Chris's car, a lift that adds hugely to her street-cred at school. Chris and I agree to stay in touch.

THURSDAY, AUGUST 1ST, 1991

Miriam has been clearing out her wine cellar. Last night, to our astonishment, she produced a 1964 Moët and a 1918 Sauternes. It was like drinking heaven. This morning, my head is surprisingly clear.

I reach the lake at 6.55am, planning to write up my diary, perhaps just sit quietly for a few minutes, and then do what I've been promising myself for some time, settle down on the north bank bench and have a good read, just like people in novels do beside lakes. I've brought a copy of À la recherche du temps perdu, in translation of course.

Tempted by the stillness and the sunshine blazing through the trees, and perhaps daunted by the prospect of Proust, I decide instead to climb into a willow tree up by the Top Pond to watch how the Père David's deer behave when they think no one's looking. I wait for forty minutes. The only movement comes from pigeons, resettling among the branches. Knowing they're the first things to shift whenever anyone approaches, they feel like camouflage. I hear jays talk to each other, then a couple of tawny owls.

The hinds filter slowly though the trees in ones and twos, picking their way delicately into the water. Two stags appear, both magnificent, one much larger than the other. The bigger beast strides into the pond, stabs his antlers into the mud and throws huge gouts of it up, over, onto his back. The mud glints in the sunshine; gobs of it slide down his hide and slop into the water. He charges at the smaller stag, spray leaping ahead of him. There's a crash of antlers, the smaller one scrambles out of the pond and disappears into the woodland. I settle down to see what happens next, but perhaps the deer sense me, or scent me, and the whole herd lifts uneasily out of the pond and moves off into the trees.

It's now 10.30am, I'm drifting in the canoe, and both the diary and Proust remain untouched. There's a Red-eyed Damselfly on the pretty little yellow Fringed Waterlilies, and, in the middle of trying to photograph it, I look up at the sound of an ancient aero-engine. A Sopwith Camel trundles over.

I've just spotted our first Emerald Damselfly for this year. We now have fifteen species of dragonfly and damselfly at Ashton Water, up from five in 1989. A success, surely.

SATURDAY, AUGUST 3RD, 1991
120 visitors.

SUNDAY, AUGUST 4TH, 1991
140 visitors.

SATURDAY, AUGUST 11TH, 1991
90 visitors. Quite glad to know tomorrow is free and I'll be able just to relax here, although, tomorrow night, it will be the usual endless Sunday-evening crawl back into London. Kari and I are spending a very great deal of time driving up and down from London.

MONDAY, SEPTEMBER 23RD, 1991
My forty-fifth birthday. It's a year since the end of my sabbatical and I've decided to commemorate it by spending a few days sorting things out at the lake.

The early morning radio weather forecaster is droning on about rain while the sun streams in through the bedroom window. I rush out to catch what I imagine to be the last moments of sunshine for the day. It stays a lovely morning and, stripped to the waist, I'm working on the west bank when, over on the east bank, with a huge crash, an entire willow tree falls into the water. I'm still standing startled as, in the sudden silence afterwards, the ripples come sliding over the lake towards me and slap against the bank at my feet.

I'm sitting in the evening sun. I've been watching a female Emperor Dragonfly (*Anax imperator*) egg-laying, pushing her ovipositor into sedge and reed, usually about nine inches above the mud at the side of the lake. It's 6.30pm and Migrant Hawkers are still hovering in the reed bays, about a metre above the water, so different from the way they fly earlier in the season, high up, full of energy, jinking constantly after prey. A rust-red Common Darter lands on my old scarlet shirt. It feels like a blessing. May I be so happy at ninety. But, as Kari says, nothing is forever.

SATURDAY, SEPTEMBER 28TH, 1991

I've been persuaded to lead what I've rashly called a Dragonfly Safari at Ferry Meadows Country Park near Peterborough. It pours with rain. As a gaggle of us troop round the water's edge, we see absolutely nothing. I do a huge amount of talking and feel my audience gradually losing patience. Once again I face the horror of a disappearing product. Feeling wretched, I swear that in future, somehow, when we lead dragonfly walks, we need to have a roof available for days like this, under which we can at least show pictures of what visitors might see in better weather. At Ashton Water Dragonfly Sanctuary, there's the observation hut, not big, but enough to shelter ten or fifteen people. The photographs and illustrations on the walls are acceptable, but is there some way we can install video equipment in there?

So, for next season, I need to think about more Open Days for visitors, better interpretation in the observation hut, how to interest birders, and what about that couple who said they'd be keen to help and left their address in the Visitors' Book?

SATURDAY, DECEMBER 14TH, 1991

I have barely arrived in the library before Miriam swings in with a letter in her hand. She thrusts it towards me.

'Read this,' she says. 'I want your views.'

It's a letter from Nick Mould, Prince's Charles' land agent at Highgrove. HRH is constructing an aquatic plant sewerage treatment system behind the house, and wonders whether Miriam could make some suggestions for planting around the projected pond. She's already got Prince Charles sowing wild flowers. A plan is attached.

I nearly explode with excitement.

'He hasn't thought of dragonflies,' I say. 'They won't tolerate polluted water. Tell him that if he puts in the right sort of plants in his new pond, and if dragonflies then breed in it, it'll prove he's doing the right thing. It'll show whether or not a reedbed sewage treatment system really works. Better still, we could do it.'

'Well, we'll see,' says Miriam. 'I want you to make a list of all the plants you think will do, Ruary. Do it now. Take the plan upstairs. And list the dragonflies you've managed to attract to the lake since you started. Once I've had a look at what you produce, I'll write to His Royal Highness.'

Chapter 23

MONDAY, JANUARY 13TH, 1992

I take the Underground to South Kensington, make my way through the gloomy, damp, dismal "To-the-Museums" tunnel, come up into the traffic of Cromwell Road, and – fiercely observed by the stone animals above – mount the elegant steps in front of the Natural History Museum. At reception, I ask for Steve Brooks. Steve leads me from the grandeur of the public spaces into the shabby staff-only drabness of the museum's innards. As before, we sit down in his tiny office, basically a desk, a couple of filing cabinets and a big window.

I show him the final draft of my first scientific paper, "Inverted Emergence in *Ischnura elegans*", and I'm very anxious for Steve to make his comments. He's the Editor of *The Journal of the British Dragonfly Society*, a much more serious scientific publication than it perhaps sounds. He makes a number of valuable suggestions, including reorganizing the whole thing. Most of the data-collection and identification for this paper has been done by Kari and Peter Mayhew, and, by the time Steve's finished, it's clear to me that I hardly dare call myself the author of this paper at all. But the key fact remains that nearly 40% of the Blue-taileds recorded at Ashton last year climbed out of the water, clambered up stems, turned upside down, clamped on, emerged from their exuvial cases, then turned the right way up again. 'Weird, innit?' as Mike would say. I wonder if we'll ever know why.

Steve and I drift off the subject of dragonflies and have an argument about aircraft, which turns into a bet. A couple of days later, I receive a note – on headed Natural History Museum notepaper – that reads, "Dear Ruary, I owe you a pint. The fuselage of the Messerschmitt 109G is 0.5cm longer than the Focke-Wulf 190. Best Wishes, Steve."

SATURDAY, FEBRUARY 8TH, 1992

Kari and I walk down to the Sanctuary for the first time this year. It feels good to be back. In watery sunshine, I stand under the leafless willows on the west bank, worry about the amount of water tumbling down from the Top Pond into the lake, then set to work mending a break in the fence.

Kari is by the boathouse, in her wellingtons, in the water. She sweeps her long-handled net swiftly through the water plants, lifts out a dripping mass, peers at it, prods it gently with her right forefinger, frowns, dumps the muddy mess back in the water, moves on a yard or two and tries again. Not for the first time, she spends over two hours like this, and will do it again several times during the spring, each time recording whatever insects she finds.

'No luck,' she calls. 'No larvae, a few waterboatmen, backswimmers, a couple of water slaters. No newts whatsoever. One worm.'

She climbs into the canoe and goes out to Warbler Bay, paddle in one hand, kitchen sieve in the other. Finally a shout of triumph: she's found a damselfly larva. She heads back to the shore, jumps out and disappears into the observation hut. I come in later and she's squinting down the microscope.

'See the lamella?'

'No,' I say, 'you're the one looking down the microscope. Don't you mean lamellae?'

'No. It's only got one.'

I peer down the microscope and see one very long fin-shape at the end of the damselfly larva's abdomen. Normally they have three; they're external gills but they also help it swim. This one has lost two; I've learnt that they can grow them back. Kari identifies it as an Emerald Damselfly.

Miriam summons us to supper. She tells us of an eminent naturalist with a lisp, who was asked by a mayoress exactly what he studied: 'Intethtinal wormths, madam.'

SUNDAY, MARCH 15TH, 1992

Smartly dressed, Miriam and I drive across to Highgrove, Miriam insisting on keeping to fifty miles an hour all the way. We arrive exactly on time, pass through the extremely polite but firm security precautions and stand beside a big hole destined to be the pond. We discuss the whole thing with Uwe Burka, its designer, David Palmer, its builder, and David Magson, the Head Gardener. I'm fully expecting to be virtually ignored, but to my surprise they all listen to me carefully. I walk around the site, suggest a couple of changes and offer to produce a precise list of plants with a diagram of what should go where.

We're just leaving when Prince Charles himself appears, in a sweater and riding breeches. Miriam gets a kiss and I'm introduced. On the journey over, Miriam has told me what to do should we bump into HRH, and so now I bob my head and call him Sir. Evidently he's on his way somewhere, but he insists on showing us his chickens. He's clearly very proud of them; they're extremely elegant. He points out the various breeds. Then he wants our views on a small extension he's made to the main building, and takes us round to see it. I look at him, assuming all he needs is a polite noise, and am stunned to see he's expecting me to give the thing serious consideration and to say what I think.

Miriam climbs back into the car. HRH grins at me, leans forward slightly, makes a sort of prodding motion with his left hand, and asks whether Miriam herself suffers from fleas.

SATURDAY, MAY 23RD, 1992

Summer is here again and I almost dance down to the lake in the windy sunshine. I patrol along the north bank and count fourteen Blue-tailed Damselflies, three Common Blue Damselflies, three Red-eyed Damselflies and six Azure Damselflies. Bright pink Ragged Robin shines in the grass and the May trees are in full bloom, blossom blowing like snowflakes in the wind. In the quietness between gusts I hear a cuckoo. Six Mandarin drakes paddle cockily about near Warbler Bay. Martins wheel and dive overhead.

Kari comes down, sets to work with her sieve and finds a dragonfly larva. Is it a Common Darter or a Ruddy Darter? As larvae, they're extremely hard to differentiate. She goes off to put it under the microscope in the observation hut. Plants, birds, dragonflies; the lake is in happy action once more.

I get agreement from Miriam to open the Sanctuary five times this year. We fix the dates and I set about contacting the media.

SUNDAY, JUNE 21ST, 1992

HRH's pond has now filled. I give the old Bentley a good polish and Kari and I drive over to Highgrove with a selection of water plants. As we arrive, Princess Diana is leaving in her maroon Mercedes convertible. It's a glorious day and she's got the hood down. She gives the Bentley a big smile and a wave.

We set to work at the pond – its liner as pristine blue as a swimming pool – carefully positioning the plants according to the agreed plan. A Black-tailed Skimmer perches on the Purple Loosestrife as soon as it's planted. Good. Then it's time to put the lilies in the centre of the pond. They're mounted in baskets that need to sit on the bottom, in the very deepest part of the pond. I hadn't thought about this. We discuss various ways and conclude that there's only one thing for it. I glance nervously at the discreet green security cameras, strip down to my underpants and wade in. It's impossible not to notice the suppressed smiles on the faces of the policemen as we leave.

Subsequently, the *Daily Telegraph* hears about this incident, not from us. In the Peterborough diary column, it claims that I must be the only person ever to have swum in water personally passed by the Prince.

SUNDAY, JULY 12TH, 1992

Close to the north bank, Kari finds and identifies a dragonfly exuvia. It's a Migrant Hawker. This is really important because it establishes proof that this species is definitely breeding in the lake; and it's such a beautiful insect! It's called a Migrant because when English names were first created, it was thought that this species flew in yearly from France. That needs a moment's thought: it means they were considered capable of flying across the English Channel, an enormous distance for a little insect. As it happens they are indeed capable of doing so, indeed they do it every year, but they also breed in this country.

Eddie Anderson from ITV comes with a team and makes a little film. We get dragonflies on TV for the second year running. And Sarah Blunt has rung from the BBC Natural History Unit in Bristol to promise us national radio space. Good again.

THURSDAY, JULY 16TH, 1992

I escape from London for a week and arrive to find a Migrant Hawker dashing about above the lake, jinking and zooming after midges and mosquitoes. I'm so pleased we decided to choose the Migrant as the emblem of the Sanctuary. If we ever have to move – nothing is for ever, as Kari says – the emblem can stay. And right now, we can look forward to seeing them from today until September.

Puttering down with the Fergy and trailer, I bring three railway sleepers and manhandle them into position over the point where the Polebrook runs gently from the Top Pond down into the lake. This makes a solid bridge, replacing the slightly doubtful stepping stones over which so many delicate house-guests' shoes have tripped.

SUNDAY, JULY 19TH, 1992

First Open Day of the year. Sunshine, thankfully. Into Pierre, the tired old Citroën Dyane, and off to put up directions to the Sanctuary. I've strimmed all the way along the path from Polebrook and opened a substantial parking space at the bottom of the field. We've hammered notices into the earth pointing out to visitors that they need to follow the path round the field to the red flag. By 10.30am, cars are arriving.

My first trip around the lake at 11.00am is very well attended. I show people how we've attracted dragonflies to the lake by planting a variety of water plants: three sorts, tall stemmed ones like irises, surface-coverers like lilies, and oxygenators under the water like stonewort. I tell them that most of a dragonfly's life is spent underwater. It's interesting to see how many are surprised by that. I show them dragonflies in action, hunting, mating and egg-laying. And I appeal for help. I spot Henry and Lynn, that couple from last year, here again. They carefully put their names and phone number in the Visitors' Book once more. I apologize and curse myself for not contacting them. They tell me they originally rang Miriam back in September 1990.

We count just over a hundred visitors, and ten species of dragonfly and damselfly.

TUESDAY, JULY 21ST, 1992

Twelve hours of very heavy rain. I walk down beneath dull and lowering clouds. The Pole brook is in full spate, water everywhere, blasting out of the Top Pond, cascading down, spreading a huge light brown flood stain out into the darker waters of the lake, lifting and pushing the three newly-laid sleepers out to bob aimlessly about like big black fish. A local group is coming on Thursday. Help!

By 8.30am the lake has risen five inches and I set to work clearing the overflow, a job I hadn't expected to do until the autumn. By 12.15pm the water has reached the overflow and by 1.15pm, water is pouring down it. I go down again at 6.30pm and find water is overtopping the banks in four places. I spend the rest of the evening digging earth from the bank behind the overflow, creating extra offtake capacity. I walk back up to the mansion in the dark, collapse into bed and wonder what I'll find tomorrow.

WEDNESDAY, JULY 22ND, 1992

I climb into Pierre, doing duty as a jeep, and it takes me down to the lake. As the engine dies, I sit still for a moment and listen. There's a sound like a castanet, no, not quite: two pebbles rapped rapidly together, five times, followed by a sort of squeal, like a shoe turned sharply on a dance floor. I recognize it. I heard it whilst dozing in my hammock a few days ago: it's a Ruddy Duck. I grasp my camera, creep along the north bank. Sure enough it's a Ruddy, talking to its mate. I get a shot of both.

The overflow is doing its job and only tiny amounts of water are leaking from any of the other points. I relax and sit down on one of the several log stools we've set out overlooking the plant pen in the north-west corner of the lake. It contains Greater Pondweed, much prettier than it sounds, a fine surface-coverer with its fat spear-shaped leaves. It's a good spot for future visitors to sit and watch odonate activity. Polebrook church strikes eight. What a change from yesterday. There's a blaze of yellow in the east and not a cloud in the deep azure sky to the west, deepest around the ghost of a moon. Out loud, I say, 'My soul He doth restore again.' Must be a memory from school.

Time to go out in the canoe, shepherd the floating sleepers back to land, then begin the job of getting everything straight again, ready for Thursday.

THURSDAY, JULY 23RD, 1992

I'm still working on putting things to rights. I've got another hour to finish off when I hear a call from close to the red flag.

'Hey! You there! Are you the Ranger?'

It's the pre-arranged group, far earlier than we'd agreed. I can see them coming round the side of the field. To my horror, I spot most of the women are dressed in fawns and pinks; several have lightweight white shoes. The men are in various shades of pale brown and light grey. I glance nervously at the soggy banks. One of the ladies nudges her husband and points at my wellingtons.

We set off, north bank, west bank, south bank, with me singing the praises of dragonflies; all goes reasonably well, most shoes still fairly dry, until we reach the point on the east bank where the water is still running down from the Top Pond. Though I've rescued the sleepers, I haven't yet managed to rebuild them into a bridge. We confront the yard-wide muddy stream. Desperate, I have a brainwave. There's a very large flat stone on the far side.

Perfect for a stepping stone. I splash through the water, seize the stone, swing round and throw it into the middle of the mess. It hits the water at an angle; time stops as a tidal wave of mud lifts gracefully into the air and plasters itself over white trousers, pink cardigans and buff windcheaters.

SATURDAY, AUGUST 1ST, 1992
Arrived last night late and exhausted after a hard week, but 225 visitors and ten species today.

SATURDAY, AUGUST 15TH, 1992
Sixty visitors. Fewer dragonflies. Rain on and off. We need somewhere under cover to take people when it rains so we can talk to them even if it's raining. The observation hut is too small. Not looking forward to journey back to London tonight.

SUNDAY, AUGUST 16TH, 1992
The Dragonfly Party. Miriam invites ninety-four eminent scientific and entomological personages, plus other guests. The extremely impressive list of names and addresses is set out on a large Sasco planner board. I keep it. During the course of the day, I march 120 people round the lake.

SATURDAY, AUGUST 29TH, 1992
Frantic clearing up this morning before opening time and only sixty people. Dull weather again.

SATURDAY, 5TH SEPTEMBER, 1992
Two hundred people, and still seven species whizzing around: Brown Hawker, Migrant Hawker, Common Darter, Ruddy Darter, Common Blue Damselfly, Blue-tailed Damselfly, Emerald Damselfly.

THURSDAY, SEPTEMBER 10TH, 1992
Kari and I drive over to Highgrove once again to see how things are progressing. Four Common Darters are whizzing about, and two pairs are mating and egg-laying. I send in a positive report

but point out we'll need to see whether the eggs breed through the larval stages and emerge as adults. Only then can we be sure we have succeeded.

MONDAY, SEPTEMBER 14TH, 1992

Home again in my Perthshire glen, I perch on the flat top of the standing stone outside my cottage. It's a champagne morning, all the colours so strong. The heather's still out, the ling, the fox-gloves, the tormentil, the rosebay willowherb, and both purple and white yarrow. A peregrine is sitting on the fence over by the road, still as a statue.

In the back garden, a Common Hawker – easily spotted by the yellow lines along the front edges of its wings – hovers up and down the telegraph pole, presumably feeding on midges. A black and yellow Golden-ringed Dragonfly zooms over the hedge and perches briefly on a rose. We don't have either species at Ashton. They prefer acidic water. So do we; our tap-water comes straight off the hill behind the cottage.

Time to think. Over the summer we've had just under a thousand visitors to Ashton Water Dragonfly Sanctuary, even better than last year. We've been able to show them that fifteen species of dragonfly and damselfly have made it their home. Back in 1989, there were only five species recorded there. So, we've proved our point. We can get both dragonflies and humans to come. But the big headache is the weather. We desperately need a bigger roof over our heads. And then I remember empty Ashton Mill. What about it as a Dragonfly Museum? I need to talk to Miriam.

FRIDAY, NOVEMBER 12TH, 1992

I give a talk at the Wildfowl and Wetland Centre at Peakirk, a tiny village between Spalding and Peterborough. I remember being brought here by my mother when I was about thirteen. The turning off the main road was near the black-and-white sign that used to indicate the limit of the 'Soke of Peterborough', a phrase that used to make my brother and I laugh, at least until our father hit the bottle.

Anyway, at that age, one sort of goose looked much like another to me. I'd have been much happier had she taken me to Peterborough station and let me watch the Gresley and Peppercorn Pacifics ease through the covered platforms, their safety valves lifting. My love of trains goes back much further than my adoration of dragonflies.

But I don't mention that to my audience, and in any case I know my mother would be very proud of me now. Afterwards, as I make my way back to the car in the dark, a bespectacled smiling young man rushes up to me, introduces himself as Stuart Irons, and asks to help at the Sanctuary. I've already made contact with Lynn and Henry Curry, the couple who offered to assist last year. So that's three volunteers ready to share a love of dragonflies and help get things ready next year.

FRIDAY, NOVEMBER 19TH, 1992

I've spent two days padding up and down the wet streets of Oakham hawking Ashton Water Dragonfly Sanctuary calendars round possible outlets. They're beautiful calendars, though I say so myself. I don't think anyone has ever produced a dragonfly calendar before. It's really thanks to Kari: as Head of Marketing at Canning, her role involves close liaison with printers and publishers. One of her printing outfits, Jaguar Impressions, is run by Trevor and Sue Leal. Trevor and I share a liking for beer and I've got him interested in dragonflies. He's a keen photographer, has seen my work and offered to produce a calendar of my dragonfly images. The result is a large, beautifully produced glossy number, and the profits from its sale are to go to the Sanctuary.

Selling them has been harder than I thought; I'd somehow imagined that quite a few people would like nice dragonflies on their walls but it seems that people responsible for purchasing in bulk are not among them, or at least not those in the Peterborough area. Undaunted, I have traipsed as far as Oakham, where a kindly bookshop has taken three and sent me to see Tim Appleton, boss of the British Birdwatching Centre just down the road at Rutland Water.

I'm not sure that a birder will appreciate dragonfly calendars but I launch into my spiel. Tim gazes at me, bemused and, possibly out of pity, buys ten. We are to meet again.

I've made my pitch to Miriam about creating a Dragonfly Museum at the Mill. Now I need to be patient. It took three years to get permission to set up the Sanctuary. Will it take another three for a Museum?

THURSDAY, NOVEMBER 26TH, 1992

Canning's departmental heads, including Kari and I, have been called together for a meeting at Canning Place, the original base of the organization and the reason for its name. It's a cosy Georgian building on the corner of a small street tucked into the right angle between Gloucester Road and High Street Kensington. It has many happy memories for me. It's where I trained my first group, where I subsequently ran endless courses, and where later I managed the super-expensive one-to-one training operation.

We gather in the lounge. I plonk myself down on the only sofa and note that the carpet stain beside it – left over from an accident during a Brazilian Cachaça-fuelled party – has still not quite faded.

Our senior partner stands up and says he has very bad news. At that moment, there's an enormous flash of lighting and a crash of thunder. It matches the mood perfectly. The recession has hit us hard, he says. Well, we're all too aware of that: things have never really recovered since that awful participant-free week in January last year. We're going to have to downsize, he says. It won't be on a last-in, first-out basis: redundancy packages will be offered to anyone willing to leave. Could we all think carefully about which members of our particular teams we might consider approaching about voluntary redundancy.

I glance across at Kari. She's looking at the carpet but I know what she's thinking. And I know she knows what I'm thinking. Throughout the subsequent discussion, everyone assumes we're all talking about our teams, but for Kari and I, the key phrase used was 'offered to anyone'. I think we've just been presented with our get-out-of-jail card.

We slip off along the road to the pub and, over a drink, decide we need to make sure the offer really is open to all. If so, dare we take what amounts to one of most serious decisions we're ever – ever – likely to take? It would be like the pair of us strapping on slightly threadbare parachutes and jumping out of our aircraft. We talk for a very long time.

Next morning Kari goes in to check with the senior partner that this really is the case. It is. She gives notice there and then. Tears well up in the senior partner's eyes. I'm the next person through his door.

Chapter 24

WEDNESDAY, MARCH 3RD, 1993

I'm still working at Canning. I haven't fully escaped yet. Kari has, and she's already successfully selling her miniatures. For me it's a morning's work in London, one-to-one, training a woman from an Italian political party. She's the only Italian I've ever met with a voice locked in a grating, stentorian monotone. I cycle back to the flat, pack a bag, jump into the car and head for Ashton.

Before leaving the flat this morning, a letter from Miriam plopped onto the mat. She was responding to my continued pressure last weekend for using Ashton Mill as a museum, a place to publicize dragonflies, to operate in conjunction with the Sanctuary. I'd approached her during the only chance I had, in the middle of a hectic family afternoon and, as her letter now puts it, "It's impossible to discuss this when the children are roller-skating." She agrees that "it is very important (underlined) we make an effort to link the Mill and Dragonflies." Anxious not to lose a moment, I've rung her. After the usual two hour drive I'm at Ashton in time for tea.

I'm ready to dive in but Miriam wants to talk about other things: who to invite to the Dragonfly Party in July; her being ill when the Countryside Commission people came; the study of birds in Senegal; a letter to E.O. Wilson about the membranes of ants' waists; the ineffectiveness of predation as a solution to disease; generalists versus specialists; how rats' intelligence changes at night and how they might take over the world 'given the odd million years'; how to enliven ageing cake with sherry; how pleased she is with a magazine article on Prince Charles's wild-flowers; and how surprised she'd been to find a mouse in her bath.

By the time I broach the subject, we're sitting in virtual darkness, the room aglow from the big log fire. There are complications as regards a dragonfly museum, she says, insofar as she's been discussing plans for a restaurant at the Mill. Her Fish Museum has been defunct for years, and clearly both the Mill and the adjoining tearoom need to be used but I'll have to wait and see what happens.

'I'll put you in touch with Coulson,' she says. 'He'll help.'

She means Adrian Colston, golden-haired Director of the Northamptonshire Wildlife Trust, and she's forgotten I've already met him several times.

THURSDAY, MARCH 18TH, 1993

I get a letter from Highgrove. There's been a flood, and effluent has been washed into the pond, turning it the colour of tea. The pond has been carefully flushed through with fresh water and it's now clear, but can I come and have a look?

FRIDAY, APRIL 16TH, 1993

Down to the Sanctuary to see what has happened during the weeks of spring. There are tiny shoots in the wildflower meadow. Lilies are already showing growth. There's no sign of Water Speedwell yet, or Water Figwort, but Starwort, Amphibious Bistort, Water Forget-me-not, Water Mint, Greater Pondweed and Marsh Sow-Thistle are all doing fine. Good. What a change from three years ago.

The lake is very full and there are signs of leakage and incipient green algae. I get to work on protecting the east bank between the Top Pond and the lake.

SATURDAY, MAY 1ST, 1993

Kari and I drive over to Highgrove. They've obviously taken a great deal of trouble to put things right, and now they'd like to bulk out the number of plants round the edges. I send a list of recommendations and offer to do the work. No sign of adult dragonflies. Too early.

WEDNESDAY, JUNE 9TH, 1993

Up at 6.00am in London and off to Ashton by 7.10am. Upon arrival, I go down to the lake immediately and set to work clearing up and strimming the paths. I work until my mouth is so dry I'm unable to swallow. Up for a quick lunch then down again for some 'Haytering'; it's a word we Sanctuary volunteers have come to use, like hoovering (a Hayter is a brand of four-wheeled mower, very tough, very heavy).

I spot Blue-tailed, Common Blue, Red-eyed and Azure Damselflies, and a Broad-bodied Chaser perched on a reed stem in Chaser Channel. Characteristically, it shoots into the air, grabs a mosquito and almost in the blink of an eye lands again on the same stem.

I beaver away until I'm ready to drop and then, with thunder approaching I go back up to the gardens and drop into the swimming pool. Delicious. Broccoli supper and bed amid flashes of lightning and great booms of thunder.

THURSDAY, JUNE 10TH, 1993

I drive down in Pierre the Citroën, climb out and decide just to sit by the lake awhile. I catch sight of a Large Red Damselfly (*Pyrrhosoma nymphula*). Wonderful. I'd been wondering why we hadn't seen any; they're pretty common. So now we have sixteen species.

I drive back up to meet Ray and Kay Thompson, whom we first met at the Olympia show in 1991. Ray has very kindly offered to make a short introductory video for the Sanctuary. We intend to show it in the observation hut. Ray has selected key sequences from his own extensive video work on dragonflies and now he films atmosphere shots around the lake. I've written the script and we agree I should be the presenter, too. We set to work. It goes well, very few takes, and a lot of laughter.

We drive into Oundle for lunch, then back to the lake for Ray to do some more filming of dragonfly behaviour. Kari has secreted tea and cake in the observation hut; and from his heavy camera bag, Ray produces a bottle of champagne.

FRIDAY, JUNE 18TH, 1993

There are still a few weeks' more loose ends to tie up at Canning but it's been decided that there's to be a leaving party for myself and another colleague tonight. I'd somehow expected something different. Typical Canning leaving parties have short, sad speeches sandwiched between a great deal of noise, laughter and drink. The subtext for most people present is, 'We're staying, we're doing the right thing, we're fortunate.' But perhaps my colleagues at Canning suspect that in this particular case the two leavers are the lucky ones. For once, I stay sober, despite listening to a very moving farewell speech about what I've done for the outfit.

What I don't tell my colleagues is that I have another meeting that very evening with an old friend from Germany, Hans Polkowski, a man I first met fifteen years ago. I was running a training course for Bosch in Switzerland. We were the same age and took an instant liking to each other, each recognizing in the other, I think, qualities of hard work, ingrained contrariness and absolute refusal to take life seriously.

Hans is now a Senior Vice-President, Head of Personnel for the whole of the Bosch organization, in other words about 220,000 people. As a newly self-employed trainer, I need work. Hans is on business in London and, by an extraordinary coincidence, is staying in the Halcyon Hotel, precisely two minutes from our flat. He knows nothing of my decision to leave Canning, but the moment he hears of it, he instantly offers to put me in touch with some of his people. We clink glasses.

SATURDAY, JUNE 19TH, 1993

5.30am. Rain, rain, rain. I'm woken by the mansion's burglar alarm. I dash down the stairs, sprint round the corner and hurry into the main part of the mansion to check whether Miriam's all right. She's fine; she's just saved quails' eggs from boiling dry and gone through a security-alarmed door to do so. That she smashed her specs yesterday and left them somewhere in the greenhouses doesn't seem to have slowed her down much. At least she's moved fast enough to stop Oundle Fire Brigade returning.

Kari and I are due at Highgrove on Monday to put in the water plants. Late in the afternoon I realize that unless I act quickly I'll have to strip down to my underpants again. Might Peterborough have a small inflatable boat somewhere? I dash into town and, getting steadily wetter, try various shops. No luck. Finally, in a service station, I locate a lurid lime green and orange children's boat. I can just fit in, but it'll look shockingly tasteless at Highgrove. Nothing for it now. Luckily Halfords is open late and I buy a tyre pump that works off the cigarette lighter in the car. In the rain, I carefully check that the pump works and that it connects properly to the boat. It does. I don't want anything to go wrong.

SUNDAY, JUNE 20TH, 1993

Henry and Lynn Curry and Stuart Irons join us at the lake and make the whole business of readying the Sanctuary for visitors so much easier. It's a wet day, we strim grass, Hayter paths, mend the fence, cut down briars and nettles, trim back reed and haul a fallen poplar out of the way. By lunchtime we're filthy. Kari brings a veggie stew down to the observation hut. We wolf it down, drink beer and chortle at the state of ourselves.

MONDAY, JUNE 21ST, 1993

Kari and I arrive at Highgrove and are checked by the polite, seemingly relaxed but super-alert policemen. We park close to the pond and hump our various plants to the water's edge. We're delighted to spot Large Red and Common Blue Damselflies, Broad-bodied and Four-spotted Chasers, a Black-tailed Skimmer and an Emperor Dragonfly. So that's seven species recorded at the Prince's pond. But we're shocked to spot fish in the water, rudd. And there's a bit too much blanket weed, though in among it we find ten Emperor larvae. We're just about to exult when one of the policemen, Tudor Davies, a keen dragonfly person, one of our fans, comes and tells us that they've been put in from another pond. Blast. And someone else put the fish in; they thought it would help.

We position our plants and then it's time for the extra lilies. I go back to the car, get the boat out, connect it to the pump and plug the lead into the cigarette lighter. The boat starts to inflate quickly and satisfactorily. There's a pressure gauge on the top of the pump and, having worked at Michelin, I'm used to these. The boat is looking pretty well inflated now but the gauge is still reading marginally above zero. I've just decided to give it a minute or so more when the boat explodes with an ear-shattering bang. I've never seen policemen move so quickly.

FRIDAY, JULY 13TH, 1993

Tim Hill arrives with a team from Lee Valley Country Park. Tim is responsible for conservation and habitats in the Park; he's read about our efforts at the Sanctuary, is keen on dragonflies, and plans to create a second dragonfly sanctuary in the Lee Valley. I march them round in the sunshine, tell them what we've done and then we go to the pub. At first I suspect the whole thing may just be a team jaunt, but by the end of lunch and after a lot of penetrating questions, I'm fairly sure they're serious. Tim asks me how to contact Chris Packham.

SATURDAY, JULY 14TH, 1993

Our first Open Day of the year. Everything's ready and the lake is a sheet of white buttercup-shaped Water Crowfoot.

At a talk in Holland Park in February, I negotiated a small second-hand generator in lieu of payment, and this – hidden out of sight under an enormous bulk Kellogg's Cornflakes box among the willows by the Top Pond – is now powering Ray's introductory video, showing on an ancient TV mounted on a table in the observation hut. Miriam has provided the old TV, and Ray and Kay have generously donated the video player. We usher people in and worry about crowding.

Edward Gee, a local farmer, is part of the group and he approaches me at the end of my talk, which I finish off with my customary appeal for help.

'This is great,' he says. 'Had you thought of widening your audience a bit?'

'How do you mean?'

'I'm involved in organizing the East of England Show. What about a stand there? Next weekend?'

We leap at the chance, but it'll mean a lot of hurried preparatory work.

A very quiet dark-haired young man hovers on the edge of things and hangs on after most people have gone. He spends a great deal of time on our makeshift landing stage, peering into the reeds, studying damselflies. His name is Henry Stanier and he too offers help. We've had 150 people today.

FRIDAY, JULY 20TH, 1993

We set up our exhibition at the East of England Show. Daughter Catharine helps. We've taken a great deal of trouble over our stand. It boasts large photographs of dragonflies, detailed information about their life-cycle, an identification chart, dragonfly calendars, dragonfly plates, small tanks with live larvae, and a microscope. It hasn't been easy to get interpretational material printed quickly and colour photographs blown up. We've spent hours with Letraset and had to wait three days for our enlarged photographs. The organizers have even excavated a little pond for us and we've spent hours carefully transferring plants from Ashton Water into our new pond. Today, miraculously, dragonflies actually appear and perch as if to order. The stand is a terrific success. We hand out leaflets, recommending people to dig ponds, and talking to farmers and estate owners about ideal dragonfly habitats. It's exciting to find ourselves in conversation with so many interested people.

I complain to Edward Gee that the Duke of Gloucester didn't come to our stand; he was ushered swiftly past. Edward promises the Bishop of Peterborough tomorrow instead. Bishop Bill

Westwood duly arrives in full dress, purple waistcoat, gaiters and all, and is genuinely interested in what we do.

SUNDAY, AUGUST 15TH, 1993

It's midday and I'm at the lake. Everything is damp and misty, a blue-grey stillness, just the gentlest susurration from the poplars. I keep blinking and checking my glasses but it's not my vision, it's the atmosphere. Two voices, a man's and a woman's, carry from Polebrook.

I have a clear sense of the brevity and value of the day. I have to go back to London this evening, back to work. How many times have I done the Sunday-evening drive back from here during the last decade? I have the same feeling as when I used to be allowed home from school on occasional Sundays for a few hours. I treasured every second of those bittersweet days, the joy of bowling along on my beloved bike, the pleasure of a proper Sunday lunch.

School terms lasted months not years; and now I'm finishing up commitments at Canning. Only a few more weeks and I'll be completely free. Am I afraid? Yes. Am I excited? Yes.

I watch Azure, Blue-Tailed and Common Blue damselflies flit by, catch the sound of pigeons in the warm mistiness, and think about putting transmitters on dragonflies. Perhaps we could then properly answer how far they go and how fast they fly.

Yesterday was our seventh and last Open Day of the season, and we've averaged 150 people per day. The weather has been on our side. It's been very good to have volunteers to help. Just as we're closing, two people, both hefty, come up to me: Sheila and Ian Wright. They've been full of questions during our walk round and they too offer help. 'We know absolutely nothing about dragonflies,' says Sheila, 'but we can lift heavy things.'

TUESDAY, SEPTEMBER 7TH, 1993

Another visit to Highgrove. Kari can't come. She has a cuddly Liberty's rabbit, unimaginatively called Rabbit, and she brings him down from the flat and puts him in the passenger seat in her place. I solemnly strap him in, promise to hide him before arrival, promptly forget all about him and set off. I reach the police check-point inside the gates and sit quietly while the bonnet is opened and a long mirror searches under the car. The two policemen finish examining the vehicle, then one them comes over, puts his head in my window and with a straight face says, 'I see the rabbit's all right, sir.'

There are goldfish in the pond now, as well as a great deal more blanket weed. I offer to bring a friend – soon – and remove it.

SATURDAY, SEPTEMBER 11TH, 1993

Late from London last night, and not down to the lake until 10.00am today, camera in hand. The Water Crowfoot that covered the surface in a carpet of little white flowers has now almost vanished. I take photographs of the lake in the sunshine, watch a Brown Hawker patrol along the west bank and try unsuccessfully to get a shot of it. Frustrated, I sit down on the bench near the boathouse and glance at my wristwatch: it's 10.25am.

There's a commotion in Chaser Channel: it's a male Migrant Hawker attempting to couple with a female. They spin up into the air, locked together like a flying heart, and land in a black-berry bush behind me. I creep towards them, get several shots, then settle down to watch what happens. Abdomen to abdomen, the male pumps sperm rhythmically into the female. They stay coupled for nearly half an hour, then at 10.55am the female starts tickling the male's rear wings with her front legs and at 10.58am she decouples herself and just hangs, held by the male's claspers still clamped round her neck. Then, still in tandem, they fly off together towards the water, over the reeds, out of sight.

It's a sunlit morning crammed with dragonfly action, as if they're making up for lost time.

THURSDAY, SEPTEMBER 16TH, 1993

I have dragooned my best friend Mike into taking a couple of days off from flying for Rolls-Royce to help me take blanket weed out of the Highgrove pond. This is our second day at it and we've dragged a total of one and a half tons of blanket weed out, hauling it onto the bank yesterday, leaving it overnight so its various inhabitants (including dragonfly larvae) could crawl back into the pond, and today hefting it with forks onto a big four-wheeled trailer. We're shattered. We decide we both deserve knighthoods; sadly no one is about, at least no one with a sword or a cushion. But at least we've seen Common Darters skimming in, and two pairs egg-laying.

MONDAY, SEPTEMBER 20TH, 1993

Kari is elected as a Member of the Society of Limners. The two miniatures that swing it for her are, first, a kingfisher – she's caught the gorgeous orange and turquoise plumage perfectly – and, second, our lovely cat Tuffy. I've watched two or three people stretch out their fingers, about to touch the exact depiction of Tuffy's fur, as if they need to check it isn't real.

MONDAY, OCTOBER 18TH, 1993

I'm finally free of Canning, and it feels a bit odd, but Hans Polkowski has put me in the frame at Bosch. I still need income so I might as well carry on doing what other people think I'm good at; and precarious though it may be, I shall be my own boss and will arrange my own time. So now I'm in Stuttgart, among the vast gloomy offices of Feuerbach, making my pitch to Dr Kettgen, the man responsible for language training at Bosch. I think he knows I'm staying with his boss's boss, so it's a bit strange, but he seems genuinely interested in what I have to offer and asks me to submit a proposal for training in Scotland. Will this be a source of income, I wonder.

SATURDAY, OCTOBER 23RD, 1993

It's the last long evening of the year. Tonight the clocks change. I spent this morning trying to write a proposal for Bosch, got tied in knots and decided to unwind by going down to the lake and rebuilding the sleeper-bridge and strengthening the main dam. Then I felt impelled to start clearing out the overflow and got cracking. What sort of unwinding is that? But it took my mind off Bosch for a bit, and when I came back and started again at the typewriter, things seemed much clearer.

Anyway, with the long sun slanting across the world now, it's too good to stay indoors. I cycle down the avenue that leads east out of the estate. Planted well before the mansion was built, the avenue used to boast a twin ribbon of magnificent elms, but, now lined with horse chestnut trees, it's still stately. I speed through the open East Lodge gates and out onto the long drove road, pale as toffee. The fields have been ploughed, the sharp brown sides of their clods shine in the sun, and I sniff in the deep smell of loam. I stop at the junction above Warmington, gaze across the Nene valley below, then look back across the high plain reaching away under a huge gilded sky to the Giddings.

Up here, life is still busy with the day, but, below in the vale, the church towers and steeples of Oundle, Elton, Warmington, Nassington and Fotheringhay are settling into the dusk, bedding down for the night, a study in tweedy darkening browns.

Heading back towards Polebrook, I turn off onto Stanborough Hill. Escaped Père David's deer now rest just outside the fence, close to their family within. I look down to the lake. The poplars are in silhouette. Turning, I see the evening sun play on the wood; each branch and leaf stands out and, as I run my eyes along the wood-edge, the shapes get sharper, the shades subtler, and the scarlet berries sparkle. I look and look.

SUNDAY, OCTOBER 24TH, 1993

Though nothing is decided, I've been given permission to work in the Mill. In anticipation I've already transported three unwanted items up from Canning in London: a battered old desk and two ancient grey filing cabinets. I drag them one at a time up the narrow stairs onto the little windowless mezzanine, then up the final three steps into the enormous dusty main space above the engine house. It's crammed with all the material from a Seventies archaeological dig, including bedrolls, shovels and wheelbarrows. There are countless shoeboxes of artefacts and a skull or two.

I set up my office in the corner facing the stairs. It's cold and a bit grimy, but it's a start. I finish my proposal for Bosch, then go downstairs and out into the sunshine to eat my sandwich. I hear the piping of kingfishers from the millpond. I creep over, peep over the wall and come eyeball to eyeball with a young one. Wonderful! And surely an omen.

Later, after much sweeping, and with a raging headache, I open the luccam – a sort of aerial porch originally used to load grain into this upper storey – whose twin doors, now guarded by railings, open into mid-air. I look out at the sunset, so early today, and listen to the kingfishers still whizzing about. Rooks and doves twitter down for the night. Time to stop.

WEDNESDAY, OCTOBER 27TH, 1993

Tea with Miriam. Today it's war stories, beginning with life at Bletchley Park, Miriam threatening to tell Churchill that the secretary who packed the red box that held his daily decoded German Ultra messages was only earning £4 per week. In other words, were the secretary so inclined, the greatest secret of the war could be easily be betrayed for the price of a pair of silk stockings.

'What about the very fact that you knew about this Ultra stuff, Miriam?'

'We thought we'd all be shot once the job was done. Shall I tell you something?'

'What?'

'Bletchley had a very narrow, very secure entrance. You needed an extremely rare red-white-and-blue pass to get in. I once went through and, instead, showed my vivisectionist's licence. The man with the fixed bayonet never noticed.'

She moves on to a story about a fellow entomologist, a Mrs Gent, whose son, also a keen insect-fancier, was fighting with the Desert Rats. He found several fascinating specimens and wrote to his mother asking whether she might send him some ethyl acetate so he could preserve his finds. Miriam says she persuaded Richard Meinertzagen to get Russell Pasha to send an armoured car with a bottle of the stuff to Mrs Gent's son's unit. I'm sure she'd have rung up Lawrence of Arabia had he still been alive.

Her stories go on and on; many of which I can't remember. What I can't forget is what fun, how stimulating – and how sometimes slightly scary – simply being with Miriam was.

SUNDAY, OCTOBER 31ST, 1993

Another tea with Miriam, along with several visitors, including Simon Marks and Ian Redhead, Miriam's doctor. More war stories. Miriam losing her memory for four minutes immediately after the bombing of Bristol. Opening and reading sealed orders marked. "Not to be opened until the Germans are within ten miles." Hiding the rifles of the local Home Guard unit who'd all gone off the pub and left their weapons in a barn. Receiving a telegram stating, "Expect German landing from dawn till dusk" and then another, "Correction: should read dusk till dawn."

Simon Marks offers to pay for the re-thatching of the boat-house. It's still got its protective polythene covering but it doesn't look very attractive. Ian Redhead says he knows a young chap just setting out on his thatching career, suggests he might be prepared to do the job and gives me his address.

SATURDAY, NOVEMBER 13TH, 1993

I now have a quote for the thatching job from Graham Carter, the man Dr Redhead recommended. I've taken a liking to young Graham: he was apprenticed to an ageing thatcher and has inherited many of the mannerisms and speech patterns of the older man. This sets him apart from people of his own age and lends him an unusual sort of charm.

SATURDAY, DECEMBER 11TH, 1993

Graham has set to work down at the lake during the week. When I arrive from London, there are four ladders up the almost-finished boathouse roof, scaffolding round the outward water-side, and Graham's tools are neatly laid out on a large board on the bank beside great bundles of clean-cut reed.

Graham's absolutely focused on his work, working with extraordinary precision and concentration, humming quietly to himself. I decide that, come what may, he'll be the man to re-thatch my cottage in Scotland. He shows me a reed dragonfly he's made, and says he intends to mount it on the boathouse once it's finished.

I walk back up the track to the mansion. It hasn't been a bad year: the boathouse re-thatched, plants doing really well both in and out of the plant pens; decent paths right round the lake; an introductory video made; seven Open Days; a small force of volunteers recruited; over a thousand visitors to the Sanctuary, sixteen species of dragonfly recorded; and a serious chance that we may get a National Dragonfly Museum based at the Mill.

Above: Ruary building a plant pen at Ashton Water; Kari clearing
Azolla from the millrace, National Dragonfly Museum.
Below: Ashton Water after it was fenced off, 1990.
All photographs © Ruary Mackenzie Dodds unless otherwise noted.

Above: An Azure Damselfly (top) and a Large Red Damselfly.
Opposite: A Banded Demoiselle (above) and a Migrant Hawker.

Above: A Broad-bodied Chaser (left) and a Four-spotted Chaser.
Left: Migrant Hawkers mating.
Below: A Golden-ringed Dragonfly.

Above: A Ruddy Darter (left) and a Brown Hawker laying eggs (both pictured at Ashton Water).

Below: A Blue-tailed Damselfly (left) and an Emerald Damselfly.

Clockwise from top left: Volunteers building the Museum walkway; Chris Packham cutting the ribbon at the Museum, 1996; Bill Oddie on the Dragonfly Project stand at the British Birdfair, 2011; Volunteers digging the Museum garden pond.

Top: Ruary with Chris Packham and the BBC Springwatch team after receiving the 'Order of the Geek' award, 2009.
Bottom: Ruary leading a Dragonfly Safari at Wicken Fen, 2012.

Above: Ruary in 1990.

Part Four

The National
Dragonfly Museum

1994 - 2001

Chapter 25

WEDNESDAY, JANUARY 19TH, 1994

Kari's working very hard on her miniatures now and they're selling well. Today she receives a letter from a wealthy American businesswoman who's absolutely delighted with an owl she's bought; and Kari is equally delighted that she's dared to put the price higher than she thought might be acceptable. If measured in raw paid-by-the-hour terms, however, her pieces are still ridiculously cheap.

I know nearly nothing about art but I'm quite ready to comment on what Kari does. She clearly finds it useful, as useful as do I when she reads drafts of what I write. It doesn't mean we always accept what's said – indeed there are arguments – but I think we're very lucky that we both value each other's views. There've been no arguments so far about what I'm currently working on, though, just thoughtful help.

SATURDAY, MARCH 5TH, 1994

I arrive at Ashton, a bundle of nerves. I've typed up and sent Miriam a three-page proposal – with diagrams attached – about the Mill. I've stuck my neck out.

THE NATIONAL DRAGONFLY MUSEUM AT ASHTON MILL
* The Museum will be the only dragonfly museum
outside Japan that concentrates solely on
dragonflies, their conservation and their
significance in the pattern of biodiversity.

Its aim is to show as many people as possible that dragonflies are fascinating insects, that they are unique and endangered and that almost everyone can help them.

* The Museum will be a practical way to show people the challenges of species conservation, habitat conservation and biodiversity.

* The Museum will provide an all-weather introduction to the world of dragonflies. It will encourage people to become involved and will advise what action they can take. It will recommend further sources of information and reference. It will emphasize the international aspect of conservation and biodiversity whilst at the same time starting work in one's own back yard.

* The Museum will be a permanent source of publicity for many conservation bodies including national and international dragonfly societies.

* There will be considerable emphasis on recorded video material of both adults and larvae, in particular live action sequences. There will also be programmed live shows and live larvae in tanks.

THE WALL DISPLAYS WILL HIGHLIGHT:
The Life Cycle of the Dragonfly
Dragonflies: Sensitive Indicators of the Environment
Dragonflies' Endangered Inter-relationship with Man
Extraordinary Flight Capabilities
Wall Chart: Identification of British Dragonflies
Worldwide Distribution of Species
What is Biodiversity? Why is it Vital?
Where and When can I see Dragonflies?
How Can I Help?
 Pond-digging
 Monitoring
 Research Suitable Aquatic Plants

Selection of National and International Photographs
The Dragonfly Societies: Information
Dragonflies in Art

FLOOR-SPACE WILL INCLUDE:
Large video monitor, video player, and video camera
  with macro attachment
Viewing area, minimum 30 seats
Two large tanks for live dragonfly larvae
Locked cases of specimens, with anti-collection notice
Locked case of dragonfly books with library under
Locked case of dragonfly artefacts and jewellery

SALES ITEMS WILL INCLUDE:
Museum brochure
Calendars
T-Shirts
Sweatshirts
Tea towels
Selected British dragonfly products

OUTSIDE THE MUSEUM:
* On the east side of the millpond, a planked platform
  for viewing dragonflies and examining examples of
  aquatic plants; three plant pens to protect fragile
  plants from wildfowl predation.
* On the east side of the millrace, a similar planked
  viewing platform.
* East of the millrace, parallel drain to be cleared.
* East behind the Mill complex, overgrown area to be
  cleared and made dragonfly-attractive.

It's a massively optimistic set of objectives, of course it is, but
I've talked the plan through with the volunteers and we reckon
it's achievable, over time. I'm sure Miriam will have discussed it
with her children, and now I desperately want to know what she

and they think. I walk into the library and she immediately gives her approval, but she says Charles, who, though he lives abroad, actually owns the Mill, will need time to consider the proposal.

We troop off to lunch at the Chequered Skipper: Miriam, her daughter Charlotte, Charlotte's daughters Miriam and Naomi, Kari's great-niece Nica and her mother, Barbara. They're all gentle with me. I'm momentarily under the impression that they've spotted how much work I've just given myself, but I'm suddenly and deeply touched when I realize they're actually aware that Kari's away in New York and I'm missing her terribly. Yes, I'm certainly missing Kari, a lot, but beneath what I hope is a calm exterior I'm jumping for joy at the prospect of setting up a Dragonfly Museum.

Miriam has soup while I chew my way through a vast mixed grill. We share our dislike of scientific jargon in articles intended for general consumption. We discuss the words 'stenoecious' and 'euroecious' and agree we don't really understand the meaning of either.

SATURDAY, MARCH 19TH, 1994

I've set up a work party with the volunteers, and we meet by the lake in pouring rain. We've developed a technique that we call aqua-strimming: the victim wriggles into waders, wields a strimmer and stands in the lake clearing reed-shoots from Chaser Channel, the open area between the north bank and the parallel line of reeds. It doesn't matter who does the job, it's impossible not to lower the strimmer from time to time to water level and spray everything in sight – operator included – in freezing black filth.

The boom that stretches across the lake to prevent deer encroaching needs several of its posts straightening and, in view of my experiences with a sledgehammer in the Canadian canoe, one of the volunteers has brought a small, possibly more stable, boat. With icy rain hissing on the water, Trevor Leal and Henry Curry set out from the north bank like a couple of explorers. They reach the boom over by the south bank, Trevor starts hammering a post, and shouts that the boat's fine. Two minutes later, there's another shout. They've sprung a leak. They paddle back across the lake, sinking slowly, Henry desperately using his hat as a baler.

SATURDAY, MARCH 26TH, 1994

It's a very wet month but undaunted the volunteers meet again. We decide to transport several heavy items from the observation hut to the Mill. Peter Scott comes down from the gardens with the Fergy and trailer, slipping and sliding through the ruts and the mud.

'I've got the tractor down,' he says, 'but I don't think it'll go back up with a load on. I'd be better driving up the field towards the cricket pavilion.'

So we manoeuvre the Fergy down Fir Avenue, the track leading down to the western gates by the red flag. We watch Peter set off. Halfway up the field, the Fergy starts to slide backwards, its big back wheels churning in soaking stubble. Trevor, Stuart and I tramp uphill, rain spitting in our faces, and start to push. The Fergy suddenly gets a grip and its offside back wheel sends a wall of mud over Stuart. He grins, a sudden split of white in a totally brown face. He licks dirt from his lips, spits, and tries to clean his glasses on his sodden sleeve.

Each time the volunteers come, Kari makes sure there's hot food for lunch and I nip to the pub beforehand and fill up a glass demijohn with local bitter. Henry Curry finds a sticky label, writes "Ruary's Rocket-fuel" on it and puts in on the big fat bottle.

FRIDAY, APRIL 15TH, 1994

Dr Kettgen from Bosch, together with his colleague Herr Gutzan, arrives in Scotland for a personalized language training course with me. Gerhard, as I now call him, wants to see what I'm made of. We work together at Farleyer House, a luxurious hotel close to my home. I've gone to endless trouble to make sure the course material is just right, the training room is ideal and their accommodation is perfect, but I'm still wracked with nerves.

FRIDAY, MAY 13TH, 1994

Kari hears that she's won the Scott-Kestin Award at the Hilliard Society. Of the pieces she sent in, I think her one of a wildcat is superb, but I suspect it's the one of Moonie, Miriam's old and nasty-tempered sheltie, whom Kari has transformed into an elderly canine, eyes filled with love, that does it.

Messrs Kettgen and Gutzan thoroughly enjoyed their course up in Scotland and want me to come and work in Germany. So Kari and I are both finding our feet. I sometimes wonder if we'd have had the courage if it wasn't for our experiences at Ashton and our time with Nica.

WEDNESDAY, JUNE 8TH, 1994

Kari and I sit in the Randolph Hotel in Oxford. Miriam's son Charles arrives. I've met him several times before. He's very thoughtful, pleasant and encouraging. We discuss the whole project. I describe my meeting with the local planning people, the local fire brigade and a local security company. He agrees that we can have an initial five-year token-rent lease and can set up a registered charity. His lawyers will draw up a lease. We're very grateful. Without his agreement, no Museum.

Elated, we finish our coffee and drive on to Highgrove. Too much blanket weed again and we're asked to remove it once more. We spot two Common Blue Damselflies but fail to find exuviae.

THURSDAY, JUNE 9TH, 1994

I pick up a massive bunch of keys from the estate office and drive down to the Mill to survey my new domain. Nothing is forever, I know that (and Kari keeps reminding me) but I'm determined to do my very best to make something really special here.

I park Pierre in the little courtyard, search for the Yale key to the small door marked "OLD MILL, WAY IN", and sit quietly in the car for a minute. This is the place where I felt so strange a year or two back. Now I know why. It's no longer just the place where I'm lucky enough to have my 'office'.

I let myself into what used to be the battery room, where the big lead-plated glass sulphuric acid accumulators were stacked in tall racks. Locals still have memories of coming down here to have their little wireless batteries charged up. When the place was a Fish Museum, this was where visitors entered the building; maybe we could use it in the same way and have a gift shop in here too.

There's a glass door through to a small workshop that has racks tailored for long-gone tools, a zinc-sheeted bench – sporting an enormous ancient vice – with heavy black drawers underneath. I slide open a drawer; it's crammed with mangled bits of ancient electrical equipment. At the far end of the room, a pair of thief-damaged doors leads out onto a rotting catwalk over the millrace. I step along it gingerly and fumble for the key to the engine house. Inside the door, there's a small glass-paned office with a broken wall-mounted speaking-tube telephone and a tiny, varnished desk fixed to the wall. There's a plastic chair, completely out of keeping with everything else, and I sit down and try to imagine what it must have been like to be the foreman here.

Immediately opposite me, across the grubby but still elegant black-and-white tiled floor, are the two massive Gilkes lowland river turbines. They're flanked by two Blackstone oil engines, both with big twin flywheels. Running along the ceiling, there's a belt-driven driveshaft, although the belts themselves have disappeared. Immediately outside the office are the two electricity generators; they'd have been connected by the belts to the turbines, or, when there was insufficient water power, to the Blackstone engines. Away to the right in another part of the hall are three huge water pumps, also linked to the driveshaft. They look like ship's boilers, tipped upright.

Everything is coated in matt black paint. I find out later that Miriam ordered this paint job, sadly after a break-in during which nearly all the brass fittings and instruments were pinched. I stare upwards and note that the driveshaft pulleys still have their brass-and-glass lubricators in position. Obviously none of the thieves had the courage to clamber up the precarious little metal ladders that lead to the aerial walkways.

I remember how intriguing and sad everything looked on my first visit. It looks the same. I'm sure we can do something. Perhaps, cleaned up, with interpretation boards, and with the outside catwalk made safe, all this could be of added value to what we can offer to the public. We can clean up the beautiful Victorian floor for a start. I sit on one of the concrete plinths, gaze at one of the Blackstones, and think how marvellous it would be to get its twin flywheels whirring round again. But, with a twenty-six horsepower engine made in Stamford in 1937, we're unlikely to find anyone who would even know where to begin.

Retracing my steps, I go back through the battery house and out into the courtyard, wrestle with the padlock on the white gate, unlock the big sliding door into the Fish Museum with its dusty stuffed fish on the walls and cabinets of various ways of fishing from around the world, and leap in the air as the jangling alarm takes me by surprise yet again. I grope upwards for the 'alarm off' button above my head and catch my breath in the silence.

I climb the steep stairs onto the grubby junk-filled mezzanine and take the final few steps up into the enormous space originally used for storage of grain. It subsequently became a carpenter's shop, and now it's where I've established my 'office'. It will be an ideal space for displays and I've drawn detailed plans (included in the proposal to Miriam and Charles) of where everything will go. But I'm worried about how visitors will be able to get up here. At the moment there's only the very steep set of wooden stairs I've just come up.

I go down again and walk outside. Besides her Fish Museum, Miriam assembled a collection of bygones, mostly agricultural equipment from the estate, much of it left out in the elements. A beautiful primrose yellow pony trap has rotted where it stands and now leans drunkenly on broken-spoked wheels. There's a rusty grey Fergy, a hay-bale elevator with flat tyres and no engine, and a collection of ploughs, harrows, seeders and harvesters, all of which have clearly seen better days.

Rummaging among the jailer-size bunch of keys, I eventually open the padlock that secures the stable door to the nearest of two ranks of outbuildings that run parallel to the millrace. Inside is a dusty, cobwebbed but complete set of blacksmith's tools, a forge, two enormous power saws, a group of ancient forks and spades, and an entire thatcher's display. Some of the descriptive labels are still in position, others have been rearranged creatively by mice; all are faded almost to illegibility. We can bring this back to life, I'm sure, perhaps get Graham Carter to restore the thatcher's items, maybe even find a blacksmith.

The other set of buildings was once a dairy and still has the stalls for the cows. It's divided into three spaces but houses very little except for a big blue-barrelled water cart, whose red-spoked wheels have also collapsed. I reckon we might be able to use this area for a workshop, a cinema, and ... something else? We'll think of something.

I go back out through the white gates, cross the courtyard and unlock the gate into the tearoom garden. It's overgrown and untidy but with a fair amount of work could look very nice. The hedges have gone mad.

I let myself into the tearoom kitchen. It's revoltingly dirty, and both domestic cookers are ingrained with muck. The fridge is more green than white and there's mould on several surfaces. Two steps up and into the first of the three public rooms with their dark wooden floors and 1970s tables and chairs. There are several more bygones in here, various dairy items and a magnificent butter churn. Damp patches stain the ceilings and in some places the wallpaper is hanging off. I open the 19th century French widows and take two steps down into the garden again. The door to the outside loo is stuck fast. I force it open to find that it's been used by a tramp; the floor and the walls are encrusted with shit. In any case the loo won't flush as the water's turned off. Which of the volunteers will ...? Me, probably.

Engine house, fish display, blacksmith's forge, bygones, tearoom. None of these have anything to do with dragonflies, but they're now my responsibility and they may well attract visitors. I climb back into Pierre and drive down to the lake for a think. I sit on the bench on the north bank and ask myself if I'm ready for this. It'll be a huge change. I'll be leading a team.

I'll be administrating an organization. I'll be negotiating with countless other bodies. If it's to be a registered charity, I'll have to set it up and then be beholden to trustees. I'll have to hunt for funds. Endless bloody forms. Another phase of my life will begin. When I drive up to Ashton, there'll be little time for sitting here by the lake, and even less to note down experiences as they happen. We now have two areas to work on, the Sanctuary and the Mill. The Sanctuary needs as much work as it ever did; we plan eight Open Days this year, so it must continue to look its best.

Do I really want this? Almost all of me says yes. Yes, because it's a unique chance to enthuse many more visitors about dragonflies. Yes, because it's a brilliant way to move dragonflies up the public agenda. Yes, because I have a tough little group of willing volunteers and it's a chance for them to create something special, to feel the magic of making what seems impossible possible, just as I have here at the lake. Yes, because I have Kari's support. Who else, quite apart from offering to run courses on larval identification, would agree to run a tearoom? There's tiny part of me that says no; it's the bit that's afraid of failure. But yes, most of all, because if I don't do this, no one else will.

SUNDAY, JULY 10TH, 1994

I drive down to the Lee Valley Country Park for the official opening of the country's second Dragonfly Sanctuary. I've never been a guest of honour before. It's a very nice feeling, especially as all it involves is standing about and smiling. The star of the show is Chris Packham – immaculate white T-shirt and black trousers this time – who gives another impressive pro-dragonfly speech backed by an enormous dragonfly banner. Local children do a dragonfly dance while we chat in the sunshine and eat snacks. Tim Hill is the man behind this. When he and his team came to Ashton last year I wasn't absolutely sure how serious they were. They were. They have strong local support, they're near London, and the Country Park has excellent dragonfly habitat, including both flowing and still water spaces. Good.

SATURDAY, JULY 23RD, 1994

It's an Open Day and I'm taking the afternoon tour round the lake. Just as I've been holding forth to a group about the lovely thatch on both our little buildings, a man points to the tall pointed finial on the top of the observation hut roof. It's completely rotten.

'Why wasn't that replaced when it was re-thatched?' he asks.

'We got a quote,' I say, 'but it was hideously expensive.'

'Would you like me to make you one? For nothing?'

He's true to his word. Two weeks later I meet him and his wife in a pub in Elton one evening and he hands me a large parcel. He will accept nothing except half a pint of beer. And four days later, once I've given the new finial three coats of Ashton blue paint and borrowed a ladder from Peter Scott, there it is, on top of the observation hut. I fail to note the kind man's name in my diary.

Another couple, the Hermsens, offer to make us plates embellished with Kari's Migrant Hawker dragonfly design. They're beautiful. What's evident, again and again, is just how much people appreciate what we're doing and how often we receive offers of help.

One request in particular takes me by complete surprise. A lady comes up to me after a tour round and asks about the machinery at the Mill. Would it be possible for her father to be allowed to look at it? No, he's not here and he's too shy to ask, but he's very interested. I agree to meet him if he contacts me.

FRIDAY, JULY 29TH, 1994

I still manage to seize the occasional quiet moment by the lake. This afternoon I decide to take the Canadian canoe out to have a look for exuviae. Aided by Peter Scott, I've restored the wooden platform inside the boathouse and it's very satisfying to unlock the door, step inside and choose which of the three craft neatly moored inside to use.

As I undo a rope, I hear a fluttering from above my head. It's a big dragonfly, caught in the cobwebs in the rafters beneath the thatch, too high to reach. I seize one of the long kayak paddles, stick one end into the mud in the bottom of the boathouse, and then raise the paddle carefully towards the roof. The dragonfly clings to the muddy surface of the blade and I very slowly tug it free of the cobwebs. I lower the paddle and edge backwards out of the boathouse. I stand the pole against the wall outside in the sunshine and gently ease strands of spider web from the dragonfly's wings. I'm expecting her – she's a female Brown Hawker – to hurtle off into the blue, but she stays on the black edge of the paddle blade. I run back to the observation hut for my camera. The dragonfly is still in position when I gallop back, breathless. I take a shot of her, lean forward, ease a couple more threads off, then she lifts and swoops away over the lake.

SATURDAY, JULY 30TH, 1994

My best mate Mike has come for the weekend and dutifully stands among the small crowd ready to be taken round on the first tour of the day. Mike, Kari and I have driven down from the mansion in Pierre. Having been metropolitan for virtually her entire life, Kari has never needed to learn to drive, but, no longer living in Holland Park, she's going to have to, indeed wants to, and the combination of little Citroën and loads of open space here at Ashton is proving very useful.

It's a lovely day, the Citroën has its roof rolled back and Kari has made a good job of bringing us down. Suddenly she's forgotten something and needs to go back to the mansion. She decides she'll risk her first solo drive, climbs in, waves confidently and drives away. I launch into my talk beside the observation hut and I'm still talking five minutes later when Kari reappears, on foot, frantically beckoning to me. I have visions of a bent Citroën. It's impossible for me to leave the group, but Mike quickly spots something's wrong, detaches himself from the group, and goes over to her. As I lead the group off down the north bank, I see the two of them walking off up the hill.

Later, when the tour is over, they reappear in the Citroën. The car looks fine and they're both convulsed with laughter. Apparently, Kari had set off, driving perfectly, but had got confused about the route. She'd veered off the track into the wood and driven on until she noticed that the trees on either side were coming closer and closer. She only stopped when one was right in front of her. Mike says he's had an almost impossible job to get the car reversed out. This is not the first time that Kari has demonstrated she's navigationally challenged, though it it's certainly the most extreme. At least she doesn't get cross and blame other people as Miriam does in similar circumstances.

SATURDAY, AUGUST 3RD, 1994

It's one of our Ashton Water Dragonfly Sanctuary Open Days. A rather distinguished-looking man in a blue blazer and a panama hat joins my first group of the afternoon. I'm sure I know him from somewhere but can't place him. Has he been at one of Miriam's parties? Somehow I don't think so. Anyway, I walk the group round, and the man asks several very thoughtful questions then comes up afterwards to thank me for the tour. Unable to quell my curiosity I say I'm sure I've seen him before but can't place where.

'At the East of England Show last year,' he says. 'I'm Bill Westwood, Bishop of Peterborough. May I write you a small cheque?' (Bishop Bill stayed in touch with us, always encouraging, and continued to send us annual cheques, even after his retirement to Beverley.)

SUNDAY, AUGUST 14TH, 1994

We've just finished our eighth and last Open Day and have averaged just under 150 visitors per day. Once again the weather has been on our side but we can't rely on it, and the observation hut is clearly too small to accommodate more than about fifteen people at a time. Sometimes we've had to ask visitors to watch the Introductory Video in shifts. We must have more space. Dare we open the Museum next year? I'm sure Miriam will be happy, but how can we possibly get it ready in time? Do we have enough troops and willpower to manage it? There have been some lovely moments of kindness during the season, these quite apart from the extraordinary generosity from the volunteers both in time and useful bits of equipment. But a Museum opening next year? It would be a huge leap.

TUESDAY, AUGUST 16TH, 1994

Mike and I take another great dump of blanket weed out of Highgrove pond. We see three Common Blue Damselflies, five Common Darters and three Emperors. To find three Emperors on a relatively small water space is a surprise. We find damselfly exuviae, proof of breeding, showing that even with the blanket weed, there's now no doubt that the water that has been through the Highgrove sewerage treatment system is of good quality. We've made our point.

SATURDAY, SEPTEMBER 3RD, 1994

Among the people that I've consulted about the possibility of setting up a Dragonfly Museum are four key members of the British Dragonfly Society: Norman Moore, Philip Corbet, and Jill and Ronnie Silsby. Today I receive a note from Jill offering the Society's help with Museum expenses. So the BDS are the first organization actually to offer financial help. It's a great vote of confidence.

FRIDAY, SEPTEMBER 23RD, 1994

My forty-eighth birthday. I'm set for another day of sorting stuff out at the Mill, but, before I go, I walk alone in the sunshine down to the lake. I've just returned from a short stay home in Perthshire, during which I had the luck to photograph a Common Hawker on the telegraph pole at the bottom of the garden. I still prefer the Common Hawker's Linnaean name, *Aeshna juncea*. They look so attractive with their prominent yellow stripes running along the fronts of their wings.

I'm approaching the boathouse and peering vaguely along the water margin. A dragonfly lands on a reed just on the other side of the steps down to the Boathouse. I guess it's the usual, a Migrant Hawker. I lean carefully and slowly over the wall and look at it hard. It's an *Aeshna juncea*, bright yellow wing-stripes. I'm absolutely sure no one will believe me; *junceas* only like acid water and there's none around here for tens of miles. But then I recall Norman telling me he'd dug acidic pools at Woodwalton Fen and that, although their nearest know habitat was forty-six miles away in Norfolk, *junceas* had turned up. Of course I don't have my camera with me, and the dragonfly dances along the outside of the reeds and shoots away into the sky. Well, we can't count it as a breeding species but at least we can say that we now have a total of seventeen species recorded here at Ashton Water Dragonfly Sanctuary. And on my birthday, too.

I do a people count: we've had 3,500 visitors since 1991.

THURSDAY, OCTOBER 13TH, 1994

Kari and I are in the gigantic *Rathaus* in Frankfurt. A small army of Rothschilds have been summoned to attend the opening of the Jewish Museum and this is the big ceremony. The place is crammed with TV crews and journalists. We sneak in and try to hide near the back but Kari is spotted and we're dragged to the front and stuck in the middle of a long row. I find myself studying the back of Lord Rothschild's neck.

I don't have time to work out who the German President is before everyone goes quiet and sits down, and an obviously important musical personage starts to play the piano on the stage. He's chosen a slow, quiet piece. I'm instantly seized with the worst coughing fit I've ever had. It begins slowly but builds into virtual apoplexy. There's nothing for it but to stand up, stuff my red hankie in my mouth, barge my way down the row, and try to get out of the hall before I ruin the recital completely. What I haven't realized is that the entire hall is now jammed with people, large numbers standing in the aisles. Most draw swiftly aside and allow this big bearded man to push his way through them and stumble towards the doors. The hitherto invisible grey-suited German security squad instantly surrounds me and blocks the exit. They must think I've planted a bomb.

Time stops. I have about three or four second before I cough my guts up all over the polished floor. What to do? Give in to a coughing fit that will drown the piano and cause a thousand heads to turn and wonder what on earth's going on at the back? Grapple with Germany's finest and risk death? I actually lay hands on the crew-cut Wotan-like bloke right in front of me when a woman beside him says one word, and he turns and opens the door. Then I'm outside, hanging onto the bannisters, coughing and retching.

I wonder what the word was.

FRIDAY, OCTOBER 21ST, 1994

I've been reading through the wodge of bumph sent to me by the Charity Commission. Several people I've talked to have shaken their heads about setting up a registered charity single-handed: very complicated, terribly time-consuming, really ought to use a lawyer, and so on. But the people at the Commission have been extremely helpful. Apparently I need a minimum of two more trustees. After careful thought I decide to ask Jane Baile, Miriam's foster-daughter, and Justin Warhurst. Jane's a very independent spirit and runs Prebendal Manor, a successful mediaeval museum not far way. She's wise in the ways of visitors and knows everyone worth knowing in the local museum world. Justin is treasurer of Plantlife, is a very canny accountant and is married to my niece. I write to Jane and Justin and to my delight they accept, although from her own experience Jane worries about what I've let myself in for.

THURSDAY, NOVEMBER 3RD, 1994

The die is cast. I send off the Charity Commission application forms for The National Dragonfly Museum. I wonder how long the process will take.

SUNDAY, NOVEMBER 27TH, 1994

Our first trustees' meeting. I break the news that I've had a surveyor come and look at the property. His name's Brian Eames. I've known him for a long time. He's done a great deal of work for Canning, and several times we've stood together in the rain on various London roofs as he's told me the worst. Last week, Brian drove up from Kent, spent nearly a whole day checking every nook and cranny, and then sent us a report. He charged us nothing. He's the first of several be-suited professionals who give their time to us freely. Wonderful. But he reckons the main Mill building will need at least £40,000 spent on it over the next ten years just to keep it watertight. Charles' draft lease make us responsible for this, and I've already checked funding with Colin Rae, the local Historic Buildings man, who tells me we could only get a 25% grant for the work.

I agree to go back to Charles to get the responsibility changed and to ask him at the same time for a longer lease. Most fund providers I've approached so far regard a five-year lease as risible. Ten just about OK. Twenty-eight is the standard.

SATURDAY, DECEMBER 3RD, 1994

It's a fine sunny day and we've been working like hell down at the Mill. We're replacing roof tiles and broken glass, running new electrical cabling, installing lighting, cleaning drains, and painting the place inside and out. Volunteers and BDS members have donated cookers, cabinets, cupboards, seating, shelves, hoovers, lighting, tables, desks, a television and a VCR.

Kari has made an enormous veggie lasagna and I've been to the supermarket for beer and soft drinks. It's vital for volunteers to feel they're going to be fed and watered and not to have to worry about making sandwiches the night before. It's also much friendlier than having everyone sitting round at lunchtime munching glumly out of polythene boxes.

People seem to appear when we need them. We've been desperate for a proper carpenter to fix doorframes, doors and windows, and so Heather and Mick Twinn have press-ganged their friends Pam and Evan Peacock into coming along. Evan is a full-time carpenter and sets to work willingly on complex tasks well beyond the rest of us. I spot him peering closely at the Fergy TD20, too.

Last week I met the local Health and Safety man and he vetoed any chance of using the big space above the engine house for our displays: severe fire risk, dangerous access and no fire exit. It's a listed building so even if funds were available we couldn't put stairs and a lift on the outside. A spiral staircase down into the engine house? No, not acceptable. I've double-checked this with the local Listed Building people and they say the same. So we've had a re-think and asked Miriam whether we can use the space downstairs instead, where the dusty stuffed fish live. I've suggested we move the fish into the former dairy. I knew we'd find a use for it. She's agreed, but she still wants everything cleaned, restored and displayed.

We've whitewashed the dairy and shifted everything across, including the massive Victorian cabinets. One team is now concentrating on laying out the fishy exhibits as interestingly as possible while a second team is starting on cleaning what will be the main Museum and the inside of the battery room. There's dust and dirt everywhere but Lynn Curry is already talking of setting up the gift shop.

The archaeological collection has been stored upstairs in the loft, along with a massive architect's drawing board, and this has left the main space above the engine house free for our use. Today, we've set out trestle tables in the newly cleared space, and ranged chairs down both sides. The chairs have come via Adrian Colston at Northamptonshire Wildlife Trust, and the tables from Canning. We've taken over the defunct tearoom, re-papered all three rooms, and restored the ageing electric cookers to working order. Henry Curry and I have attacked the shit-encrusted outside loo and made it presentable once more. Henry's fearless approach to plumbing has enabled us to turn the water back on, too.

Fearless approaches seem indeed to have become the norm. First, a heavy cabinet reaches the top of the stairs, suddenly swings over and threatens to tumble down on its pushers' heads. Second, someone carrying a large tank ignores warnings about the state of the catwalk over the millrace and yells as their right foot disappears through the rotting woodwork towards the water below. Next, a patch of dead ivy the size of very large carpet is triumphantly cut free from the outside toilet roof, slides rapidly earthwards, and pushes over – and momentarily buries – Stuart Irons. There've been several other moments when I've simply had to look away.

This morning Kari has made yet another veggie lasagna and I've been to the pub to fill two demijohns with beer. We've brought over plates and knives and forks from the tearoom, carried them upstairs and laid everything out as grandly as possible. It's time for lunch. We sit down and I look along the tables. I've got something very important to say.

Among the volunteers, I make a special note to watch the reactions of those that have worked hardest both here and at the Sanctuary. They're all here: Peter Scott, Henry and Lynn Curry, Mick and Sue Parfitt, Mick and Heather Twinn, Sue and Trevor Leal, Ian and Sheila Wright, Henry Stanier, Stuart Irons, Pam and Evan Peacock, Ray and Kay Thompson.

I wait until we've almost finished, replete with lasagna and beer, then stand up. I know, I say, that up to now all our decisions have been collaborative but I'm now making one that's not for discussion. Yes, we still have a huge amount of work to do, but, wait for it, I've set a date for opening to the public: Thursday the 8th of June next year. We'll open from 2.00pm to 5.00pm every Thursday and Friday afternoon, and 10.30am to 5.00pm every Saturday and Sunday right through until the 1st of October. The tearoom will open every afternoon while we're in action. And we'll do eight Open Days at Ashton Water Dragonfly Sanctuary, too.

There are several gasps, a couple of shaking heads; but there are also approving noises and determined looks. Can we do it, I ask. Henry Curry and Mick Parfitt reach simultaneously for 'Ruary's Rocket Fuel'. We can, we will.

Chapter 26

THURSDAY, JANUARY 5TH, 1995

Pierre the Citroën is rusting fast, it's getting old and its tired suspension really isn't fit for the job of transporting stuff back and forth any more, up the pot-holed drive and down the muddy wintry track to the lake. Kari and her sister Berit offer to subsidize us for a second-hand Land Rover. Wonderful. What a generous – and timely – donation.

So after several searches we've lighted upon a 1983 model, a bright red former Royal Aircraft Establishment fire engine, sitting in the open air at R.J. Land Rovers in Sawtry. I really like fire engines, and the prospect of being able to drive about in a fairly practical one is delightful. It has a noticeably low mileage but, not being mechanically brilliant, I take Billy Nall over to have a look at it.

Billy has a workshop up in Ashton village and has helped us out on several occasions. He looks under the bonnet then asks for our prospective purchase to be raised on a ramp. He pokes about, and emerges from underneath muttering to me: 'Buy it, buy it.' When I get him out of earshot of the R.J. staff, I ask him what makes him so definite. 'I'd swear that mileage is genuine,' he says. 'It's hardly been out of its fire station. It's never been driven off-road, certainly. When you drive the rough stuff, the front and rear differentials always get a knock or two. The ones on this thing are unmarked.'

Thus we acquire 'Fire Nine', which, from the paperwork left inside, we discover was its original RAF Thurleigh call-sign. It was part of the team researching the feasibility of using 'ski-jumps' to launch Fleet Air Arm planes from aircraft carriers, 'Harriers from Carriers'. Fire Nine still has its hoses, its fire-fighting tanks, its ultra-high pressure BCF foam wand, its aerodrome maps, its taxiing bats, its protective gloves, its public address system, its tall wavy aerial, and, best of all, its flashing blue lights and two-tone out-of-my-way air horns. We dispense with the tanks, fit a sensible van-type rear body, and keep all the toys.

Fire Nine begins years of faithful, practical service for another aerial cause, dragonflies. Appropriately, it retains the RAE coat-of-arms on both doors, blue shields with the motto '*Alis Apta Scientia*' (Knowledge and Skills for Wings), surmounted by what look like winged dragons. Henry Curry is extremely knowledge-able about a wide range of fauna. He cleans his glasses, peers closely at the coat-of-arms, straightens up and says,

'They're actually dimorphodonts.'

WEDNESDAY, JANUARY 11TH, 1995

I finally meet Dick Witt, the man who got his daughter to ask about the Mill machinery last summer. He's tall, craggy, stooped, bespectacled and very quiet. I lead the way into the engine house and Dick studies the right-hand Blackstone carefully.

'See that?'

'What?'

'That crack.' He edges his finger along a fissure that runs the length of the water jacket surrounding the cylinder. 'When they stopped using this, they left it with the water in. They didn't drain it down. Come the next hard frost, the water expanded and that was that. Wrecked it. Remember the days before anti-freeze, when cars used to get cracked blocks in the winter?'

'I do,' I say. 'It happened to my brother's Allard.'

Dick moves over to the left-hand engine. He's silent for a while, just bending, staring and tapping, then, 'This one's gone, too.' More silence. 'Not so bad, though.' Then the magic words:

'Would you like me to try to get it going for you?'

'Oh, I would,' I say, 'I really would.'

Dick gives the engine a pat. 'Well, I was apprenticed at Blackstone's before the war. So I know a bit about these.'

I think back to that moment last year when I sat on the plinth over there and wondered whether we might …

'You'll need to help me, mind,' he says. 'I'm seventy-eight.'

FRIDAY, JANUARY 13TH, 1995

Working with Dick to get the monster Blackstone going, my contribution seems to consist of helping him clean things, lift things, carry things and pull jammed things out of other things. It's Dick who works the miracles: do I know anyone who can stitch-weld cast iron to mend the water jacket? Of course I don't but I get a quote. It's several hundred pounds. Dick knows someone too, though, and he gets it done for free. So now we have a fully functioning water jacket once more.

But today disaster strikes. We finally get the engine to pieces, and find the foot-high big end for the connecting rod is completely worn away and needs its chrome re-metalling. That stumps Dick; if it stumps him, it stumps me, so we stop work. The game's up. End. Blast. Well, only a few people knew we'd even started. We sit and drink tea and smile ruefully at each other. It's been a good experience. Dick asks if he can have the big end. Why not?

WEDNESDAY, JANUARY 25TH, 1995

I come down to the mill and, to my surprise, Dick's van is parked in the courtyard. He opens the tailgate and there, shining in the sun, is the big end, beautifully re-metalled.

'Dick! How on earth?'

'Had a brainwave. Took it to the Nene Valley Railway. They're used to big engines.'

'I can't believe it! What did it cost? How much do we owe you?'

'Oh, they didn't worry about that. Did you ever get a chance to look at those pulleys?'

SATURDAY, FEBRUARY 11TH, 1995

Jane, Justin and I hold another trustees' meeting. I report that I've approached twenty-six possible fund-providers and followed up with ten of them. We're clearly going to have to go back to Charles and get a ten-year lease at least. But things are moving forward with the Charity Commission, though we're not there yet. Volunteers have been coming virtually every weekend and we're making very good progress. I show Justin and Jane my ten-week plan for getting the whole place ready for Dragonfly Day on 3rd June.

SUNDAY, FEBRUARY 19TH, 1995

A volunteer weekend. In the tearoom, we re-stain the wooden floors, mend three tables, acquire and clean two more fully operational fridges. Kari spends hours scouring the insides of the two cookers and is taking her role as future tearoom commander with her usual attention to detail. She has a tiresomely long list. We pay our first visit to Booker's, the food wholesalers, and among many, many other things, we invest in a set of seriously large pots and pans. She has also researched the whole business of scone production. I'd no idea it was a subject for research, but after hours of study Kari comes up with an easy-to-do recipe that knocks the socks off everyone who tastes the finished product.

Over in the engine house, Dick's hard at work. A couple of other volunteers are now helping him. The Blackstone engine will be cooled by water in the newly stitch-welded water jacket. We've deciphered how it was designed to work: when the water gets hot in the jacket, it will rise – *should* rise – up a pipe into the top of two tall drum-shaped tanks mounted outside, above the catwalk, to be replaced by cool water flowing down a second pipe from the bottom of the same pair of tanks. It's supposed to work on the same principle as a domestic back boiler, a thermosyphon: hot water rises and is replaced by cold. Our assumption is that if the water was left in when the engine was last used, the system must have been working. So, with luck … But the tanks have been without top covers for years and we have no idea how much rubbish has accumulated in them, or whether they can still hold water, or whether the water will flow properly round the system. There's only one way to find out what's in the tanks.

Trevor mounts a ladder and disappears down into Tank One. There's a lot of muffled swearing and then filthy black gunk starts to fly over the side. Henry Curry, hit on the head by a clump of twenty-year-old leaves, throws most of it back. More swearing. Laughter. By the end of the weekend we've cleaned both tanks, filled them, found out they only leak a bit, and lidded them in corrugated iron. And inadvertently flooded the engine house in the process.

SATURDAY, MARCH 4TH, 1995

Another volunteer weekend. Dick and I have re-assembled the Blackstone and he thinks we should have a go at starting it. The problem is how. Dick fuels the beast up and oils round – Sid at the farm has kindly allowed us oil and diesel – while I martial a gaggle of the burliest volunteers. We divide into two groups and lay hands on the two flywheels. Dick shouts and we start to spin the wheels as fast as possible. Nothing. Six tries later, we're all lying on the floor, gasping and glaring at the silent machine.

I drive up to Billy Nall's shack and dragoon him into bringing down a cylinder of compressed air. In order to start a monster like a Blackstone you really need a massive supply of compressed air to shove the piston round and round until the diesel ignites and the thing starts to run. Both engines have heavy cast iron air bottles beside them for just this; they look exactly like black torpedoes standing upright and they weigh about the same. But are they in good enough condition to take modern air pressures? They've been standing there since 1937. So we hook up Billy's cylinder and try again. The engine leaps round but refuses to fire. Billy scratches his head and looks at the label on the cylinder. His mouth drops open. It's not compressed air, it's compressed gas. Oops. Fortunately for us, it's inert: argon. But, though we're still alive, we're no further on. We all look at the air bottles. We need at least one of them to work. But how on earth do we move them around, let alone get them tested?

MONDAY, MARCH 6TH, 1995

Dick appears with a neat two-wheel trolley designed specifically for transporting the air bottles. It transpires he designed and welded it up, at home, yesterday. Much later he mentions that he's had to handle actual torpedoes in his time. During the war, he says, he worked in Portsmouth on Vosper engines for RAF rescue launches and Royal Navy torpedo boats. But he says no more. It doesn't need much imagination to realize what he must have been through. Quite apart from the constant bombing of the naval dockyard, the engines he'd have worked would have come back from action in the Channel: shell damage, blood, body parts …

'Can you unbolt the bottle from the wall?' he asks. 'I want to have a look at it, back home. See what you can find in the meantime.'

We wheel the air bottle out into the yard, manhandle it into the back of Dick's truck and he drives off. I phone round and then head over to a diving centre near Whittlesey, but their compressed air canisters are laughably small compared to ours. Then I locate a supplier in the desolate ex-industrial wasteland that is outer Corby and make the first of several visits involving single-handed wrestling with torpedo-size air cylinders in cheerless surroundings.

FRIDAY, MARCH 10TH, 1995

Dick is already parked as I roll the Land Rover into the courtyard. The tailgate of his pickup is up and inside is the air bottle.

'It's fine,' he says.

'How do you know it's fine, Dick?'

'I tested it.'

'You what? How?'

'I pumped water into it under pressure. Took it way over the pressure we need. It didn't explode.'

'Christ! What if it had …? Where were you, while it was filling? I hope you took cover.'

'No.'

'You didn't?'

'No. No point. Well, not at my age. Can you bring the trolley?'

'Did Ann know what you were doing?'

'Eh? She's looking after the terrier this morning. Got the keys? Not much time today.'

SATURDAY, MARCH 11TH, 1995

This afternoon we release compressed air into the Blackstone oil engine. It gasps several times and then – oh joy – thumps into action. I'm afraid the chimney might be stuffed with nearly fifty years' worth of dead birds, but I walk outside onto the catwalk and watch as little puffs of smoke huff into the sky. It's a very good feeling.

Our first job is to switch the exhaust into the air bottle pipe, and pump the bottle back up to proper pressure ready for next time. If ever we forget this – and we regularly do – I'm lumbered with yet another journey to outer Corby. Who cares? The mill has a heart beating again.

THURSDAY, APRIL 27TH, 1995

A letter arrives from the Charity Commission. We're finally a registered charity. It's been relatively straightforward, taken under six months and been free of lawyers.

The Bentley has gone. There's no question of running a registered charity and a tired expensive old Beast at the same time. It has passed to Adrian Dence, a man who can afford to look after it in the style to which it ought to be accustomed. We miss it terribly. There aren't many cars that can take you from Peterborough to Perthshire and let you step out at the other end very nearly as full of energy as when you set off.

I take Fire Nine – an entirely different sort of motoring – into Oundle and apply at the local bank to open a charity account in the name of The National Dragonfly Museum. There's a pause, and, behind the glass screen, a number of slightly incredulous whispered conversations. The bank manager summons me into his office. He's a classic old-school type, fractionally scruffy, a chain smoker with heavy black glasses. He's intrigued, amused and sceptical.

'Have you ever run a museum before?'

'No.'

'Or a tearoom?'

'No. But …'

He grins at me over his specs and authorizes the account.

SATURDAY, APRIL 29TH, 1995

Another trustees' meeting. Jane shows us how to attract local attention. Justin helps us to organize our finances and their attendant paperwork. We now have funding from the British Dragonfly Society and from the East Northamptonshire District Council. Good. We're not panicking. Yet.

I also report that Kari has agreed to fund the purchase of a Leica Wild Microscope, with a matching camera and a large TV monitor. For the second time, she's burgled her own savings. This kit will enable entire audiences to see exactly what would normally only be visible to one person peering down the microscope. Steve Cham, a serious dragonfly enthusiast, works at Leica and gets us a discount, but Kari's generosity – very nearly £5,000 – means we can be really effective in getting the message across to visitors about the extraordinary larval lives of dragonflies. We've had the brainwave of putting a live dragonfly larva in a dish, sticking it under the microscope, and getting it to perform.

'Well,' says Kari, 'it was either a new kitchen for the flat, or a decent TV-Microscope set-up for the Museum. No choice really.'

SATURDAY, MAY 13TH, 1995

English Nature has agreed to support us. They will fund sixteen interpretation boards to the value of £7,000, provided they approve of the texts and provided I do all the liaison with the supplier. I write simple texts that I hope will be understandable by eleven-year-olds. Terry and Tim Dutton, a Walsall-based father and son team who run Insight, suppliers of interpretation material, are extremely helpful and produce beautiful, well-designed, blue-edged birch-ply boards. The wood comes from a sustainable source in Ireland.

Upstairs in the Mill there are several enormous sheets of reinforced hardboard. I have no idea what they were originally made for but we commandeer them, paint them white, suspend them from the rafters in our Museum space and, with Evan's careful carpentry, hang the interpretation boards on them. The result is a series of spacious bays that enable several visitors at a time to read each board in comfort. We mount floodlights to further brighten each bay.

Evan has also solved another problem. We're unsure how to mount the massive TV monitor that Kari has bought for us. It needs to be high enough for, say, an entire class of schoolchildren to watch it. It's far too heavy to fix to the wall. Evan arrives with pre-cut timber (we don't ask where the wood comes from and he doesn't charge us) and assembles an eight-foot-tall stand complete with shelving for a video-player and spare kit. He leaves us with the minor detail of how to get the monster TV monitor actually onto the stand. It takes four of us with a great deal of faith in each other to manhandle the beast upwards into space and finally, after a couple of heart-stopping lurches, onto the top of the stand.

SATURDAY, MAY 20TH, 1995

A small team from the Northamptonshire Wildlife Trust arrive and join us in the construction of an observation platform jutting out into the millrace. It's all done in a day, in time for us to stand triumphantly, drinks in hand, in the evening sunshine to watch damselflies laying eggs in the rushes on either side of the platform. It will be perfect for showing youngsters what they would normally only be able to see from a boat.

SUNDAY, MAY 21ST, 1995

Ray and Kay arrive and we make an introductory video for the Museum. Just as when we did the same job at the Sanctuary, a certain amount of drink is taken. They present us with a TV and a video machine on which to show the finished product. We clean out one of the little rooms close to the entrance, lay gravel inside, put up suitable signs, set out plastic chairs – hand-me-downs from the Canning School – and check it all works.

SATURDAY, JUNE 3RD, 1995

The National Dragonfly Museum opens to the public. I've managed to get quite a bit of local publicity and visitors flood in. I hadn't thought of the complication of the opening coinciding with Miriam's Dragonfly Party. I'm torn in two as I need to be up at the mansion and down here at the Mill, but there's no need to worry as the volunteers run the day perfectly whilst I float about, smiling vaguely. Lynn has the gift shop looking really attractive and does a brisk trade in sweatshirts, tea towels and related dragonfly items. Henry mans the TV-Microscope – he's copied and extended my initial demonstrations – and enthralls successive groups of visitors with the astonishing sight of a dragonfly larva shooting out its labial mask and attacking and consuming a bloodworm. Dick sets the Blackstone going, Evan talks to children about farm machinery, and Mick Parfitt and the others take visitors out onto our observation platform to show them dragonflies in action.

Kari has recruited two youngsters from Oundle, Sam and Charlotte Sears, to work in the tearoom and today, having drilled them to a pulp, she leaves them to it and joins me in yo-yoing up and down between the Mill and the mansion. Sam and Charlie perform excellently, handling serving the public and feeding the volunteers.

I spot the local bank manager sipping coffee and tucking into a scone in the tearoom garden.

THURSDAY, JUNE 8TH, 1995

We said we would try opening on Thursday and Friday afternoons and this is our first time. It's a risk because all the volunteers have full-time jobs, so these weekday afternoon sessions will be solely down to Kari and I.

This morning we went into Peterborough and bought all the perishables for the weekend. In the summer temperatures, milk and cream are the key things to look after and the Land Rover now has a large coolbox aboard. After lunch, Kari and I drive down to the Mill in good time, she to the tearoom, me to the Museum.

Kari's scones are now tried and tested. They're quick to make and delicious. She gets cracking making several trays of them and laying everything out ready for the visitors. At 2.00pm, she swallows hard, goes out into the garden, opens the gate, puts out the "Tea Room Open" sign, walks back to the building, mounts the stone steps and throws wide the elegant French windows. The die is cast. She's alone in the face of … no one.

So she goes back into the kitchen to finish her preparations. She's in the little storeroom when she hears footsteps coming up the three stone steps and in through the French windows: many footsteps, many, many footsteps. She straightens up and curses me. Must be a coach party and obviously I've forgotten to tell her. Well, she thinks, there's nothing for it, I'll just have to go through and take their orders. She fixes a smile on her face and breezes into the main tearoom. It's full of sheep. It takes some time to herd them into the garden, for Kari to clear up the mess and for me to find the local shepherd. The rest of the afternoon is busy with human customers but otherwise uneventful.

FRIDAY, AUGUST 5TH, 1995

It's almost exactly two months since we started at the Museum. Thursday and Friday afternoons have become a strain, Kari and I doing them alone for most of the time. In my case, I'm doing something I really want to do, talking dragonflies and machinery, but running a tearoom is hardly Kari's calling in life. Every minute making scones means time away from what she really wants to do, make a living out of her art. And Thursdays and Fridays are often very quiet, so being in the tearoom just in case visitors appear is doubly frustrating.

We're good at talking things through. It's saved us more than once. Now it's clear that, what with the Museum and training courses with Bosch, my stuff is taking priority, so we go and sit by the lake with a bottle and have a long discussion. She wants to know how I'd feel about her doing a two-days-a-week painting course at Edinburgh College of Art, Fridays and Saturdays, from October to March. It will mean being apart a fair bit. Well, we're used to that now, and I'll have to drive her to and fro. Of course I agree, but it's really important to have talked it through. She puts 'Assistant Curator, National Dragonfly Museum' on her application form.

WEDNESDAY, AUGUST 7TH, 1995

Philip Corbet rings from his office in the Biology Department of Edinburgh University. Would we like to have his collection of dragonfly specimens as a donation? Are we sure we can take care of them? They're fragile. How will we curate them? The cabinet is in Edinburgh. It's Victorian and has three sets of ten drawers. Can we collect it? He gives the details and measurements. It's the size, shape and weight of about half a billiard table. I put the phone down and have a think, then go outside and measure the Land Rover. The cabinet will fit almost exactly. But the problem will be getting it through the rear door. I ring Philip back and ask him to double-check the exact measurements. He simply repeats what he said before. He's a very precise man. So I go back and measure again. The cabinet will go into the back of the Land Rover with half an inch to spare on either side. I thank him and tell him we'll collect it in the spring. It's going to be a long careful journey south.

Another phone call, this time from the local bank. They're getting rid of a small safe. Would we like it? I drive into Oundle and it takes two of us all our strength to lift the little green monster into the back of the Land Rover. We install it behind a fridge in the tearoom food store and hide its big elegant brass key in one of the cookers. The bank manager is on our side. I suspect Kari's scones.

SUNDAY, SEPTEMBER 24TH, 1995

It's a beautiful evening. Most of us have turned up for our last day of the Museum's season. We're sitting in the tearoom garden gazing out over the millpond. We've done it. We've run our first season. And we have really won. More visitors than we could have dreamed of – 2,500 – and the beginnings of a regular clientele at the tearoom.

What I proposed to Miriam last year has actually happened. I mentally run through the list for what's yet to be done. Several items are still outstanding. We need two more observation platforms. We need a demonstration pond. We need more interpretation material: for example, we haven't got a worldwide dragonfly distribution board (but we've got a brilliant one on dragonfly vision instead) and it would be great to have more activity and information in the engine house. And we need to address how to get visitors flowing easily through the whole place. At the moment they buy their tickets and then, in order to reach the main museum area, they have to walk straight out of the door they just came in. But all in all …

We break out the champagne. Later in the evening someone takes two photographs: Henry Curry, saucepan on head, two Greene King beer cans projecting from it, Viking helmet style. Ruary, wearing a red traffic cone like a dunce's hat.

Chapter 27

SATURDAY, JANUARY 13TH, 1996

I've just completed my time sheet. It shows I worked for forty-six and a half weeks out of fifty-two for the Museum last year. Surely it's been too much fun for that?

FRIDAY, MARCH 1ST, 1996

Driving down to the Mill in the late afternoon, my head is full of small preparations needing to be made before the arrival of the volunteers tomorrow. Our volunteer list has forty-five names on it now, though of course not everyone turns up each time. We're planning to build a garden pond; the rubber liner is sitting behind me in the back of the Land Rover, along with a small water pump. I pull into the courtyard to find a blue Kawasaki motorbike, gleaming and powerful, sitting outside the Mill entrance. No one's about, so I wander over and give it a look.

'That's mine,' says a large leather-clad, rosy-faced man, appearing from round the corner of the Mill. 'Like it, my Kwacker?' It's not really a question, but then he asks, 'Know anything about this place?'

Motorbike Man looks a bit middle-aged to be riding such a monster but he's certainly got style. We chat and I tell him we've got a much bigger machine inside. Would he like to see it? He grins. 'Lead on, then.'

An hour later, we're still talking. He's seen the generator hall and been suitably impressed. I've apologized for not having a nice glossy brochure for him to take away, and he's now listening patiently while I extol the virtues of dragonflies.

When I stop talking for a moment to let him examine the jewellery in the 'Dragonflies in Art' cabinet, he says, 'I haven't introduced myself. I'm Michael Turner. I'm Marketing Director for Anglian Water. We're water people and you tell me dragonflies spend most of their time under water and it has to be good quality. That's how we feel, too. You say you haven't got a brochure. Would you like us to help you with that? Maybe we could help with more signage, too? You seem a bit short.'

Prejudiced by media reports of the rapacity and inefficiency of water companies, I unashamedly enquire as to Anglian's precise policy towards river water quality and conservation. Michael treats me to as enthusiastic a harangue about water as I've just given him about dragonflies, and repeats his offer of help. I tell him it's fantastic, and I'd like to think about what we really need. He gives me his card and says to ring him. I check with my fellow trustees that they approve of a connection with Anglian, then ring Michael with a shopping list. So begins a long and happy relationship with Anglian Water.

SATURDAY, MARCH 2ND, 1996

We erect a large sign on the wall of the tearoom, to catch the eye of cars driving towards Oundle. It sports our Migrant Hawker logo and in big letters it says, "THE NATIONAL DRAGONFLY MUSEUM". Though it doesn't say so, it was supplied by Anglian Water. A local worthy passes in his car, stops, reverses and asks whether we got permission to erect the sign. I tell him we just put it up. He harrumphs and drives off. I decide to wait until someone comes and orders us to get permission, or take it down. No one comes. Ever.

We set to work digging a hole in the rough grass between the forge building and the millrace. There are nineteen of us and by the end of the day we have a fine garden pond, already full of water pumped up from the river. Our guide has been the *Dig a Pond for Dragonflies* booklet, written by Norman Moore and produced by the British Dragonfly Society. Up in the mill loft we've found a ghastly old carpet, originally yellow but faded to dirty cream and covered with the sort of stains that would shock a cleaner and intrigue a detective. So, once we've got the hole dug and laid a layer of smooth sand, we slide the carpet in and put the liner on top.

Dumped in the undergrowth at the far end of the site is a pile of cream Barnack limestone, presumably left unused when the wall beside the road was built. We clear the brambles away, clean the stones, transport them, and lay them all round the edge of the liner, a discreet protective barrier. Only seriously mischievous children will be able to fall in now. The pond will be a perfect way to show visitors how easy it is to dig a pond and attract dragonflies to the average garden. Not everyone will have nineteen people to dig it, though.

WEDNESDAY, APRIL 17TH, 1996

Kari and I drive south from Perthshire in the Land Rover. It's one of many journeys to and from Scotland in this vehicle, a rather different experience from journeys in the Bentley. Fire Nine doesn't go very fast, the seats are stiff, upright and uncomfortable, it has no radio, it roars. Other than glancing in the rear view mirror at large trucks coming menacingly closer behind us, there's nothing to pass the hours except watching the fuel gauge steadily drop until it's time to find yet another petrol station. But we still love our red Land Rover.

Today we divert into the busy Edinburgh traffic and thread our way to the University Biology Department to pick up Professor Philip Corbet's collection of dragonfly specimens for the Museum. Here he is to meet us. Last August we spoke on the phone and he explained that they're housed in a very large Victorian wooden multi-drawer brass-knobbed cabinet. Philip has organized a team of helpers, including Professor Aubrey Manning. It isn't every day you see two professors staggering across a car park weighed down by a vast piece of furniture. We offer it up to the back door of the Land Rover. It looks as if it won't fit.

'Did you remember the door has sticking-out hinges?' asks Philip sharply. I do my best to look serene whilst frantically trying to recall whether … I haven't thought about it since last August. What on earth are we going to do if it doesn't go in? The cabinet slides in with just the tiniest space on either side.

THURSDAY, MAY 30TH, 1996

An Anglian Water vehicle arrives with box after box of glossy A5, sixteen-page, beautifully designed and laid out full-colour brochures. We've included a very neat dragonfly identification chart by Charlotte Matthews, and my photographs have been supplemented by better ones from Henry Curry, Andy McGeeney (President of the BDS) and Steve Cham (the man who got us a discount at Leica). I've written the text, and it's been read in draft, laughed at, partly rewritten and checked thoroughly by publisher/proof-reader Kari. It's been a challenge to think of the right sort of language to choose. I've aimed for a style that I hope will be cheerfully readable by eleven-year-olds.

What is so special about dragonflies?
They are very beautiful
They don't sting
They eat mosquitoes, gnats and midges
They are fantastic flyers
They are amazing to watch
They can warn us about water pollution

Why so bright and so fast?
Dragonflies are the Jump Jets of the insect world. But if you compare the way a Harrier flies with that of a dragonfly, it's like comparing an elephant with a ballerina! There is no manoeuvre a Harrier can do that a dragonfly can't do better.

Size for size, they are also much faster. They can fly up to 40 mph and can cover 15m in less than a second from a standing start. In the insect world 40 mph is terrifyingly fast. It means they can seize their prey in microseconds and easily escape from hungry birds. The males fight each other too, for females and territory. So like the fighters of the First World War, they need to be brightly coloured to see who's who. Some of their colour schemes make birds think twice before attacking. For example, the female Broad-bodied Chaser is the same colour and has similar markings to a hornet.

Explaining the difference between damselflies and dragonflies, their life-cycle, habitat loss, encouraging people to dig ponds, to put local native water plants, to record what they see, to join the BDS and so on was relatively easy, but I found it hard to get across the importance of biodiversity.

What is biodiversity?
Biodiversity is a word that sums up the idea that on this planet there are a truly enormous variety of life forms. Plants and animals are all interlocked in one way or another. This linking is very fragile. Quite often what happens to one species can have serious effects on another.

Why is it vital?
All over the planet, humans are changing the face of the Earth. We are changing habitats to suit us. As this happens we reduce or destroy habitats for other species. So plants and animals are disappearing at a startling rate. It is terribly important to protect the variety of species all around us. If we fail, we risk the loss of many more species – maybe finally even humans!

Where do dragonflies fit in?
The number of species in the British Isles has been falling mainly due to human activities. Here is an example. In several counties in the south of England, there used to be a beautiful dragonfly. It was called the Orange-Spotted Emerald. As rivers were 'improved' and river quality went down, it started to disappear. By 1950, it was seen only on one river in Hampshire. When a sewage plant was built beside the river, it disappeared

completely, another casualty for biodiversity in the British Isles. Fortunately, the Orange-Spotted Emerald still exists on the Continent. However there are similar examples of species vanishing and numbers dropping from all over Europe.

If we do not make sure the water quality in our rivers stays good (and gets better) the number of dragonflies will continue to drop and we will risk losing more species like the Orange-Spotted Emerald.

Much of the text described the Mill itself.

Ashton Mill – No ordinary mill

If you look carefully at the outside wall of the Mill, near the millpond, beneath the brickwork you can see the stonework of an earlier mill. Indeed there have been water mills here for over nine hundred years. The Domesday Survey in 1089 describes a thriving mill complex, its wheels and millstones grinding corn into flour. The rent at that time was £2 and 325 Eels per annum! Peterborough Abbey owned these mills for about five hundred years, until the Dissolution of the Monasteries in 1539. The Abbey also owned a bakehouse here, no doubt baking bread from the freshly ground flour. If you look again along the pond side of the mill, you will see that an extra storey was added probably in the late 1700s. The Luccam, the projecting white structure at the top of the wall, contains sack-lifting gear and was probably added at the same time. Ashton Mill continued to grind flour until the end of the 19th century.

Conversion

In 1900, the first Lord Rothschild converted the mill into an electricity generating station and water-pumping works. All the mill machinery was removed and massive girders were put in to strengthen the building. The new machinery was installed by Walter Morris Thomas, an engineer with an extraordinary grasp of the rapidly developing technologies of the day. The system was modelled on a much larger one on Lord Rothschild's estate at Tring. The machinery was designed to harness the power of the River Nene in order to create hydro-electricity and to drive water pumps. The equipment has been out of action for about fifty years but we hope to restore it to its former glory in due course.

What is so special about the Mill machinery?

The generating hall is a time-capsule of leading-edge, turn-of-the-century technology. In 1900 the use of dynamos, batteries and electric lighting was still very new. Practical hydro-electric systems and oil engines were even newer. It is very rare to see vintage hydro-electric, diesel-electric, water treatment and pumping systems in the same building. Everything was built to the highest standard. One glance at the floor will confirm that.

The Farm Machinery Collection

It is amazing to think that fifty years ago these machines were so common that most people wouldn't give them a second glance. Now, it is hard for us to understand what they did. We hope eventually to have details of what each machine can do, and perhaps a video of some of them in action. We also plan to restore the 'Fergy' to working order.

The Room of the Five Craftsmen

Here we have gathered all the equipment from five different crafts. If we could find a blacksmith, a saddler, a thatcher, a woodman and a basketmaker, these people could walk in, pick up the tools and start work. We plan to have demonstrations by local craftsmen from time to time.

The Fish Room

The Mill complex was originally converted to a museum by Miriam Rothschild in 1981. It was primarily a Fish Museum and its aim was to publicize the importance of water quality. A few years earlier there had been a cyanide spillage into the River Nene from a factory upstream. Large numbers of fish had been killed.

The Fish Room retains the items collected by Miriam Rothschild. These include unusual fishing baskets, salmon rods and flies and a fenland punt. The room also contains a collection of preserved fish from Walter Rothschild's Natural History Museum at Tring.

During the season we display live local fish in oxygenated tanks.

Renewable resources, conservation and The Dragonfly Museum

Here at Ashton Mill in 1900, at a time when people thought little about finite energy resources, Lord Rothschild chose the best and most advanced technology and used it to harness a renewable resource. He did this at Ashton for his younger son Charles, to whom he gave the estate.

Charles Rothschild in turn showed equal far-sightedness. Because of his efforts at a time when people thought little of protecting habitats for species, Charles Rothschild is now widely regarded as the father of modern nature conservation.

We feel sure that father and son would be pleased with our continuing work at the National Dragonfly Museum to show you, through dragonflies, the importance of biodiversity and conservation.

Besides the ton of brochures, the Anglian Water van disgorges a set of signs, big ones for the outside walls of the Museum and the tearoom, and small ones for directing visitors round the site. At a stroke, Anglian have made us look professional. They have also sent us a cheque.

SATURDAY, JUNE 4TH, 1996

A large pile of timber is sitting in the tearoom garden, already sawn and cut to size. Today we begin work on building a second observation platform in the millpond. It will be a terrific addition. Visitors will be able to stroll down from the tearoom and watch dragonflies in action over the pond.

We've been looking carefully at this pond. There are the remains of a jetty just below a gap in the garden wall. Evan the carpenter has already made a small white gate to fit this gap; it keeps young children from straying down from the garden into the water. But now we look closer, it's clear that the pond isn't really a pond at all. It's the head point of the mill outflow and, though its northern end is now blocked by enormous fallen willows, in the old days when the river was the best system for freight transport, it would have been possible to bring a boat in here from the main river and tie up below the garden wall. Back then, the tearoom would have been the miller's house.

If we're to build our platform, we may have to find and remove the original posts of the jetty. During the course of the day we do indeed find these posts and they're a devil to remove, stuck as they are in slimy black ooze. But eventually the job's done and we set about constructing the platform.

One of the problems is how to drive new posts into the mud. I'm busy elsewhere when a decision is made that perhaps a stepladder should be brought into play, and a sledgehammer wielded from the top of it. Mick Parfitt mounts the steps, sledgehammer in hand. Leslie McCombe holds the ladder and Stuart Irons holds the post. Mick takes a mighty swing, misses the post, hits the ladder and falls off. Luckily the ladder is already moving sideways as he swings, which means that Leslie's actually being pushed away as the sledgehammer descends, and it merely brushes her shoulder rather than smashes her skull. All three fall into the black mud.

Mick is one the most loyal of the loyal volunteers, ready to do absolutely anything, but this is not the first time things have not gone well for him in situations like this: last year I came round a corner to find him hopping up and down on his right leg, clutching his left foot having hit it very hard with a hammer. However, his readiness to stand by us, whatever we do, through thick and thin, makes him a true friend.

SATURDAY, JUNE 22ND, 1996

We are open and busy. The weather is beautiful and, as we've already noticed, the moment the sun comes out, visitors arrive. It's extraordinary. There's no interval; it's instantaneous. Dick Witt is pottering about in the generating hall, setting the Blackstone engine thumping from time to time. And Peter Mayhew's father Derek is working on getting the forge working again. He's actually a senior manager in a concrete company, but a bit of blacksmithing will be relaxation, he says.

Evan and Pam Peacock have enlisted the help of another engineering-minded family, Roger, Jenny, Darren and Amanda Margrave, and today they've started work on restoring the little grey Fergy that has been sitting disconsolately in the open air just inside the Museum gates for years. They've moved it under cover into the little garage at the end of the Fish Room building and are already dismantling it. It's going to be great to have a working Fergy; it will set off the rest of the farm equipment collection just right.

Evan mentions that if we can get the tractor going, he might be able to liberate a Fergy-compatible grass cutter from somewhere. It would save having to bring the Hayter down from the mansion garden every week and hours of stumping around behind it. There's someone he knows, he says, at a local district council; it might take some time. I offer payment and he suddenly goes vague.

SATURDAY, JUNE 13TH, 1998

Today is the Grand Opening, due to take place at 3.00pm. It isn't every day that Chris Packham and Miriam Rothschild will appear together. It's a great combination and will bring in a really wide spectrum of visitors. There's been a lot of publicity and there are police 'No Parking' cones all the way down to Ashton Roundabout.

Unfortunately, Miriam's lovely nephew Amschel died earlier in the week. She feels she oughtn't to be (and doesn't really want to be) on parade so soon after the event, so she won't come. But she invites Chris to lunch. We sit in the dining room, sun pouring in through the mullioned windows, Chris very smart in perfectly pressed black shirt and shorts, and he and Miriam get on extremely well together. They talk biology. I guess he's about the same age as Miriam's nephew.

Chris, Kari and I drive back down to the Mill with a good hour to spare before the big moment.

'Where do I cut the ribbon?' says Chris.

'Across the gate, here,' I reply.

He squints at the gate. He's obviously done this before.

'Should we just check for width? And have we got scissors?'

Which is when I realize I've forgotten to buy a ribbon.

Henry Curry offers to go. 'I can take the short cut', he says, 'over the river and across the fields.'

'You're both needed here,' says Chris. 'I'll go. Is there a shop in Oundle?'

Henry directs him down the little footpath to the town. He disappears and just over half an hour later he saunters back round the corner, white ribbon in hand. I suspect he may have run quite a bit of the way. He makes a brilliant speech. It's clear to his listeners that he knows a great deal about dragonflies and he's very much in favour of what we're doing. The day is a great success.

SUNDAY, JUNE 14TH, 1996

A small, serious, bespectacled, white-haired elderly man, slightly hunched, bends over one of the dynamos in the generating house and asks a series of questions far beyond my electrical pay-grade. He straightens up and says that the pre-First World War carbon brushes are ruined ('Are they? Right.') and he might have some replacements in his loft. His name is Ron Cook and he used to work on dynamos for the BBC at the big transmission station at Daventry. When I was little, I remember seeing 'Daventry' on the green and orange illuminated dial of the radiogram in the lounge at home. Along with 'Hilversum' it seemed a million miles away. Now, here's a man beside me who actually worked there.

SATURDAY, JUNE 22ND, 1996

Kari is extremely nervous. She hates standing up in front of groups of people and today she's running our first Larval Identification Course. She's spent ages designing the format and preparing diagrams for the participants. Like other members of her family, being nervous makes her irritable and I'm anxious that she'll bite some innocent volunteer's head off. Or worse, a participant. She doesn't. Well, only mine. The course goes extremely well. She has also set up a Larva Room, next door to the gift shop. With its three bubbling tanks, the place is a great draw for the kids who love peering through the glass and spotting dragonfly larvae moving among the water plants.

SUNDAY, JUNE 23RD, 1996

We can't keep doing this: earlier this afternoon, I started the Blackstone in front of an admiring crowd and forgot to blow the air bottle back up. No air, no engine. And Corby is closed on Sundays. But today we've managed to sweet-talk the local fire brigade into coming along with their compressor. Here they are in full yellow gear, big red appliance thrumming outside, air hose snaking through the gift shop. I don't think they'll come a second time; mustn't forget again. They were grateful for the crate of beer, though. It took off, into the cab of the fire engine, quicker than a Ruddy Darter.

THURSDAY, JULY 11TH, 1996

It's a quiet Thursday morning and there's an Environment Agency Land Rover parked outside the Mill. Three men are standing beside it. I get chatting to them and we walk along the millrace together, towards the weir. We talk dragonflies, how some like moving water – like the Banded Demoiselles they can see at this very moment fluttering among the club rushes – and how some like still water. And how it would be great to have both sorts of water space. I mention Ashton Water Dragonfly Sanctuary and say how nice it would be, ideally, to have a little lake like that just here, on the western side of the millrace. I sense them glancing at one another and they suddenly become serious. What sort of lake would I want? How big? Where exactly? They introduce themselves as Tom Youdan, Terry Hill and Andy Wright. They say they'll need their Conservation Officer, Emma Tidmarsh, to come along and have a look. They might be able to help.

SATURDAY, JULY 13TH, 1996

Roger and the tractor team arrive with two lovely surprises. First, they have restored and are now returning a bright red turn-of-the-century Royal Daylight oil cabinet for the generating hall. It stores new oil and has a system for filtering old oil for re-use. It glows, and it will be very practical and economical. And second, terrific news, a portable compressor to blow the air bottle up if necessary. It's only on loan, mind. And the single-cylinder Lister stationary engine that comes with it is a pig to start. It's good news nevertheless: no more burly men in yellow helmets in the gift shop.

THURSDAY, JULY 18TH, 1996

A note from Miriam, on headed paper, is slipped under our door. "I desperately need to borrow some mousetraps. They are eating my butterflies."

FRIDAY, AUGUST 2ND, 1996

Daughter Belinda, now twenty-four, arrives from London. She's been up before, but this time she's riding pillion on the back of a New Zealander's motorbike. It's lovely to see her and to meet Richard. He's the strong silent type, with a dry sense of humour and an obvious love of Belinda. They are both battling their way in the mayhem of London, she in a call-centre, he as a cycle courier ('Yeh, no. We're quicker than motorbikes. We get through smaller spaces.'). We spend time looking round the Museum then go back to the mansion. We're living in the main part of the house now and have been allowed to use an extra bedroom, ostensibly for family and friends, although Kari has commandeered most of it as her microscope laboratory. Its décor is essentially pink and it has two single beds. I notice Belinda and Richard glance at one another.

WEDNESDAY, AUGUST 14TH, 1996

Sheila Wright (the traditionally-built lady who, back in 1991, said she could lift heavy things) clumps up the wooden stairway and pokes her head round the door of what we have now come to call 'the office', the huge space above the generating hall that houses three ancient desks and six filing cabinets scrounged from the Canning School. It also has an odd-smelling sofa and two easy chairs spotted and rescued from a council lorry en route to the tip. These three are grouped round the double-doors beneath the Luccam, so that on quiet sunny days we can open the doors and gaze out at dragonflies whizzing over the millpond.

'Right,' says Sheila, 'what do you want me to do?'

I'm a bit nervous. I'm very aware that she's a don in Business Studies at de Montfort University in Leicester. I take a risk.

'Can you take dictation?'

Sheila laughs. 'I used to, about a hundred years ago. If you insist. But hang on. How much do you know about that computer in front of you?'

'It does what I want it to,' I say, defensively.

'Can you write e-mails?'

'Other people did that for me when I was at Canning. And it was a different sort.'

'Well, would you like me to show you?'

'I'll need to write down exactly what you say.'

She draws up a battered former Wildlife Trust chair. 'All right. Here. First, press this.'

I write on my pad "Press 'Click'."

Sheila never lets me forget that. But from then on I have total and unwavering support for the horrible business of administration and form-filling for fundraising. Sheila wades through the paperwork and frees me to cajole, bully, and persuade the ever-growing team of volunteers.

MONDAY, AUGUST 19TH, 1996

Emma Tidmarsh has visited. I've got permission from Miriam and Charles, and today the Environment Agency JCB has arrived to create a 'bund' – a bank to you and me – that will give us a two-acre lake. A pipe has already been sunk between the millrace and the planned pond, and we've been presented with a long turnkey that reaches down from a small manhole in the bank to control the stopcock on the pipe. So we will have total command of the water level in the lake. It's a very generous gesture of support from the local section of such a large nation-alized organization. I ask them how we can best publicize their kindness, and they say not to bother, it's fine. Maybe get something for the digger driver? I already have.

WEDNESDAY, AUGUST 21ST, 1996
Warren Gilchrist arrives. He's a tall, upright, bluff, retired naval commander. He's very important for us, as he sits on the board of the John Spedan Lewis Trust, which is the fund-providing arm of John Lewis. I'd never heard of them until Bridget Chamberlain, their Secretary, rang us. She'd read of our work. Could we send in an application and could someone come and have a look? I have duly completed a formal application together with seven support sheets and a summary.

Support Sheet 5 lists the publicity we have achieved so far this year.

Broadsheets
The Times (half page)
The Independent (three pages in the Weekend section)
The Sunday Telegraph (double column)
Peterborough Citizen (quarter page)
Peterborough Evening Telegraph (two pages)
Stamford Mercury (half page)

Magazines
Country Life
Country Living
BBC Wildlife
Countryside
British Wildlife
Old Glory
Network 21
Link

Garden Design
Anglian News
Conservation Foundation Press/NGO Press Officer Circular

Television & Radio Interviews
BBC Television, John Craven's Countryfile
BBC Television, Look East
Anglia Television News
Central Television News
BBC Radio, The Natural History Programme
BBC Radio Northamptonshire
BBC Radio Cambridgeshire
Canadian Broadcasting Corporation

Warren Gilchrist marches about, ceaselessly questioning. He must have been just the same when inspecting his ship, and I feel very much like a lieutenant, albeit, as the tour continues, a reasonably trusted one. As he drives away, I wave goodbye with my right arm and cross the fingers of my left hand behind my back.

SATURDAY, SEPTEMBER 7TH, 1996

Kari comes zooming out of the tearoom kitchen and seizes me by the arm.

'You've got to do something about Iona. Or I'm going to kill her.'

Iona is Heather and Mick Twinn's young daughter. She's developed a reputation as a little devil and while her parents work on other jobs she tends to gravitate towards the tearoom, probably attracted by the delicious smells, but also certain that it's a place where she can get maximum attention.

'She's just stuck her dirty fingers over a whole tray of scones,' says Kari. 'I've had to start again. No sooner had I warned her, than she was all over the baked potatoes. I can't stand it. Do something.'

So I do. But it doesn't stop Iona accidentally-on-purpose falling into the garden pond later in the day. From then on there's always a slight frisson among us when Iona arrives.

WEDNESDAY, OCTOBER 8TH, 1996

We're now a fully fledged Museum and for some time we've been encouraged to join the museum establishment and obtain official registration. We make contact with the Museums and Galleries Commission and wade through a series of thick documents. I get a sinking feeling that joining is likely to tie us up in red tape and endanger our independence. Perhaps we're not so fully-fledged after all.

We're told that we need to come up with a mission statement. We want to get the message across to the general public that dragonflies are beautiful, fascinating and in trouble, and that almost anyone can help. But we're advised by those-in-the-know that words like *beautiful* and *fascinating* are not quite the ticket – and that there'd be a worry about mentioning *volunteers*.

I'm horrified. I can't just erase the volunteers. They *are* the Museum.

My fellow-trustee Jane Baile and I have tea with Miriam at the mansion. She asks what is causing me to frown, and Jane tells her.

'I don't think,' says Miriam, 'you should be too frightened to retain your independence.'

THURSDAY, OCTOBER 24TH, 1996

Charles Lane sends through our lease. It's for ten years. Well, it's not twenty-five, but it's a lot better than five and it means we can operate here at least until the autumn of 2006. Nevertheless, if we can't get the lease extended it's going to be very hard to raise serious funds. So far, we've been astonishingly lucky. We've received support from English Nature, Anglian Water, East Northamptonshire District Council, Northamptonshire Wildlife Trust, the British Dragonfly Society, the Environment Agency and of course Kari de Koenigswarter. We have neither asked for nor received funds from the Rothschilds but, put simply, without Miriam and Charles, we wouldn't exist.

SATURDAY, OCTOBER 26TH, 1996

Trustees' meeting. We agree that complying with the many constraints that would need to be put in place were we to join the
museums establishment 'should not be a priority at this time'.
We have other more pressing matters, the most vital of which is
to maintain the morale of the volunteers and to safeguard their
commitment to future projects. So, once again, the die is cast. We
stand alone.

WEDNESDAY, OCTOBER 30TH, 1996

Kari receives a formal invitation from the Llewellyn Gallery in
London to show six of her miniatures in an exhibition entitled
'A Million Brushstrokes.' Kari usually wants me to double-check
her replies to things like this, so we walk down to the observation hut and sit at the table looking out over the lake. On the official response form she writes, "We have been happily busy at the
Dragonfly Museum." We agree that being a successful miniaturist
and running dragonfly courses is a long way from Canning.

She grins. 'And I can run a tearoom, too.'

We both know that Miriam's idea of a lingering death would
be to have to run a tearoom in Biggleswade. No, we don't know
why Biggleswade especially.

THURSDAY, NOVEMBER 28TH, 1996

A cheque arrives from John Lewis.

Chapter 28

Spring is here and Lynn Curry has suggested a volunteer outing. Here we are at Woodwalton Fen. I'm friendly with Alan Bowley, the Reserve Manager, and he's very kindly agreed to take us round. Few of the volunteers have been able to resist a walk through such an astonishing piece of pristine fenland with the man who knows the place as well as anyone alive, and so we're a fairly large party.

There are several children with us, one of whom is Iona. She knows it's an adults' thing and she's promised her mother Heather to be good. Some of the group have never been to Woodwalton before and are truly surprised to see, deep in the fen, Charles Rothschild's thatched bungalow on stilts. Kari points out the marks on one of the concrete support pillars showing the height of the water during various flood years. The marks are startlingly high, but not high enough to flood the bungalow. Her grandfather was prescient in many ways.

Alan takes us up the wooden steps, into the dark rush-matted interior with its big beech wood armchairs. He gives us a short talk about Charles Rothschild and calls him the father of modern nature conservation. Wellingtoned and anoraked, we all trudge out into the fen. It's too early for dragonflies but there are several really unusual plants, Marsh Sowthistle and Fen Ragwort, for example. It's satisfying to hear Henry Stanier tell Alan, quietly but proudly, that we have Marsh Sowthistle at Ashton Water Dragonfly Sanctuary.

Alan leads us out past the ditch where back in 1989 Kari and I first met Paul Whalley and he told us that if we were serious about dragonflies, we'd buy monoculars; they now dangle round our necks. On we go, eastwards, along ancient half-buried duckboards to a tall hide overlooking a substantial piece of open water.

We climb the steps in single file and form up in the hide.

'Everyone quiet,' says Alan in a stage whisper. 'Now we wait. Watch out for a very big hawk. Long tail. Easy flight. Wings usually in a gentle V.'

Only a handful of minutes pass, scarcely enough even to make Iona impatient; the bird appears.

'Male Marsh Harrier!' blurts Alan, then, in a whisper, '*Circus aeroginosus*. See? He's got something in his talons. A vole? Maybe we'll see a food pass if the female is … yes, look!'

The bigger female has suddenly appeared from below. She now swoops upwards and, turning right upside down, takes the vole from the claws of the male: two big elegant birds in silent harmony. We watch in awe. Even Iona is impressed.

We tramp back the way we've come and head out onto a clearer area of the fen near the western end. Alan stops suddenly.

'Ah! Good! Gather round, everyone, please.'

We form a respectful circle, not quite sure why.

'Now,' he says, pointing downwards. 'See this? It's a Fen Violet, a *Viola persicifolia*.'

We all look down. It's a smallish, pinkish job, fairly similar to an ordinary violet, a bit paler maybe, sitting all by itself.

'It really is extraordinarily rare,' says Alan. 'Woodwalton is one of the very few places you'll find it in the whole country. It prefers lime-rich soils, so it's very unusual to find it in basically acidic conditions such as these.'

We gaze, a ring of respectful silence, at the solitary little flower. A small person suddenly steps into the centre of the circle, reaches down and … pick.

None of us have seen Heather lose her temper with Iona before. It's quite spectacular.

SATURDAY, JUNE 14TH, 1997

The start of another season. We've given up on opening Thursday and Friday afternoons. It simply wasn't economical and it was something of a strain for just Kari and I.

Charles Lane has contacted us recommending we develop an internet site. I tell him we'll do it this winter, and wonder whether such a thing will be of any use. Perhaps internet sites are just a fad ...

SATURDAY, JULY 13TH, 1997

It's the fourth weekend we've been open this summer. Despite Leslie McCombe's near-death sledgehammer experience last year, she and her husband Keith are still turning up to volunteer. Ironically, Keith works as a Safety Officer for the local Parcelforce depot in Peterborough. Perhaps not unconnected with the sledgehammer incident, he's offered to carry out a Health and Safety survey and to draw up a Process Document for the whole Museum, in particular the generating hall. Dick has manufactured and installed a large protective grille to – as Henry Curry puts it – 'protect the spinning flywheels from the visitors', and it has a door through which only volunteers may pass. But there's already been a heart-stopping moment when an over-enthusiastic young volunteer came perilously close to losing a hand.

For a week or two now, Keith has been looking speculatively at the pulleys on the driveshaft that runs along the ceiling of the generating hall. Parcelforce is in the process of moving premises. They're leaving a building that contains similar pulleys to these ones and, more importantly for us, canvas belts of the correct width. Today Keith opens the boot of his car, presents us with a Protocol Folder for Health and Safety at the Museummuseum, and uncovers several neatly-rolled bundles of canvas belting.

We set to work stringing them up, stapling ends together and oiling the pulleys, then get the engine going. The belts flail and slip helplessly, unable to grip, until Dick drives home to Maxey and returns with a large can of Stockholm tar. We slap some of the stuff onto the belts, more onto ourselves, and by the

219

end of the day, as the volunteers gather to watch, the driveshaft rumbles round once more. After over forty years of stillness, here it is, working as good as new.

Ron Cook has been working on the dynamo, devising a way of drying its coils, damp from years of disuse. He gazes up at the turning pulleys, pushes his specs up onto his forehead, grins gently, and says, 'Shouldn't be too long now. Have you seen what I've done? Look.'

He points to the wooden partition behind the right-hand dynamo. Two big glass-fronted brass dials, an ammeter and a voltmeter, glitter. It's taken him months of painstaking work at home to get all the black paint off and set them working again.

SUNDAY, JULY 14TH, 1997

Late afternoon and I'm talking to a visitor in the gift shop when I hear a puttering noise from the tractor shed. It's the Fergy. They've got it going again. Roger Margrave drives it victoriously into the courtyard. And after a few test runs they let me climb on board and I chug off round the side of the Mill along the footpath to the river. I manage to stop it, three-point-turn it, and bring it back to the courtyard without stalling. There's a small round of slightly ironic applause; and a big celebration in the tearoom garden after we've closed.

SATURDAY, JULY 19TH, 1997

The Sanctuary is open today and tomorrow, as well as six more days this year. It's really a palaver to man both sites effectively, quite apart from the labour involved in managing both places. Endless grass-cutting and hacking back vegetation. But the lake still works its gorgeous magic on visitors and remains a splendid place for them to see dragonflies in action.

SATURDAY, JULY 26TH, 1997

Professor Philip Corbet arrives to deliver 'Dragonflies and Man', the first of what we have decided will be a series of annual Corbet lectures. We take a discreet risk and set out an array of chairs upstairs in the office. If there's a fire, there's only one escape route, made of wood. No one seems to notice. Philip speaks to his audience exactly as if they're his colleagues yet somehow avoids any sort of technical jargon. We sit enthralled. I think back to the time in rainy Leeds when I first met him and we shared sandwiches.

FRIDAY, AUGUST 8TH, 1997

Ron Cook comes over in the afternoon and gets cracking on the dynamo once more. I leave him to it and go back upstairs, only to be disturbed by a van driver. He's from Anglian Water and he's brought seven beautiful freestanding interpretation boards for the generating hall. I only wrote the texts and supplied the photographs a fortnight ago. I take them into the hall and set them out; they look great and they'll save a lot of explanations. Ron is too pre-occupied to pay much attention; they're not an engineer's concern. I go upstairs again but, after a while, Ron calls me down into the generating hall and asks me to set the Blackstone going. Once it's in action, he calls, 'Move the belt over onto the drive pulley and let's see …'

I shunt the lever that shifts the belt from its idler pulley onto the drive pulley on the main shaft, and immediately the belt leading down to the dynamo starts to turn. The dynamo starts to hum and Ron flicks a switch.

'Look!' he shouts over the racket of the engine, pointing upwards.

A bulb above his head has started to glow and begins to brighten.

'There's a lot more work yet,' he yells. 'Switches, wiring, lamps, that sort of thing, now. But we'll get there.'

SUNDAY, AUGUST 17TH, 1997

Jolting side by side in the red Land Rover, Kari and I bump down the long track from the mansion to the village, over the perfunctory speed bumps, onto the main road, and round to the Mill. I swing into the little courtyard, switch off the engine, take out the key, attached to its jailer-size bunch, and clip the keyring with a karabiner clip to the left-hand belt-loop of my trousers. It's a gorgeous day; it's going to be very busy. We sit relishing the quietness for a moment, then climb out.

In the tearoom kitchen, Kari gets started on a pasta lunch for the volunteers and scones for the visitors. I walk across the courtyard, unclip the bunch of keys, and begin the somewhat laborious process of unlocking the multitude of Museum gates and doors. Nine different keys, not including the three Land Rover keys (ignition, front doors, rear door) the three house keys (Chubb, Yale and inside door), oh, and two keys to the observation hut and the boathouse down at the lake.

Gradually the volunteers arrive and gather in the tearoom kitchen for a preliminary cup of tea. I march about giving out tasks. Sandy Whittingdale agrees to help Kari chop onions for the lunchtime lasagna. Two people need to help Lynn set up and man the gift shop. The Smithy doors need re-painting in Ashton blue. There's more woodwork to be done on the observation platform in the millpond. Dick Witt will need someone to help him lift part of the second Blackstone engine into place. The cinema needs to be swept clear of the leaves and dust that blew in yesterday. The grass paths around the Museum grounds need mowing. The tractor team (not here yet, they're coming from Dunstable) want an extra pair of hands to divide the recently-rescued Ferguson FE35 in half for gearbox work. Someone else will need to hook the big yellow grass-cutter – yes, it's here, on loan of course – onto our lovely newly-restored little grey TD20 to clear the track to the footbridge over the river and down to Ashton Lock.

Francis Chiverton is our youngest volunteer. He's a teenager, as keen as mustard and very sensible. To his delight, I let him drive the Fergy. He clambers onto the tractor seat, frowning with concentration, and sets off round the side of the Mill to cut the grass.

By the time the first visitors start to trickle in we're ready. We've fished out a couple of larvae from our tanks and Henry has agreed to do Larva Demonstrations while I tell people about the wonders in the generating hall. Our system is to wait until we have a reasonable number of visitors, then announce that there'll be a Larva Show and, once Henry's finished, I take them through to demonstrate the Blackstone.

Visitors gather in the main Museum space and Henry does his stuff, explaining how extraordinary dragonfly larvae are. He puts a dragonfly larva under the big microscope and its image instantly appears, monstrously large, on the big TV screen. He focuses down on their eyes, each with 10,000 lenses and photo-receptors, then their wing-cases neatly enclosing the wings ready for later adult flight, and explains how larvae breathe through their backsides. We always make something of that; the kids love it. 'Don't try this in the bath …' and so on. Then he drops a red bloodworm into the dish and hopefully the dragonfly shoots out its labial mask and feeds the bloodworm, sausage-like into its jaws. The water goes pink. Henry plays the sequence back in slow-motion. It's a sight no one forgets.

After the Larva Show, I lead the visitors through to the generating hall. They stare at the immaculate black-and-white tiled floor and the array of massive Victorian machinery, the engines, the generators, the turbines and the pumping gear. I tell them how, when I first visited this place, I used to dream of getting some of the stuff going again; how, on one of the dragonfly tours round the Sanctuary, a lady came up afterwards and asked if her father might come and see the machinery in the Mill. He was too shy to ask himself, she said. How I'd subsequently met Dick Witt, already in his late seventies and we'd gone into the engine house and he'd looked at one of the two huge Blackstone oil engines and said: 'Would you like me to get this going again?'

I release air from the air bottle with a sudden hiss and the great flywheels start to turn. I have to time it exactly right for the engine to fire and for the wheels to start to spin. I then use the engine's exhaust to pump the air bottle back up, before easing the belt onto the drive wheel and watching the wheels on the driveshaft on the ceiling begin to spin. Then, I shift the lever across, and the belt to the generator starts to turn, and we're making our own electricity. It's only one bulb at the moment but the visitors' faces literally light up.

It's just after the second show of the morning. I'm on the cat-walk over the millrace pointing out a Common Darter to a small boy. He's peering through the mesh that stops youngsters from falling into the water. I straighten up and, as I do so, one of my keys catches in the mesh, rips the belt-loop free from my trousers and flips the whole bunch over into the millrace. The water is brown, opaque and a good ten feet deep. One or two of the keys have duplicates; most, of course, don't. Three of us spend nearly an hour fashioning hooks and wire and trawling about in the mud below. Nothing. I feel as if my world has stalled.

But here are another group of visitors to talk to, and for me to pretend the magic is just as usual. I eat no lunch and spend any free moment I get guddling about fruitlessly in the depths. I notice Francis has disappeared.

'He's gone home,' someone says.

'Did he finish the grass-cutting?'

'Sure. All done. Happy as Larry.'

I wonder if he's all right, though. It's out of character for him to vanish without explanation. I have to find these keys. No luck. By now I'm really worried. More visitors. More talks. I'm in the gener-ating hall on the third talk of the afternoon, hands clasped firmly behind my back in scholarly fashion, and have just reached the point where I'm saying 'And then the dream began to come true …' when I feel metal being pressed into my fingers. Lots of little bits of metal. I grasp them and … it's all my keys, safe on their big keyring.

I spin round and there's Francis, grinning from ear to ear. I finish my demonstration and, as the visitors smile at the twin-kling light, I ask him how he did it.

'Went upstairs to the office. Rang Mum. Got her to come and get me.'

'You live in Stamford, Francis!'

'Yep. Far side. She came and got me. Went home. Took one of our big loudspeakers to bits. Got the magnet out. Strung wire through it. Brought it back here. Lowered it into the millrace. Up they came.'

I hug him.

SUNDAY, AUGUST 31ST, 1997

Princess Diana has been killed in a car crash. We remain closed. I'm a bit shocked by the hysteria I see on the TV in the evening.

SUNDAY, SEPTEMBER 14TH, 1997

There are only two weekends to go before we shut up shop once again, but both the millrace and the millpond have become covered in an unpleasant reddish scum. It's Azolla, sometimes known as Duckweed Fern. It's extremely invasive; it covers the surface so thoroughly as to leave total darkness beneath and thus kills off any oxygenating plants below. The only way to deal with it is to get into a boat and scoop it out with a sieve. So any of us who have any spare time do exactly that. Kari does it best. She's much more stable in a kayak than she used to be.

SUNDAY, SEPTEMBER 28TH, 1997

Our last day of the season but we're still fighting Azolla.

TUESDAY, SEPTEMBER 30TH, 1997

Kari and I drive over to Highgrove, worrying whether the Prince's pond has also been struck by Azolla, and very conscious of it being only a few weeks since Diana's death. As we pull in, Nick Mould, HRH's man in charge of the pond project, is standing in the little car park chatting to a gardener. Nick, bespectacled, quietly humorous, perceptive, immaculately dressed, has supported us from the start and it's always nice to see him. The three of us stand by the pond. A Southern Hawker zooms about, and Kari gets to work sweeping a sieve through the plants on the margins. She finds both damselfly and dragonfly larvae, demonstrating once again that the Prince's reedbed sewage treatment system is working fine.

There's horrid bad news, too. No sign of Azolla, but the pond is covered in blanket weed mixed with Crassula, another – even worse – invasive non-native species, often brought in on the feet of water birds. We say we'll send him recommendations. Sensing our anxiety, Nick says he'll discuss the pond with David Magson, the Head Gardener, and takes us off on a private tour round the jaw-droppingly elegant garden.

It's time to head for Scotland and a rest.

Chapter 29

SATURDAY, FEBRUARY 7TH, 1998

The River Nene is in flood and the Mill buildings – Museum area, gift shop and generating hall – are under six inches of water. The volunteers arrive and it's all hands on deck with mops and buckets. Thank heavens we moved everything vital upstairs when we packed up at the end of last season. Worse, a water pipe in the tearoom roof has burst, brought part of a wall down and wrecked our redecoration work. Henry and Lynn Curry discovered the damage on a routine caretaker visit while Kari and I were up in Scotland. They had to summon up courage to ring us. Today we all make a start on putting things right. It's going to be long job.

THURSDAY, APRIL 9TH, 1998

I'm standing alone on the bank between the millrace and the lovely little lake made for us by the Environment Agency. The margins have grown in and already it's started to attract dragonflies and damselflies. I'm trying to come to terms with the shattering news that it's going to have to be destroyed.

Miriam has remembered that the old well beside it should have been checked. It's something none of us – including Miriam – thought about. When we received permission to create the lake, we had no idea the well might still be of any use. But Miriam has had the water checked and there's a possible risk of contamination. I've argued hard, several ways, and lost, so that's that.

I've talked the thing through with Caroline Tero and others at the Environment Agency and they freely admit that they saw no importance or value whatsoever in the well, or risk to it. But if that's what the landowners say, so be it. They say they will remove the bund at no charge and they offer to contribute £1,000 to the digging of another pond further away. But they won't be able to do the job a second time and there can be no pipe from the river. Once was enough, they say. It's still a very kind offer.

It's very hard to believe that this key part of the Museum's habitats will have to go. It's actually heartbreaking.

SUNDAY, APRIL 28TH, 1998

It's early morning, the start of the second day of a work party. Henry Curry and I are standing in the mud at the edge of the mill-pond. We're building the walkway from the tearoom garden to the visitors' car park. It's an extension of the observation platform we built two years ago. And we're in trouble. Two massive fallen willow trees lie in our path. A gang of us have sawn off the main branches but try as we might we simply cannot shift the trunks. We've even tried slinging a rope round one of them and hauling it with Fire Nine. Even using the Land Rover's four-wheel drive and the lowest gear in its secondary gearbox, Fire Nine merely grumbled and dug a hole for itself. Oh for a chainsaw and someone chainsaw-trained.

Chris Gerrard, who works for the Northamptonshire Wildlife Trust, was here yesterday giving us a hand. He's one of so many folk who turn up, lend a hand, and go again. Before Chris left he said that had he not been committed to another voluntary job today, he might have been able to come and chainsaw through the willow trunks that were causing us so much hassle. Pity.

There's a shout from behind us and here's Chris coming towards us, wearing a red safety hat and carrying a chainsaw.

THURSDAY, MAY 7TH, 1998

John Dickinson from Central Television is here at the Mill, making a short documentary about our work. Kari, as our Artist in Residence, is filmed, painting a watercolour on the observation platform. She's agreed to do this on condition that she doesn't have to say anything; this from the woman who spent years going to acting classes in New York.

SATURDAY, JUNE 13TH, 1998

Our first day of the season. Henry Stanier's father, Bev, offers to run for us in the London Marathon. Henry himself has been keeping careful records of dragonfly species seen at the Museum. We're up to fifteen. No Emperor and, of course, no Common Hawker. So the Sanctuary is still winning.

Lynn Curry is busy setting out the gift shop. Since 1995, aided by her sister-in-law Sue Parfitt, she has assembled an amazing variety of dragonfly–related products, but this year she has excelled herself. There's something for very nearly everyone, sweatshirts, T-shirts, model dragonflies, stationery, books, jewellery, even dragonfly exuviae. Kari and her sister Berit have produced a series of superb dragonfly designs for the clothing. Besides being images of great beauty, each dragonfly is accurate down to the last wing-vein. I quail at the thought of how many hours Berit must have put in on that task, up in her apartment on the fifteenth floor of a Greenwich Village skyscraper.

SATURDAY, JUNE 20TH, 1998

It's 3.00pm. The police 'No parking' cones are set out all the way down to Ashton Roundabout once more. In the crowded and sunny tearoom garden, Miriam sits in her wheelchair in a bright floral dress, green headscarf shoved back to show a widow's peak of silver hair, a black bag on her lap and a pair of scissors in her hand. She has just made a short speech and now, flanked by Andy McGeeney, President of the British Dragonfly Society, and by two blue-rinsed gold-chained lady dignitaries from Oundle and East Northamptonshire District Council, she whirrs forward and cuts the white ribbon stretched across the little gateway. Our new walkway to the visitors' car park is now officially open.

It's not just a convenient and safe route for people – including those in wheelchairs – to avoid the crazy drivers who treat the Oundle to Polebrook road as a British alternative to the Mille Miglia, it's also a wonderful way to see dragonflies in action over the millpond. We've built in two viewing spaces that jut out into the pond and added a large dragonfly identification board. This is the official opening, but the walkway has been finished for a week or two, and already we've found that on lovely days like this visitors tend to come to a standstill, hardly out of their cars, hands resting on the still-new rails of the walkway, gazing in silence at the millpond and the Mill. And, happily quite often, dragonflies. I'm convinced there's something mildly therapeutic about watching dragonflies, and that visitors sense it too. Is it the combination of stillness, silence and sudden speed?

SATURDAY, JUNE 27TH, 1998

Andy McGeeney, tall, alert, distinguished, comes back to deliver the second our series of annual Corbet lectures. It's entitled 'What's the Point of Dragonflies?' It's brilliant. Just like last year, tickets for the event have sold very well but this time we've decided not to pile everyone upstairs into the major fire risk area above the generating hall, and so we've arranged all the chairs in the cinema. That's a very grand title for what is basically a small barn with an Anglian Water-donated projector slung on a beam, and a screen on the wall opposite. On days when we're open, we have Dr Georg Ruppell's wonderful film about dragonflies, *Jewelwings*, on a loop in there. Andy's talk is as always stimulating and intriguing.

SUNDAY, JUNE 28TH, 1998

I'm torn in two. A man called Andrew Barton has brought in a framed collection of fishing flies made by him and his mate Ron Clayson. Tied to represent various damselflies, they're a blaze of colour beneath the glass. Would we like them? A gift? Could I show him where we'd put them? Meanwhile, a coachload from Cleveland has arrived, half an hour early.

SATURDAY, JULY 4TH, 1998

Kari's at it again:

Course – Larvae Identification For Beginners – 4th July 1998
    Maximum ten participants
    Fee £30, lunch included
    10.00am – 5.00pm.
        Tutor: Kari de Koenigswarter.

The aim of the course is for participants to be able to identify larvae to genus and understand the basic steps of 'keying out'
to species. The course will consist of a plenary session with the
TV-Microscope link, one-to-one guidance, self-study periods and
depending on the weather, a hunt for exuviae in our dragonfly
habitats.

Fired by the success of that first course in 1996, Kari ran two
courses like this last year. She has set a framework for courses
that will run for nearly twenty years and has trained Henry Curry,
Henry Stanier and Stuart Irons to run them. All three of them
have emerged from their training with renewed respect for her.
She simply will not let them get away with anything remotely slip-
shod. Don't I know it.

MONDAY, JULY 6TH, 1998

The Mill roof, an enormous expanse of Collyweston slate, is going
to have to be renewed. Charles Lane has obtained funding for it,
and it will be fantastic, but it will have to be done while we're
open. It won't wait until the autumn. Today the men start work
and we begin a two-month-long battle with dust and scaffolding.
We'll be too busy to grieve the loss of our little lake, now just an
enormous brown scar.

SATURDAY, JULY 11TH, 1998

Kari has gone one step further and decided we need to run a different sort of course:

These courses are educational, they bring us publicity, and they make us money. (Stuart, aided by loyal volunteer and plant expert Karen Buckley, will still be running the course nearly two decades later.)

SATURDAY, JULY 25TH, 1998

Tomorrow we open the Sanctuary for the first time this season. We've decided to reduce the number of Sanctuary Open Days to three, but it still means we have a great deal of preparation to do. Yesterday I popped down to check everything was in order for Sunday and found a dead Père David's deer on the path in the south-east corner. With nothing special needing doing at that point I hadn't been round there for over a month. Today, a team of the hardest-nosed of us, armed with spades, forks and a tarpaulin, rumble up the bumpy path from Polebrook in Fire Nine, dismount, enter the Sanctuary and approach the smelly suppurating corpse. As we try to manhandle it onto the tarpaulin it falls apart in a flood of maggots. The stink is so strong it catches our breath. One of us throws up. We retreat, tie makeshift masks round our faces, return, shovel the pieces onto the tarpaulin and eventually the poor beast is buried. There's very little banter in the Land Rover on the way back to the Museum.

SUNDAY, JULY 26TH, 1998

We're just finishing for the day, locking up and setting out white wine, beer, soft drinks and crisps in the garden overlooking the millpond when the courtyard between the Museum and the tearoom suddenly fills with blue-and-yellow Migrant Hawkers. We often get one or two whizzing about there, especially when the sun is shining in, and when it's reasonably sheltered from the wind, but this is extraordinary. More and more appear, to the point where we cease counting and just watch as the air fills with glittering wings. What's so odd is the silence. With so much movement one expects noise.

I've seen this before, once with Brown Hawkers near the Grand Union Canal at Denham, and once with Migrants at Polebrook airfield. Henry Curry mentions ants and then I remember that the airfield incident did coincide with the nuptial emergence of ants. They're an obvious source of food for the dragonflies. Henry searches about and soon discovers ants emerging from cracks in the paving stones in the tearoom garden. But it's the aerial display in the courtyard that fascinates us. And how on earth did all these dragonflies know the ants were here? We have no answer.

SUNDAY, AUGUST 9TH, 1998

For someone who loathes standing in front of groups of people, Kari has really got the bit between her teeth:

COURSE:
Larvae Identification Follow-Up – 9th August 1998
Maximum ten participants
Fee £30, lunch included
10 .00am – 5.00pm.
   Tutor: Kari de Koenigswarter.
   This course is available to those who have previously completed the Larvae Identification for Beginners Course. It will enable participants to further develop their identification skills to include the more difficult species.

THURSDAY, AUGUST 20TH, 1998

In a heavily loaded Fire Nine, Kari, Catharine and I drive through Oakham, on our way to the British Birdwatching Fair at Rutland Water, ready to set up our stand. It is of course a risk to appear at an event strictly aimed at birders, but mindful of Norman Moore's dictum that "Dragonflies are the bird-watchers' insect" (*Dragonflies*, Corbet, Longfield and Moore, 1960) we've decided to go for it. Besides, adult dragonflies are at their very best in July and August, precisely when birds are at their quietest.

I haven't seen Tim Appleton, the Birdfair's boss, since November 1992 when he rather quizzically bought a handful of dragonfly calendars off me. But he hasn't forgotten and he makes us very welcome. It's going to be a strain because we need volunteers to man the stand here for the next three days, as well as keeping the Museum going back at Ashton. We've brought loads of stock from the gift shop; enough, we think, to last us through Friday, Saturday and Sunday. And volunteers Mick and Heather Twinn have obtained an entire mobile exhibition-board system from somewhere, complete with lighting, which will make our lives very much easier.

SUNDAY, AUGUST 23RD, 1998

We're shattered, but the Bird Fair has gone incredibly well. People have shown enormous interest, especially in adult dragonflies, and gone berserk for dragonfly books and sweatshirts. The dragonfly larvae in our little tank have been a source of fascination for the kids, and women have been delighted with the dragonfly jewellery. What we thought was enough stock for the weekend had run out by Friday evening. Bill Oddie appeared and made very nice noises. We arrive back at the Museum to find that the team there has also had a bumper weekend. We agree to do it all again next year.

BANK HOLIDAY MONDAY, AUGUST 31ST, 1998

It's 'Country Jobs of Old Day', our busiest day. We've decided to celebrate all our different collections of tools and equipment. So today Graham Carter is giving thatching demonstrations; Derek Mayhew, dressed in blue overalls and a magnificent leather apron, is bashing away at the forge; the Fergy is in action; Darren and Amanda are operating the corn grinder, milling oats into porridge flakes; and we have a small collection of stationary engines thudding away. The whole event is attracting a great deal of attention, and has produced several new volunteers who are solely interested in the Victorian hydro-electric system in the generating hall. We decide to make it even bigger next year.

SUNDAY, SEPTEMBER 6TH, 1998

We've only just unlocked and it's still quiet, but it's sunny and it'll get busy later. We've managed to stay open every weekend whilst the entire roof of the Mill has been replaced. It's been a real struggle but the workmen have told me that next week the scaffolding will come down.

The tractor team is here and I'm suddenly confronted by the entire Margrave family, Roger, Jenny, Darren and Amanda. They hand me an old yellow blanket with something flat bulky and heavy inside. I unwrap the object. They've made us a new weathervane, a big dragonfly in silhouette, to replace the flying fox that used to swing above the Luccam and which recently blew down in a storm. We found the fox, as sharp as an axe, in the bushes beside the Mill. Had anyone been beneath as it fell, it would have decapitated them. The new weathervane is a truly wonderful present but there's a catch: sorry, but none of them are prepared to climb up and put the heavy thing into position. Am I? It will need to be fixed very firmly in place. They give me very careful instructions. We study the route and the requirements through binoculars.

Armed with pliers, screwdriver and the heavy dragonfly weathervane, I climb the three storeys of scaffolding to the highest point below the Luccam, take a deep breath, step out over the gutter, edge extremely slowly up the steep slates to the ridge, and inch my way towards the outermost end of the Luccam roof. The very thought of looking outwards into space – let alone down to the ground below – makes me squirm and feel dizzy. I concentrate on checking that the weathervane mounting bracket is still firm and that the metal quadrant signs – N, E, S and W – are still properly in place. They're fine. I lift the weathervane up in order to slot it into its upright sleeve. By now it feels as heavy and cumbersome as a cast iron lamppost. As I raise it, a gust of wind catches it and tips it towards the void.

My left arm is like a vice round the stem of the heavy dragonfly, my right hand is locked under a ridge tile beneath me and my guts are turning somersaults. I stay rigid and terrified until the wind dies, then start again. On the second attempt the dragonfly slips into place, I fumble ever-so-slowly for the screwdriver in my pocket, tighten the sleeve screws up and begin to ease back down the roof towards the scaffolding. It's only when my feet are firmly on path beside the Mill once more that my knees begin to shake uncontrollably.

SATURDAY, SEPTEMBER 26TH, 1998

It's a sunny afternoon, fairly quiet. A smiley good-looking blonde woman appears with two young boys in tow.

'Hi,' she says. 'These are the Jones boys. Can we see around?'

It's an American accent. There's nothing much else on, so I spend a fair amount of time with them. We're lucky because there are one or two Common Darters still zooming about.

'Come and see the Blackstone,' I say. 'Your boys will like this.'

'Oh, they're not my boys. Ben and Ryan are my neighbours from Ringstead.'

'Oh, I'm so sorry. I thought …'

'I'm not married. Say, can you volunteer here? Do you have a book or something where I can sign in? This place is awesome. It's so hard to find places to volunteer in England. In the States, it's easy.'

Carol Bouchard writes her name, phone number and address in the book, says she'll be in touch next year, and leaves.

SUNDAY, SEPTEMBER 27TH, 1998

We close. It's been a good year. We've attracted several Natural

History Societies and even run a Discovery Day for the Northamptonshire Wildlife Trust. It's the least we could do; they've steadfastly supported us.

SATURDAY, OCTOBER 3RD, 1998

Despite the Environment Agency's offer of £1,000 towards a new pond further away from the dreaded well, it's not been possible to raise the additional £2,000 funding needed for a substantial area to be cleared down to a clay substrate and for a watertight bank built up round it. As before, it's Kari who has come to our rescue. She has agreed to pay the difference – using yet more saved money from Canning – and PJ Thory Ltd has brought a big yellow digger and excavated a new pond at a safe distance from the well. However, unlike the previous water space, the new pond is too far from the river for a pipe to be laid and we've been scratching our heads as to how to fill it with water.

Over a pint in the Chequered Skipper the other night, I mentioned the problem to Billy Nall who immediately said he knew someone who could help. Today we stand on the new bank, and beside us is a socking great red-and-silver twelve ton HBC Angus Bedford-chassis fire engine, hoses snaking out from it, in one direction to the river, and the other belching water at 450 gallons a minute onto the bare earth in the pond. Bright red Fire Nine is parked beside the thrumming appliance and the whole ensemble looks like some sort of brigade exercise. It takes the entire day, with a break for a good lunch, but then it's done. We gaze happily at a sheet of brand-new still water and start planning a planting programme.

Chapter 30

WEDNESDAY, MARCH 3RD, 1999

Today the man from Health and Safety Executive is coming to inspect the generating hall. We've done everything we should have done, but one never knows. He arrives at 10.00am and turns out to be very quiet and polite. He slips into brown overalls and examines the Blackstone, the dynamo, the belts and the pulleys, then he asks to see our Logbook and Code of Practice. I produce both. He studies them for a long time, smiles, says they're fine and what we're doing is perfectly acceptable. He sticks a small black electronic device to the side of the air bottle, tests it, and confirms it's sound. I don't mention Dick's rather scarier method of testing. We work through our safety regulations and our insurance arrangements. He returns to his car and wishes us well.

I can't quite believe it. I think I expected some sort of bloody-minded sergeant major. The Oily Rag team will be delighted when I tell them the news. They're rightly very proud of what they do. I go to the Chequered Skipper for a pint.

SATURDAY, MARCH 6TH, 1999

A volunteer work party day. And here is Carol Bouchard, the attractive blonde American, true to her word.

'OK,' she smiles. 'What can I paint?'

Several volunteers offer to show her.

I'm at my desk upstairs in the Mill and I've just made my sixth phone call of the morning. I put down my biro and lean back. Things have really changed. There's a lot of paperwork involved in operating a registered charity and hunting for funds. Running the Museum is now effectively a full-time job. I certainly couldn't do it if I hadn't learned so much at Canning and at Michelin.

The key differences here are that I spend a great deal of time applying for funding – in other words filling out endless forms asking for money – and much of the rest leading a team that can walk away whenever it likes. I'm quite happy about team leading, but the grind of form-filling and following up bores me. Most of the money that has been given to the Museum has been from organizations that have taken the trouble to send people along to have a look at what we do. The British Dragonfly Society and the John Spedan Lewis Trust are shining examples of that.

The National Dragonfly Museum is properly on the map now and is steadily gaining momentum. We've reached a point where we're not even sure about the word 'Museum'. Is it appropriate for what we do? Someone remarked that the word 'Museum' gave the impression of 'dried-up things in dusty glass cases', which is most certainly what we're not. We're kicking the word 'Biomuseum' around. It gives the idea of life, as well as curation and interpretation. Philip Corbet likes it, but he's not the general public. We'll sleep on it.

Something else: the volunteers are spending less time on platform-building, ditch-digging and door-painting and much more time guiding and helping visitors. This actually calls for a different type of volunteer, or at least one who is prepared to spend time talking to the public rather than just getting dirty.

But what we need now is serious money and that can only be got by having a longer lease. I talk the matter through with Charles Lane on the phone and tell him the National Lottery won't look at any lease less than twenty-five years. He suggests we might be able to find a mutually agreeable form of words that might cover that. On the strength of this, the trustees decide to think of the future.

They're as aware as I was back in 1986, and again in 1993, that these things take time but it's important to plan ahead. We decide to call it 'Stage Two'. If we're to realize our next aim, which is to move towards education, we are going to fund someone who can handle a reasonable amount of administration and can work with school parties. We have a person in mind.

Henry Stanier currently works for the RAF at Cottesmore in a tiresome clerical job. He's dying to find something more connected with natural history. Henry S is no longer the shy young man who spent time alone studying damselflies on the jetty at Ashton Water. Quite apart from turning up regularly for years and doing absolutely anything asked of him, he has – under Henry Curry's careful encouragement – blossomed into a confident, effective and convincing presenter of the TV-Microscope link demonstration. That's not to say that Henry Curry and I didn't hide on the mezzanine floor, above and behind the audience, holding our breath and crossing our fingers, when Henry S gave his first performance. We needn't have worried. What we want now is to find funding for him to get a more rewarding job here.

Henry S has produced some surprises, too, not least when he arrived with the entire contents of the crockery and glass cupboards of the RAF Cottesmore Officers' Mess. Apparently they were upgrading – or something – their stock and all these pint glasses, cups and saucers, teapots and Harrier pilots' personalized mugs were heading for the skip. The extra stock is very useful for the tearoom, and for our evening get-togethers; and there's something slightly surreal about drinking from a fighter pilot's personalized mug.

MONDAY, MAY 10TH, 1999

Kari receives a letter from Gill, wife of the British Dragonfly Society's President, Peter Mill. Gill is delighted with two watercolours that Kari has sent her, a Common Blue Damselfly and a Large Red Damselfly. They're much larger than her usual miniatures, but they glow. Kari says she wouldn't mind doing larger work more often.

SATURDAY, MAY 15TH, 1999

A visit from eldest daughter Anna, her husband Simon and my grandchildren, Sally and Oliver. Sally's eyes no longer resemble my father's; they're much prettier, but almost every time I look at her I remember that moment in the hospital. Oli and I start work on a railway layout up in the loft of the Mill. I had a very big layout back in Spalding and hated losing it. Up in the roof of the Mill there's easily enough space to recreate a scale third-of-a-mile of four-track East Coast main line, with a branch to an imaginary Spalding-like town named Deeping Four Spires. On bike rides in the Lincolnshire fens under the vast skies it was always possible to see at least four churches simultaneously.

One of the sad parts of spending so much time down here at the Mill is that I get to see Miriam less and less. I really miss those happy lunches and leisurely teas. She knows how busy Kari and I are, and her peremptory commands, issued by her secretary on typed, headed paper and sellotaped to our door: "COME TO LUNCH. DUCK AND PEAS" now begin to dwindle. The days of laughter, quails' eggs, Château La Cardonne, and red roses in vases on the sunny dining table are fading.

SATURDAY, JUNE 5TH, 1999

We're open once more, and yet again it coincides with one of Miriam's parties. Several grandees come down to the Museum and most of them say very positive things, but the nicest moment of the day is when Lala Dawkins – Richard Dawkins' wife – presents a mosaic tile with the outline of a dragonfly on it for display in the Museum.

A small, sturdily built, elderly man in a seaman's sweater reappears, too. Obviously not one of Miriam's party-goers, he looks very like the jolly sailor in the 'Skegness-is-so-bracing' railway poster. His name is John Wainwright and he came a couple of times last year but it's clear he loathes working with other people. This year, on earlier volunteer work parties, I've taken to giving him jobs in outlying parts of the Museum grounds and he seems to like that. I hadn't expected him to show up when we opened to the public. When he frowns, which is often, he looks extremely serious; but when he smiles, which is much rarer, the adjective 'beatific' doesn't nearly do him justice. He also likes his lunch and his beer, and is much more relaxed with the young staff in the tea-room than with us older types. The fact that his sweater could do with a wash appears to be a source of amusement for them. He has a very hesitant way of speaking and an occasional stutter. Today he produces a small pile of trees from the boot of his smart little turquoise Mini Metro.

'Oh. Um. I … er … Ruary? I … er … um… shall I plant these? Um … where? Oh, and would you like a Thuya?'

John's enthusiasm for tree-planting will stay with us. He's a classic example of a volunteer who works like a Trojan but has no wish whatsoever to interact with the public.

SUNDAY, JUNE 6TH, 1999

Sheila Wright and Henry Curry attend their first meeting as trustees. It's terrific to have them aboard, although they've effectively been aboard for the last seven years.

I break the news that Kari will not be running the tearoom any more. She's done an amazing job, coping with a job she pretty much hated for four long years, and she's desperate to spend more time developing her painting career. But she's made sure there's a rock-solid young team in her place: Sam, Charlie and Laura, properly trained up by her, brilliant at scones, and sent away for council hygiene courses, too. Kari sent me on one of those, too.

THURSDAY, JUNE 17TH, 1999

Today we're finishing up what has been a two-day job. We'd been fretting ever since we opened about improving access, and resolving the issue of visitors having to reverse out of the gift shop, go through a gate and back into the main Museum space.

Mick O'Dell, small, bespectacled and burly, keen on dragonflies, was here last Sunday with his wife, Sylvia. We were standing together in the gift shop and for some reason I mentioned our access problem.

'You mean you want a hole in this wall here?' he asked, patting the wall behind him.

'Yes,' I said. 'I've got permission from Charles Lane but the quotes frighten me.'

'Well, I'll do it.'

'What?'

'Sure. Cost you nothing. When do you want me?'

And so, yesterday, Mick turned up with a pickaxe, a reinforced concrete lintel and a set of Akrow supports; and today, we're just putting a final coat of paint on the edges of a wonderful walk-through entrance to the main Museum.

SUNDAY, JUNE 27TH, 1999

Kazuo Unno opens a display of his and his colleague Misaki Mizukami's images. They're both very successful Japanese wildlife photographers.

Carol Bouchard – and a couple of extremely willing helpers – have completely re-whitewashed the interior of the old dairy, we've fixed up lighting, and the elegant Japanese photographs look fantastic.

Henry Curry and I have been surmising about Carol. We both suspect that there's something very smart beneath the carefully maintained, I'll-do-anything, girl-next-door exterior. She says she works at RAF Molesworth, which is – as all the locals know – in fact a USAF base, one that doesn't have aircraft. What matters to us, though, is that she has repeated several times that she finds the Museum 'awesome'. And she doesn't stop for tea breaks.

On the strength of the success of the Japanese exhibition we set up an amateur dragonfly photographic competition. We're astonished and delighted at the response.

SATURDAY, JULY 3RD, 1999

Sarah Pateman, the Environmental Hygiene and Safety Officer from East Northamptonshire District Council arrives to check the tearoom, in particular our food preparation procedures. After my experience with the inspector in the generating hall,

I'm a little less afraid, and Sarah too turns out to be human. She checks the fridges, the cookers, our storage procedures and the overall cleanliness. She examines my HACCP (Hazard Analysis Critical Control Path) (Who on earth dreamed that one up? Boy, was it a pain to complete), congratulates us on passing our council courses, and presents us with a Good Hygiene award. Sam, Charlie, Laura and I do our best not to collectively faint away.

Later that afternoon, I cut myself fairly bloodily, and Laura really does faint away.

FRIDAY, JULY 16TH, 1999

Ever since we took over the tearoom in the former miller's house, the flat upstairs has been occupied. We've made a point of getting on well with the tenants and often invited them down to join us of a weekend evening. Today, Damon, the last tenant, is leaving. Kari and I have expressed an interest in moving there and paying a commercial rent. It would save a great deal of trundling back and forth from the mansion and, apart from the incessant roar from the nearby A605, it's a really delightful spot. We're also very conscious of occupying space up at the mansion. We've stayed there on and off for ten years. And we'll be a presence at the Museum at night, good for security. But it will also mean even less time with Miriam.

TUESDAY, JULY 20TH, 1999

It's the evening of the official launch of the Cory Environmental Trust in Northamptonshire, and they've chosen The National Dragonfly Museum as their venue. A small army of VIPs is expected and we've spruced everything up and laid out long tables in the tearoom for drinks and a simple evening meal. Kari makes sure Sam, Charlie and Laura look smart and ready with trays of drinks.

We have an excellent relationship with both the East Northamptonshire District Council and with Cory, and we're supported financially by both. Cory has even funded an outside loo for disabled visitors: it's now a far cry from the shit-encrusted hovel that Henry and I cleaned out back in 1994.

Everything works perfectly: I march the group round the site, point out damselflies perched in the rushes beside the garden pond. Then the dragonfly larvae do their stuff for Henry and the TV-Microscope link, and finally the Blackstone thumps into life and lights up the generating hall the better for it being evening time. We now have four DC lights hooked up.

The guests trickle back into the tearoom and settle down to baked potatoes, lasagna and more red wine. A neatly-suited, slightly pot-bellied gent snaps his fingers at Kari from across the room.

'I say! You! More wine!'

Another guest leans over and whispers in the man's ear, looking over his glasses at Kari. Aghast, the suit looks satisfyingly horrified. It's the only incident, if you can call it that, in an evening that's a great success. It's exciting to see fairly hard-nosed businesspeople genuinely interested in what we do. Even better news: Cory offers to fund a bridge over the little stream that runs through the Museum grounds, and the local council say they will fund production of 10,000 leaflets for us.

THURSDAY, JULY 22ND, 1999

The Dragonfly Sanctuary opens next weekend and it desperately needs work. Carol Bouchard offers to help and we drive from the Museum to the lake in belting rain. Carol puts on waders, starts up the strimmer and heads out into Chaser Channel to attack the reeds. I set to work clearing the paths and Haytering the grass.

An hour and a half later, it hasn't stopped pouring and I decide it's lunchtime. Given the conditions, we've done more than enough. The forecast 'gives for' better weather tomorrow. I'll come down and finish off. I manage to signal Carol to stop. She's sopping wet, hair clumped round her neck and ears. She pushes up her visor, switches off the strimmer and squints at me.

'What?'

'Let's call a halt. Lunchtime.'

'This ain't finished. I'll stop when it's done.'

She tugs the strimmer starting-rope, it roars back into life, and on she goes.

At three-thirty – it's still coming down in buckets – Carol silences the strimmer and grins at her work. We head back to the Museum, change out of wet things, and I take her to the Loch Fyne restaurant in Elton. It's the least I can do.

WEDNESDAY, AUGUST 11TH, 1999

We've now properly moved into the upstairs flat in the Miller's House, above the tearoom. Kari's up in Aberdeen on a week-long painting course at Gray's College. She's really serious now about improving her technique and doing larger pieces. She rings to talk about how spooky the eclipse was. I hadn't noticed it; I'd got completely tied up cleaning revoltingly dirty pelmets.

SATURDAY, SEPTEMBER 18TH, 1999

Norman Moore arrives to deliver the third in the series of annual Corbet lectures, 'The conservation of dragonflies at home and abroad.' Norman, who is after all the father of modern dragonfly conservation, talks very seriously about threats to dragonflies worldwide. The cinema gets very stuffy and we have to open one of the big barn doors. Norman is nearly drowned out twice, first by a truck with a hole in its silencer, and then by a gang of noisy lads returning to Oundle from a lunchtime session at the Chequered Skipper. No one except me notices. He's too interesting.

SATURDAY, SEPTEMBER 25TH, 1999

Another trustees' meeting. It's been a very good year. 'Country Jobs of Old Day' has been even better, with a splendid selection of tractors turning up and even a US Army jeep … which I was allowed to drive solo, blasting along the oak-lined road in the evening sunshine with the windscreen flat, the ghosts of those extraordinarily brave USAAF B-17 bomber pilots from Polebrook Airfield just up the road riding beside me.

Our list of volunteer names now tops a hundred and most are ready to turn their hand to anything, grass-cutting, pond clearing, giving talks, leading guided tours, making cakes, whatever. And we've had more success at our second Bird Fair; yet another cheerful visit from Bill Oddie.

MONDAY, DECEMBER 27TH, 1999

The phone rings in our cottage in Scotland. A poplar tree has fallen and smashed its way through the new Collyweston stone slates in the roof of the Mill. I get in the car and drive south. By the time I arrive Sid Jackson has made sure the hole is watertight and tarpaulined. There's no damage at all to the exhibits, just a wet sofa. It now has an additional, subtly different aroma.

Chapter 31

THURSDAY, FEBRUARY 24TH, 2000

It's freezing cold and volunteer Carol Bouchard, son Richard and I sit together in the bleak chilly tearoom, papers strewn over three tables, trying to sort out the Museum accounts for 1999. The computer upstairs in the Mill has crashed. Blessed computers, but luckily I've kept all the papers in what fellow-trustee Justin calls the 'Shoebox System'. Evidently his first ever accountancy job involved a small businessman literally shoving a shoebox full of receipts at him and telling him to get on with it. By the end of this dull cold day, the three of us have done the whole job.

It's clear that the tearoom is losing money. Carol offers to help next summer so that we can save recruiting another youngster.

'Am I saying this?' she asks. 'Am I really offering to help in an English tearoom? Me? Someone who's allergic to kitchens? Someone who puts lemon in tea? Someone whose idea of a sandwich is processed cheese between two bits of bread? Is this American really going to make scones for Brits?'

'Looks like it,' I say.

Richard looks at the floor and smiles.

TUESDAY, MARCH 7TH, 2000

Miriam and I are sitting in the library, me on the sofa, she in her wheelchair. We were – well, in truth, she was – on the subject of pyrazines, but now it's carotenoids. It's a dark evening and the fire is blazing. There's a sudden fluttering at one of the tall mullioned windows. It's a blue tit, somehow trapped inside and fighting to escape. I climb onto the window seat and try to catch it, but it panics and shoots out of my reach. I try again, twice more, then drop back down and suggest we open the windows as wide as we can, switch the lights off and leave the room.

I've hardly finished speaking before Miriam springs out of her wheelchair, darts up onto the window seat, seizes the little bird, opens the window, shoves it outside, shuts the window, resumes her seat and continues the conversation. It happens so quickly I can scarcely believe it.

SATURDAY, MAY 27TH, 2000

We're hard at work preparing the Museum for the new season. We need to deal with flaking paintwork and remove months of dust and cobwebs from the insides of the buildings. The machinery is being fettled up, the tearoom is being spring-cleaned, and, throughout the site, waterside areas need to be cleared and opened so that visitors can see dragonflies clearly without falling in.

Suddenly everything stops. A Hairy Dragonfly has been spotted on the millpond. It's a new species for Ashton. Basically a big blue and yellow job, (Sunday name: *Brachytron pratense*), it's the first of the big dragonflies to appear in this part of the country every summer and it flies very fast and low. It's called Hairy because it has substantial hairs on the thorax, the theory being that the hairs help to keep it warm against late frosts and sudden temperature drops. It's a great sight, or more precisely a great series of fleeting glimpses. No further work is done until lunchtime.

It's very important for us to know whether *Brachytrons* are just visiting, or whether they like the Museum habitats sufficiently to start mating and egg-laying. Most dragonfly recorders now regard what actually breeds in a habitat as more important than what simply visits it, so we'll watch carefully for exuviae this year.

SATURDAY, JUNE 10TH, 2000

We're open again. The damage to the Mill roof has been repaired. The honey-coloured Collyweston slates glow when the sun shines.

You'd never know now that last winter an entire poplar tree had smashed through.

It's all change in the tearoom. The last of Kari's scone-trained team has gone. It's strange not to have a member of the Sears family nipping cheerfully about. Sam had already gone off to university and now the time has come for Charlie – or Charlotte when we tease her – to go, too. Ann Tomlinson has offered to assist Carol. They begin by cleaning out and re-papering the foodstore. I walk in and – surprise – its walls are now mauve.

I'm in between talks when I'm summoned to speak to a wiry, scruffy, shirt-sleeved man with a roll-up hanging from his lower lip. He refuses to make eye contact.

'Know that pile of junk you've got in the corner by the farm stuff?'

'Yes.'

I know it very well. It's one of the jobs we haven't yet got round to, a large pile of rusting metal I've been meaning to get shifted since 1994. It contains bits of several machines. I remember picking up a cylindrical cone-ended fuel tank, like something off a Wright Brothers aircraft. It had rust-holes in it. I chucked it back.

'Did you know,' he says, 'you've got the parts for a complete Auto-Culto in there?'

'No. Um. What's an Auto-Culto?'

'A little rotavator, harrow, plough sort of thing, for small-holdings.'

'Right.'

'Shall I restore it for you? I can take it today. I'll need to make some bits.'

I find myself wondering whether he's serious. But, after all, even if he just drives off with the stuff and never comes back it'll simply save us having to move it. So he backs his trailer into the courtyard, unearths what he needs from the pile and disappears. Busy with other visitors, I don't even get his name.

SUNDAY, JUNE 11TH, 2000

Trustees' meeting. We finally get round to discussing Charles

Lane's suggestion of an internet site. They're becoming very popular, we belatedly acknowledge that. Henry Curry takes on the job.

John Wainwright arrives with a bootful of hawthorn saplings. He wants to plant them round Kari's pond, exactly where they will shade out the sun and drop leaf litter into the water. I persuade him that they'll make a good hedge along the side of the visitors' car park. He trudges off down the long millpond walkway, trees under one arm, fork in hand. He's already spent days round there, on his own, putting in armfuls of daffodils. He will take nothing in return except a hug from any of the tearoom girls, and a beer with his lunch. Kari reckons he's a secret millionaire. (She's not far wrong: he later leaves us a legacy.)

THURSDAY, JUNE 15TH, 2000

Summoned by the BBC, I arrive at The London Wetland Centre, Battersea, to do a piece for *Charlie's Wildlife Gardens*. I've never been here before and I'm very impressed. It's a huge site, right in the centre of London, absolutely ideal for dragonflies. I've seen Charlie Dimmock on TV but it'll be interesting to meet her face-to-face, which I do very suddenly now as she's walking down the track towards me. She's friendly and interested in the whole business of dragonflies in a garden setting.

Stephen Moss, the director, comes up, gives Charlie a smacking kiss and we start. The camera rolls but the soundman immediately stops us; a Boeing 747 lumbers overhead. We're directly under the flightpath for Heathrow, so this happens again and again, leaving Charlie and I to chat. We veer off onto other topics and by the end of the morning she has almost persuaded me that Australian sparkling red wine is wonderful stuff, grossly under-rated. Almost.

The London dragonflies perform exactly to order, flying, mating and ovipositing exactly as Stephen requires. Later, as Charlie and I sit drinking coffee on the decking outside the café ...

''Ullo, Charlie,' says a black-suited ratty little man, slipping close and leering.

'Hello, Willie,' says Charlie coldly, staring at the table, refusing to look up.

The man sidles off.

'Journalist,' she says quietly.

WEDNESDAY, JULY 19TH, 2000

Kari and I pay another visit to Highgrove. A female Emperor Dragonfly is ovipositing in the pond. An Empress has laid eggs in a Prince's pond. We photograph her and send HRH a copy, along with our report.

FRIDAY, JULY 21ST, 2000

Dick is working on the second Blackstone. He's almost got the massive piston head free. If he gets it out, it'll be far too heavy for him to lift away alone.

'Leave that a minute, Dick,' I say. 'The phone's ringing. I'll be back in a second.'

When I return, the piston head is sitting across the room on the turbine plinth and Dick has disappeared. He's obviously done it himself. Where is he? Has he had a heart attack? There's a scuffle from above. Dick is up on the tiny catwalk near the roof, an oil can in his right hand, his left arm hooked round the driveshaft, glasses on the end of his nose, squinting at a lubricator. How on earth can I explain to Ann if he falls?

'For heaven's sake, Dick, let me do that.'

'I'm not afraid of heights. Only just packed up flying my Microlight, remember.'

'Dick, that's not the point …'

'We need more diesel before this afternoon. Will you go and see Sid? He'll be on his lunch break soon.'

SATURDAY, JULY 22ND, 2000

Carol brings a packet of Dragonfly-brand Tea into the tearoom, very appropriate. We agree to serve it with a view to making it a fixture. I'm leaning on the outside wall of the tearoom garden, talking to a visitor, when I see Carol march across the grass with a tray, heading towards two elderly ladies seated at a table overlooking the millpond.

'Truly genuine Dragonfly Tea for y'all,' she says.

The ladies look confused.

'Pardon? Could you speak a bit slower?' says one of the ladies.

Now Carol looks confused. There's a pause.

'I'm French,' says the other lady.

'Oh! *Alors!*' says Carol. '*Ici, j'ai* ... darn it ... *du thé, de* ... what is it? ... *la libellule. Comprends?*'

'Eh?' says the French lady. 'I'm sorry ... I do not ... '

'We didn't understand your English either,' says the first lady.

SUNDAY, JULY 23RD, 2000

I lead a group of visitors out to our garden pond. There's a Blue-tailed Damselfly perched on sedge stem, and a Common Blue Damselfly ovipositing, her abdomen curled round the edge of a white water lily leaf. When the group arrives at the millrace observation platform I point out a pair of Azure Damselflies in cop among the reeds. A Brown Hawker is patrolling up and down the millrace, its copper-coloured wings glinting in the afternoon sun. Everyone falls silent to watch the big insect as it glitters back and forth.

Then we walk round the side of the building and I pause and tell them a little of the Mill's history before we head up the western bank of the millrace toward the weir. I warn people not to move too quickly. Dragonflies have superb vision. They can spot you up to forty metres away. With their bulging eyes – 30,000 lenses and photoreceptors in each eye – they can see in front, above, below, behind ... 80% of their brain processes visual information. They're superlative seeing-machines.

Off we go and, just as I'd hoped, Banded Demoiselles are dancing among the club rushes, their deep blue wings flashing in the sunshine. We stand for a while in the sound of the falling water and the sweet smell of the river, then move to Kari's pond.

Sure enough, when we reach the pond, there's a Brown Hawker female ovipositing on the one of the soggy logs we've put in specially for the purpose. And a late honey-brown Four-spotted Chaser still on the wing, speeds over the Greater Pondweed, comparing nicely with the shining scarlet of a Ruddy Darter that lifts from the grassy path in front of us and drops further away, giving us just enough time to admire before lifting again. Dragonflies can fly at over 30mph and cover fifteen metres in less than a second, from a standing start. That's almost supersonic for something that size. When I wrote the brochure I actually put 40 mph and I'm sure one day I'll be proved right. An earlier dragonfly authority, Tillyard, reckoned they did 60 mph. They have a magic protein molecule called Resilin in their wing muscles that gives them extra power and enables them be such superb aerial acrobats. It's the same stuff that gives fleas their amazing jump.

We mount the steps of the footbridge over the Nene and watch a small squadron of Azures – little shards of sky-blue neon – darting over the yellow water lilies. It's time to take the visitors back for the Henry Show and the Blackstone.

SATURDAY, AUGUST 26TH, 2000

It's 'Popping and Banging and Lights Day', and has been advertised as such. We've decided to expand the whole 'Country Jobs of Old Day' experience into a weekend, with stationary steam engines, corn grinding, the now operational hay elevator, a glittering line of red, blue and grey tractors, including our lovely newly-restored Ferguson FE35 with its unusual copper-coloured engine. We have a weaver, a thatcher, a blacksmith, a basket-maker, a leather worker, a hawk-handler, even a stone-mason, (who is in fact Alan, Francis Chiverton's father).

3.00pm: the darkened generating hall – we've put blackouts on the windows – is packed to capacity. Ron Cook gazes anxiously at his beautifully restored gauges. After fifty years of idleness, the Blackstone thumps, the belts whir, the pulleys spin and the generator is turning again. But will everything work? Will the Mill be able to make its own DC electricity once more? We know it will, of course, because we've tested it thoroughly, but for the benefit of the visitors we pretend.

Tension mounts as Ron strides over to the bank of glittering, newly polished brass switches. A thoughtful frown, a determined flick, lamps glow throughout the hall and lo, there is light. A storm of applause. It may seem a far cry from dragonflies, but all this machinery is a terrific attraction, especially for fathers who don't specially share a love of natural history with their kids. But seeing as they're here, why not watch a Larva Show? We deliver information by stealth.

And, pretence or not, it's a splendid tribute to the hard work of the Oily Rag team. Now all we need is for a corporate fairy god-person to step forward and help us restore one of the lowland-river water turbines. It would be expensive. We'd need to drain the turbine dock. Two brothers, Mark and Russell Bulley, have already descended in sub-aqua gear and verified that everything is still there. Walter Morris Thomas left cast iron slots in the upstream end of the dock for exactly this task, so that wooden baulks could be slid into place to keep the water out. To be able to make electricity once again, as Charles Rothschild did, would be wonderful. Of course the phrase 'renewable resource' wasn't coined a hundred years ago, but that's what it would be. It would fit very well with the Biomuseum's conservation message.

Biomuseum? We've decided to rename the place. We've talked amongst ourselves and to hundreds of others, including top scientists, cub groups, dustmen and duchesses. Well, one duchess. Comments ranged from professional museum people's closely reasoned arguments at one end of the spectrum, to a blunt 'They won't know what you're talking about' at the other. The general view seems to be that Biomuseum avoids the just-things-in-dusty-glass-cases image, gives the idea of a museum alive where everything depends on living things, on habitats and on people. And makes people wonder a bit.

BANK HOLIDAY MONDAY, AUGUST 28TH, 2000

It's the finale of 'Country Jobs' weekend, and this afternoon we've got the fourth in our Corbet Lecture series. We've asked Professor Chris Baines, the well-known environmentalist – and Charlie Dimmock's co-presenter of BBC TV's *Charlie's Wildlife Gardens* – to place dragonflies in a broader wildlife context.

Afterwards he stands in the courtyard, sipping tea, chatting with admirers and having his photograph taken.

We're over-run in the tearoom. Service is slow and at least three groups are getting restless. Carol comes hurtling out of the kitchen, apologizes profusely and distributes placatory packets of crisps to everyone.

SATURDAY, SEPTEMBER 16TH, 2000

There's a very bossy female middle-class voice booming out of the gift shop. Lynn will be able to handle her, I know, but I can't resist edging closer to listen in.

'Yes, well,' says the woman, 'I'll have you know I'm a personal friend of Dame Miriam Rothschild.'

'Are you?' says Lynn. 'You'll know her niece Kari, then. I'll get her for you. She's in the tearoom kitchen.'

'Oh! No! I mean, I'm not that … well, goodbye.'

As she shoots out of the gift shop door past me, I see she's a big woman but she's moving at the speed of a startled rabbit.

I finish a talk, and walk out into the sunshine to find an immaculate, brightly-coloured piece of agricultural machinery in the courtyard. It's the Auto-Culto. The gentleman with the roll-up hanging from his lip has been as good as his word. We're surprised, delighted and grateful. He's even mended the little fuel tank, last seen riddled with holes. We place it reverently in one of the sheds. It looks well, and outshines the four-wheeled Victorian bath chair beside it.

I thank the man very sincerely, and as he drives away I realize to my horror I still haven't got his name.

SUNDAY, SEPTEMBER 17TH, 2000

It's late afternoon. I walk down past the forge and along the riverbank path towards the new Cory-funded observation platform. They have also provided money for a solid bridge over the little stream close by that runs beneath the road, down through the woodland, under the forge and eventually out in the millpond. We've been digging another pond in the wood – we've already managed to tip a small digger on its side, no casualties – and I haven't had time to see how things have been going.

I decide to head for the platform first. Since it was built, Kari and I have taken to coming down here after a day's work, sometimes with a bottle of wine. We lay a couple of planks, left over from the construction, between the platform's protective railings and make a seat. We perch there as the water flows by, and watch the sun go down over the silhouette of the tall spire of Oundle church. Sometimes a late-flying Brown Hawker keeps us company. We were here last night and now I realize I forgot to remove the two planks.

As I approach I spot two figures sitting on the makeshift bench talking quietly. A mum, I guess, with a tumble of red hair and a dark blue anorak, and her daughter, wearing a light blue wind-cheater, her fair hair tied back in a pony-tail. Mum is explaining something; daughter is listening very seriously, clutching a red bag to her chest. I creep away, none the wiser but quite sure that neither of them will forget this moment by the water.

SUNDAY, SEPTEMBER 24TH, 2000

Our last day of the season. John Wainwright arrives with more trees for the car park. I have to tell him he can't plant the Thuya or Giant Red Cedars or the Wellingtonias he's brought along. They don't really fit with our local-and-native policy. It's sad. They'd be a great memorial. At a trustees' meeting today, I report that in addition to our regular donors, we're getting solid financial help from John Spedan Lewis, The Esmée Fairbairn Trust and the Bernard Sunley Trust. Other fund-providers are keen but await confirmation of a longer lease.

And, thanks to Lynn Curry and her team, we've sold more items in the shop – despite fewer people and unkind weather – and we now have an e-gift shop.

Kari comes back from lunch at the mansion and reports that she heard Miriam telling her guests that 'of course Ruary has put dragonflies on the map'. We both know she's unlikely to say that to my face. And we also know she doesn't give credit lightly.

THURSDAY, OCTOBER 5TH, 2000

It's the BBC again. They want to bring Lenny Henry along to film a comedy pilot, so of course we open specially. Lenny is very big, and quietly cheerful. He submits to a scene where he's dragged kicking and screaming into a Dragonfly Museum. Is there no publicity that's bad publicity?

WEDNESDAY, NOVEMBER 8TH, 2000

Son Richard is here again, and while I wade through paperwork upstairs he gets on with heavy stuff outside. He's now very much stronger than me; it's really annoying. He loves attacking the bigger branches of redundant, fallen willows, parts that have defeated the rest of us. He calls me downstairs, takes me through the white gate and asks whether he can have a go at an entire sycamore, very large, still in leaf, that has grown up against the wall of the forge. It now overhangs the roof and its roots threaten to wreck the entire wall.

'Well, that would be great, but where will it fall, Rich?' I ask.

'I'll sling a rope round it and pull it down over there, away from the forge and the garden pond.'

He sets to work with an axe and I leave him to it. I've got several phone calls to make.

Half an hour later, the wind is getting up and rattles the Luccam doors. Ten minutes after that, there's the sound of fast-moving wellingtons thudding up the stairs.

'Dad? Can you come a minute?'

We fly downstairs, out into the courtyard, through the white gate to the sycamore. Richard has got two ropes round it but with more than half the base of its trunk chopped away it's now swaying, the rising westerly gale pushing it dangerously close to smashing through the red tiles of the forge. The wind roars in the leaves. We cling to the ropes and, without a word to each other, realize that the two of us can't stop the tree falling for long. A vision of an enormous hole in the forge roof floats in front of me.

Richard shouts, 'Did you see that van in the courtyard, Dad? Maybe you could ...'

'Can you hold it, while I …?'

'I'll try,' he yells.

I sprint back to the courtyard. Two plumbers are sitting in a blue van, both reading *The Sun* and eating sandwiches. They instantly get the message, leap out and within thirty seconds all four of us are on the ropes hauling the sycamore – its outer branches now stabbing the tiles – into the wind and away from the roof. The tree crashes harmlessly onto the grass. The plumbers think it's the funniest thing that's happened to them for months.

Chapter 32

Our first work party of the year. We've had a letter from the local police warning of an increase in burglaries in the area, so today we're installing an alarm system. We've also inherited a complete telephone switchboard and have decided to rig up an internal phone network. Henry Curry works for BT and is utterly at home with installations such as burglar alarms and phones, so while I concentrate on fixing lunch in the tearoom – Kari's in Scotland – Henry gathers a team and sets to work.

At about 11.00am, they troop in for coffee. They've hit a problem. They can't work out how to run an aerial phone line across from the Mill to the forge; it's basically from one blank wall to another. Sure, they can use a ladder to screw fixings to each wall, but how to string the line between them, well out of the way of vehicles below? Out they go, still muttering about it. Ten minutes later, I happen to glance out of the tearoom kitchen window. Four men are clumped together, walking very, very slowly across the courtyard, holding a ladder upright. At the top of the ladder, teetering like an acrobat in a circus, is young Francis Chiverton holding a length of telephone line. I look quickly away and check on the baked potatoes. Shortly after, the group come back in, triumphant. Would I like to ring all departments to announce that lunch is served? Francis is about to say something, but is silenced by a chorus of frowns.

SATURDAY, MARCH 17TH, 2001

Our work party is cancelled. We're in the middle of the foot-and-mouth outbreak. I stay in Scotland, helping local farmers by disinfecting the wheels of vehicles entering and leaving the glen.

SATURDAY, APRIL 21ST, 2001

The committee of the British Dragonfly Society hold their formal spring meeting in the tearoom. They also donate another computer. We serve them lunch, but later we're too involved with pulling out fallen willows from the millrace with the Land Rover to notice that they've gone. I write to thank them. It's so good to have their support.

SUNDAY, APRIL 22ND, 2001

Kari and I drive up for supper with Miriam. As we sip pre-dinner drinks I glance into the dining room and see that the long table with its many chairs is set with just four places. Miriam has a very serious guest, Professor Derek Denton. We've met him before. He's about to publish a large book about animal consciousness, although right now he seems a little uneasy with Miriam's dogs, in particular Sunday, the scruffy little black mongrel that Miriam rescued from a rubbish dump in Jerusalem. Sunday's the only dog able to hold her own against Miriam's ferocious shelties. Miriam and Derek are deep in psychological conversation as we go through.

We're still fiddling with quails' eggs, listening to Miriam and Derek discussing the complexities of consciousness, when the phone rings and Miriam excuses herself, swivels her wheelchair and zooms back into the library. In her absence the conversation drops from the sublime to the banal and finally to a slightly strained silence; into which butts Sunday. She hops up onto the empty chair beside Derek, panting, tongue lolling, gazing fixedly at him. The silence continues, broken only by Sunday's frantic panting. Derek becomes increasingly uncomfortable. Suddenly he turns to the little dog and, in a very cold Australian voice, says:

'Why don't you take your consciousness somewhere else?'

WEDNESDAY, APRIL 25TH, 2001

I send out the second edition of our newsletter, the *Ashton Skimmer*, to our by-now substantial mailing list. It includes:

OUR APPEAL FOR HELP FOR THE NATIONAL DRAGONFLY BIOMUSEUM – STAGE TWO

We had a FANTASTIC response to our appeal. We have raised just under £10,000, with personal cheques ranging from £3 to £500. We hope you will forgive us for not writing to you to thank you all individually, but we want to say how delighted and grateful we are for your collective generosity. We see this as a massive vote of confidence in what we are doing, and in what we plan to do.

What's in store? Well, armed with your support, we are currently negotiating with major fund-providers. A factor which concerns them is the length of our lease. We are in discussion with our landlord, Dr Charles Lane, with a view to extending our lease. It is worth remembering that, without Charles Lane's amazing support in the form of leasing the Mill buildings to the charity, our dream of a National Dragonfly Biomuseum would not have come true. We will keep you posted about developments.

As most of you know, we plan to expand our displays, get more equipment, make our exhibits properly waterproof and, ideally, get a full-time person. So far as fund-applications go, I think it's fair to say that we have done almost all we can for the time being. The good news is that we have already had positive answers from The John Spedan Lewis Trust and the Bernard Sunley Charitable Trust. Now, we just have to await the outcome of other people's decisions. We will keep you posted.

We plan a new introductory video. Our present one is getting a bit dated. Besides the many other changes since 1995, people keep thinking that the grizzled old buffer floating around the grounds must be the introductory video presenter's elder brother.

We also plan to review our dragonfly recording procedures. Over the years, we have amassed a considerable quantity of data. There are moves afoot at national and county level towards better, more uniform recording of species. We want to play our part.

We are going to help at Wood Walton. We have plans to reopen an old farm pond. And Chris Packham is coming back (unforeseen developments permitting) … and … and … well, there is a lot happening and, clearly, there's absolutely nothing like being near water, messing about with dragonflies!

We are still a lovely, strong team of volunteers, sometimes very sorry to see an occasional departure due to changing circumstance, but regularly infused with new blood. Our collective memory of awful, terrifying, happy and hysterically funny moments grows by the year. If anything, there is a slight change of focus, in that we spend more time working with the public and perhaps less actually building or clearing. But the areas that we 'manage' have a maddening habit of managing themselves back to their preferred states. And wood will rot so; we have just renewed the catwalk to the generating hall, for example, (no mean feat, perched over a very flooded Nene). So there is still lots to do.

Thank you again for your tremendous support.

Haste ye back!

WEDNESDAY, 3RD MAY, 2001

It's a busy day of paperwork. I'm at my desk, upstairs in the Mill. Afternoon sunshine floods in through the row of windows on the south side of the big room. The old loading doors on the north side below the Luccam are open, and, above the gentle traffic roar from the A605, a coot squawks peremptorily from the millpond below. The telephone rings and I pick it up cheerfully. By the end of the call, I'm in a different mood.

Charles, our landlord, is very apologetic: farming is seriously in the doldrums and every farmer is now searching desperately for as many diversifications as possible. It isn't simply because of the recent foot-and-mouth outbreak. Profitability is seriously down over all.

The Mill building could help, he says: it could be converted into office space and could generate a commercial rent. A similar mill downstream has already been successfully converted thus. Unless the Biomuseum is now in a position to produce a commercial monthly rent, it will have to close. He's truly very sorry to have to do this to us. We could carry on next year if we wanted but we might have to move out at very short notice.

I don't have to consult anybody about whether or not to continue next year. Quite apart from the logistics, none of us will want to carry on in the knowledge that we could be closed at any moment. I go quiet for a moment, then I thank Charles for the offer and tell him we'll have to shut the Biomuseum at the end of the 2001 season, to which we're already publicly committed. We say goodbye.

I sit back, stare at the big old beams above my head, and remind myself of Kari's words: 'nothing is for ever'. So this is it. The end. I think I'm going to cry but I don't. I notice my left hand is still holding the receiver. There's no one else around and perhaps that's just as well. I stand up, walk to the open doors and look down at the millpond.

A kingfisher dashes across the water, hovers right in the centre in a blur of turquoise then scoots back to its perch. It often sits there, a slim branch overhanging the rushes, hidden by the wall from passers-by but in perfect sight for me up here. With the willows casting afternoon shadows across the pond, and the surface mirror-still, this is the sort of view that would have had Constable reaching delightedly for his sketchbook. No one is here to share it with me, no one down below on the long walkway we've built along the side of the pond from the car park to the tearoom, and now – at least from the end of this summer – no one will be.

I go down the stairs into the main Museum and look at our lovely interpretation boards, the TV-Microscope link and all the exhibits. Then I go outside, stand on the first observation platform and think of us building it seven years ago. I look upstream to the more recent platform, where, some evenings, Kari and I sit. I can't bring myself to unlock either of the two outbuildings, the forge or the Fish Room. But I wander past the gleaming farm machinery and head back through the gift shop, along the catwalk into the engine house. I gaze at the Blackstone and the generator, and up at the belts, the pulleys and the electric lamps. It's too much. All this work. All this love. How, in heavens name, am I going to tell the volunteers?

Kari is in Scotland. I ring her. We always knew it might not last, she says. Nothing is for ever, she says. Well, I knew she'd say that. We do our best to cheer each other until I put the phone down. And then I do cry.

There are very few entries in my journal for 2001. We had a highly successful season. The volunteers carried on regardless. Of course Miriam and I discussed the whole thing, but, when all was said and done, what could she do about the profitability in farming? Of course there was anger, a lot of it, with some of the newer volunteers even wanting to take legal action.

Two things remain with me: first was the amount of care and sympathy with which the volunteers approached me personally; and second was the general reaction, which was essentially: OK, what next? This response was relatively easy for the volunteers whose main interest was dragonflies. Dragonflies, after all, fly elsewhere. But it was harder for the engineering team whose years of work would now go for nothing. No, that's not true. It wouldn't go for nothing. It had a value and a love in its own right. But still.

On Saturday, September the 15th, as a mark of respect for recent terrible events in New York – 9/11 – we remained closed for the weekend. At that moment it felt as if the entire world echoed our own smaller uncertainties about the future. Carol, our only American, invited us all home and fed us Mexican food. We were steadfastly – superficially – cheerful, and raised our glasses to what lay behind us, and what lay ahead.

And on September the 22nd, we began the mammoth task of packing up. It was of course much easier to take things down than it had been to put them up, but emotionally it was very much harder. There was no anger by then, just a wish to leave things in good condition, and much sadness, expressed as so often among

British people more by what wasn't said than what was.

We mothballed the generating hall ready for when, one day, it will be recognized for what it is, a wonderful example of Victorian use of a renewable resource. There are very few, if any, other extant Victorian lowland river hydro-electric complexes that were built to generate electricity, pump water to houses, and drive ancillary machinery simultaneously. And this one is on the estate of Charles Rothschild, the man whom many regard as the father of modern nature conservation. Its time will come again.

One of the most poignant moments for me was when, quite alone, I took down the railway layout grandson Oli and I had assembled upstairs in the Mill loft. Another layout lost.

In the meantime, rising from our own ashes, we renamed ourselves The Dragonfly Project.

Part Five

A Passion
for Dragonflies

2002 - ... ?

Chapter 33

The following three annual newsletters were sent to everyone on our mailing list:

THE ASHTON SKIMMER, NUMBER 3, APRIL 2002
THE VERY SAD NEWS

I have just been looking at the 2001 *Ashton Skimmer*, published this time last year. It was full of plans for the future at Ashton, both short-term and long-term. Most of you will already know that, days after the newsletter had been sent out, the blow fell.

Our landlord, Dr Charles Lane, telephoned us to say that he felt that he could no longer go on providing low-cost accommodation to the charity. With the recent drastic changes in the fortunes of farming, he was having to foreclose on our ten-year lease. We feel it is important to stress how fortunate we have been to have had such a generous landlord. Without his kindness, the Biomuseum could not have been born, nor have run so successfully for so long. We are still on very good terms with him and hope to able to continue to store our equipment at the Mill until we find another home.

WHAT DID WE ACHIEVE?

The Biomuseum really has been a success. Much of what we have done has already been recorded in previous *Ashton Skimmers* and it is impossible, in a few paragraphs, to do justice to what the team have succeeded in doing. But here are some facts: during our seven years we attracted twenty-two thousand visitors. We put in almost four and a half thousand man-days of voluntary time. This represents more than a quarter of a million pounds worth of work. The bulk of this time was spent getting the message across to visitors that dragonflies are beautiful, fascinating and in trouble – and that the visitors themselves could help.

We did much more. We ran dragonfly education courses. We improved the existing dragonfly habitats that surround the Mill and dug three more dragonfly-attracting ponds. We built three observation platforms and a substantial ramped walkway across the millpond to the car park. We laid out 'Dragonfly Trails' for visitors, enabling them to get the best view of dragonflies in action. We also spent a considerable proportion of our time on less directly dragonfly-related things. We painted, decorated, repaired and improved the premises. We cared for and restored the existing Mill machinery and vintage farm equipment. We set up and ran an attractive and profitable gift shop. We also set up and ran a very pleasant tearoom. These sentences hide hours of backbreaking work, as those who visited and saw us in action will remember.

As volunteers, we learned a great deal, not only about dragonflies. We developed a huge range of skills in basic things like habitat management and plumbing, and also in areas such as people-handling, training, teamwork, public-speaking, and systems control. And, most important of all, we had tremendous fun.

YOUR HELP
As volunteers, we could not have done what we did without tremendous support from hundreds of people. It is almost certain that YOU are one of these people, who have given us so much encouragement over the years. We shall always be grateful for such fantastic positivity from so many directions.

A significant amount of our success is directly attributable to the British Dragonfly Society. Without the advice, guidance and generosity of experienced members of the Society, we would have struggled with major factors such as habitat creation and visitor interpretation. Without the Society's financial aid, our platforms and walkway would not have been built. And without the moral support of so many members, we would have lacked the confidence of knowing that we were doing the right thing.

We have also had enormous support from a wide range of organizations, including English Nature, World Wildlife Fund, The Environment Agency, Anglian Water, The Wildlife Trusts, East Northamptonshire Council, The Cory Environmental Trust for East Northamptonshire, The John Spedan Lewis Trust, The Bernard Sunley Charitable Foundation, and The Esmée Fairbairn Charitable Trust.

Perhaps even more touching has been the help we have received from so many private individuals. Much of the monies raised were intended for Stage Two of our plans and are still held in reserve. If you contributed towards Stage Two and feel that, in view of the changed circumstances, we should return your donation to you, do please let us know. We very much hope that you will feel as the John Spedan Lewis Trust did. When I contacted them to offer to return their donation, they said, 'You keep it. We know you'll use it wisely for the dragonflies.' We will.

THE 2001 SEASON

It was lovely that the 2001 season was our best. Despite working in the full knowledge that we were about to close, the volunteers continued to give their hearts to the Museum. We had more visitors. We sold more in the gift shop. We swung the tearoom back into profit. Our Country Jobs of Old day was a riproaring success. On Bank Holiday Monday, the 27th of August, Chris Packham gave the last Corbet Lecture, a stunning performance from the man who originally opened the Museum. So we went out with a bang.

OUR ATTITUDE AT THE MOMENT

Yes, of course, it was a shock, particularly so for those of us who had put so much work in on the engine house and the farm machinery. We are over it now and are facing the future. We do not see the closure at Ashton as the end. We see it merely as the crash-landing of our metaphorical aeroplane. Yes, it is a setback, but the crew are unscathed and in good heart, the equipment is intact and the mission remains the same. We just need another aeroplane.

WHAT NEXT?

For the 2002 adult dragonfly flying season, we have been invited by English Nature to operate from Woodwalton Fen National Nature Reserve. Woodwalton was mentioned in last year's *Skimmer*. We went over as a team to help with conservation management there. But to be allowed to work there this summer is very exciting. Eleven miles from Ashton, Woodwalton is a dragonfly heaven. It has twenty-one recorded dragonfly species. It is the site of Norman Moore's decades-long study of dragonfly community development and territorial behaviour. It is the nearest home for the Scarce Chaser (*Libellula fulva*), and many of us volunteers have made pilgrimages over there in the past to gaze at and photograph this elusive insect.

At Woodwalton, we plan to run 'Dragonfly Safaris' for the general public. These safaris will be based on the experience we have gained from running guided walks at Ashton. They proved immensely popular with the general public. Our well-established dragonfly education courses will find a new lease of life in Charles Rothschild's thatched bungalow-on-stilts in the heart of the fen.

The key thing is we are still very much alive. Please keep in touch. Come and see us at Woodwalton, if you can. It really is an extraordinary place. And remember, it takes more than the loss of an aeroplane to keep a good crew down!

Best Wishes and Thanks to you ...

* * *

THE MIGRANT SKIMMER, NUMBER 1, APRIL 2003
THE BULLETIN OF THE DRAGONFLY PROJECT
(FORMERLY THE NATIONAL DRAGONFLY BIOMUSEUM)
I began last year's *Skimmer* by looking through the edition from the year before. I've done the same this year. I see that, despite the strongly valedictory note due to the closure of the Museum, we were cautiously optimistic about our new nomadic status. Well, we had good cause to be hopeful.

SUMMER 2002 AT WOODWALTON FEN

Our first summer on the road. It worked. We were welcomed at English Nature's Woodwalton National Nature Reserve. Alan Bowley, who heads up the team there, and Andy Mason, his second-in-command, pulled out all the stops to make sure we had everything we needed. They even laid on an electricity generator for us, so that we could use our microscopes and videos.

Woodwalton is very isolated. We worried whether people would know what was happening and whether they would find us. It turned out that our education courses were almost fully subscribed and a steady stream of people arrived for our half-day 'Dragonfly Safaris'. And, despite Woodwalton being a cross between a wilderness and a maze, we didn't lose a soul!

We ran five education courses, two of which were basic introductions to dragonflies, two were larval identification courses (Initial and Advanced) and a fifth course was on dragonflies and water plants. I suspect that the number of people on the courses has a lot to do with the expertise and patience of the trainers, so the Project owes a great deal to the commitment of Henry Curry, Henry Stanier, Stuart Irons, Karen Buckley and Kari de Koenigswarter.

What was it like for people coming on any of the twelve Dragonfly Safaris? There were usually about ten folk, with two or three knowledgeable volunteers to meet them at Jackson's Bridge and guide them through the fen. The dragonflies often acted as if they were under orders. Most of the time, they foraged, perched, mated and laid eggs exactly as required. By the time our visitors arrived at Charles Rothschild's bungalow-on-stilts in the centre of the fen, they could already differentiate between Darters, Hawkers, and Red-eyed or Blue-tailed damselflies. Their eyes widened as they watched damselflies 'in cop' and learned about the life-cycle of these amazing creatures. Besides a basic grasp of dragonfly biology, we gave our visitors an eye for dragonfly behaviour and habitat.

At the bungalow, Lynn, Sue, Carol, Ann and Pam presided over our gift shop. (Thank you, ladies, for your hours spent in semi-darkness, whilst the sun blazed down outside.) There was usually a brisk bit of trade, especially in soft drinks, before our visitors sank down into a waiting semi-circle of chairs and were treated to 'The Henry Show'. Most of you will have seen it. In case you haven't, it's a demonstration with the TV-Microscope link. Our visitors discovered the unusual breathing habits of larvae, saw the wing-cases and enormous eyes, hugely magnified. Just as at the Biomuseum, the best bit of the show was the moment when the larva shot out its mask and grabbed the unsuspecting bloodworm.

Astonishingly, the weather behaved. Of the twelve safaris, only one was in dull conditions. The sun shone, and even more surprising, the horseflies seemed to have declared a ceasefire. Horsefly ceasefires are relative of course, but most of us escaped unscathed. Anticipating a marketing opportunity here, we'd laid in a stock of insect repellent. We've still got lots for next year.

It would be impossible to leave the subject of our stay at Woodwalton without mentioning the sheer delight of just being there. Quite apart from the abundant wildlife (Quote: 'If anybody else interrupts my dragonfly talk to point out another Purple Hairstreak, I'll scream!'), there was the sheer joy of being in Charles Rothschild's 1912 bungalow-on-stilts. Sitting inside quietly, beneath the thatch, you could find yourself catching echoes of earlier naturalists. If you stayed very still, out of the corner of your eye, you might catch a glimpse of Charles Rothschild himself, bent over, peering at a moth. Could that be Frohawk out on the verandah, sketching? Someone, hunched over the table in the other room, making notes ... possibly Jordan, the curator from Tring? Three people sitting on the steps discussing labial palps of Ruddy and Common Darter larvae ... Lucas, Tillyard and Morton perhaps? You listen more carefully. It's Stanier, Nelson and Curry.

Apropos of Charles Rothschild, we should put on record that his granddaughter, Kari de Koenigswarter, spent time at the bungalow designing, compiling and editing a Schools Education Pack for the British Dragonfly Society. If you want a copy, please let us know.

We developed a tradition of sitting on the verandah in the evening sun, after the visitors had gone. We would mull over the day, gaze out over the bush and listen to birdsong and aeroplanes. There'd be a bird call. The more impetuous would leap up with binoculars and hazard, 'Sedge Warbler?' The more knowledgeable would remain seated and say quietly, 'Reed Warbler.' We would sit down, chastened. The same thing would happen with aircraft. We'd leap up and stare at the sky: 'American engine ... Harvard?' A female American voice behind us would drawl authoritatively, 'Cessna A37.' We'd sit down again.

We think we won our spurs at Woodwalton. We are very grateful to English Nature for taking us under their wing. We demonstrated that we could bring the general public safely onto this precious site in manageable numbers, and provide a unique educational experience. We also showed that we can survive without a centre and still be of service to dragonflies, still get the message across to the general public that dragonflies are beautiful, fascinating and in trouble ... and that people can help.

And we have remained a team. This is truly amazing. We still have volunteers regularly driving to help from Lincolnshire, Northamptonshire, even Hertfordshire. This means that, quite apart from all the administration and fetching and carrying, we can staff our gift shop, run our courses, do our TV-Microscope show, and guide safaris without becoming (totally) hysterical. It is really lovely to be part of such a can-do gang.

During the winter Henry and Lynn Curry, Mick and Sue Parfitt and other accomplices have been giving evening talks to groups of naturalists across East Anglia and the Midlands. This can mean long evenings on top of long days, often with small audiences. These audiences usually make up for their size by their enthusiasm and such work keeps the Project flame alive during the dark non-dragonfly winter nights.

WICKEN FEN NATIONAL TRUST NATURE RESERVE
Wicken is to be our base for 2003. Some of you will recall Adrian Colston from the early days at the Museum. He used to be in charge of the Northamptonshire Wildlife Trust. In that role, his advice and help in setting things up was invaluable. Adrian has been Property Manager at Wicken Fen for several years now, but has continued to watch our progress from afar. He has been very encouraging and has offered us the use of the National Trust facilities for 2003. We plan to run courses and safaris in the same way as we did at Woodwalton last year.

It is very exciting for us. Wicken Fen, near Ely, is known nationally and is a superb place for dragonflies. It has the advantages of accessibility, clear signage from major roads and all the necessary facilities. I must add that it is a personal favourite. I have worked on BBC dragonfly programmes there, with Bill Oddie and with the Open University and, boy, did the dragonflies perform! On one occasion last year, Henry Curry and I went over there for a meeting and finished up unable to leave until it finally got dark. We sat on the bank of a pool, transfixed by the activities of an Emperor, a Brown Hawker and several Four-spotted Chasers. It was as if they were putting on a show to encourage us to come next year. We astonished ourselves by foregoing a session in the Anchor Inn!

Our objective at Wicken is to publicize dragonflies, and to provide a hands-on educational service to the general public. We also want to win our spurs with the National Trust by demonstrating that our volunteer team can provide added value to the wonderful work that is already going on there. If all goes well, we would like to consider the possibility of setting up something a little more permanent at Wicken. The various fenland restoration projects can only be good news for dragonflies, and we would very much like to be part of this.

We are really looking forward to working with Adrian and his team at Wicken. They have already gone out of their way to show they care. Come and see us if you POSSIBLY can.

WE'LL GET THAT DRAGONFLY CENTRE YET!

* * *

THE MIGRANT SKIMMER, NUMBER 2, MAY 2004
THE BULLETIN OF THE DRAGONFLY PROJECT
(FORMERLY THE NATIONAL DRAGONFLY BIOMUSEUM)
First, news of last year:
SUMMER 2003. WICKEN FEN NATIONAL TRUST NATURE RESERVE
We'd learned a lot from our successful 2002 summer at Woodwalton. As we said in the last *Skimmer*, we were very grateful to Alan Bowley and his team. But we had to face the fact that not many members of the general public knew Woodwalton and fewer could find it! (It was a long walk back to a loo, too ...) So how could we possibly find somewhere as fabulous, yet more accessible?

Wicken Fen, near Ely, is known nationally and is a superb place for dragonflies. And, compared to Woodwalton, it had the advantages of accessibility, clear signage from major roads and all the necessary facilities. Our worry was the distance from our volunteers' home area. Would we be able to operate successfully so far away?

Apprehensively, we committed ourselves: twelve safaris and four one-day courses. And the result? We found we were truly among friends. Adrian Colston's team at Wicken bent over backwards to make us feel welcome. (Quote: 'Doing anything tonight? We're all having a barbecue. Wanna come?') It is obvious that they work at Wicken because they love the place.

The two red-tiled classrooms were perfect for us, space to run our courses in one part whilst having our TV-Microscope show and gift shop in the other. (Loos en suite, lovely circular picnic tables just outside and a smashing café right there.) And more really attractive dragonfly habitats than we could possibly take people to in the time available.

We soon discovered we needed to divide our Safariers into two sections, the long-range marchers and the 'toddler-and-crock' squad. We were very concerned whether the youngsters and oldies would be able to walk far enough to see any dragonfly action. We needn't have worried. Dragonflies! You couldn't move for them! Not for nothing did an early naturalist call Wicken 'The home of ease for entomologists'! Often, the short-rangers would get no further than the brick-pit pond, returning an hour and a half later full of excitement and new-found knowledge, ready to plonk themselves down to watch a larva-feeding demonstration.

Our training courses were highly successful, too, with glowing questionnaires. Besides our open courses, Henry Curry and Kari de Koenigswarter ran a larval identification course for the Environment Agency and I ran courses for Anglian Water and the Peoples' Trust for Endangered Species. All three organizations want repeats.

So we enjoyed another astonishing summer of bright sunshine and happy experiences, essentially the same team in a different location, but quite a lot busier.

Of course, we found time of an evening to muse on earlier naturalists in whose footprints we trod. Wandering in the gloaming, we spot a dim figure moving methodically across Verrall's Fen; the ghost of Verrall himself, perhaps? Or Moberley? Or possibly the ubiquitous Charles Rothschild? All three, after all, were far-sighted enough to buy parts of the fen, long before 'conservation' became a household word. The shape comes closer and materializes into Kevin James, the Deputy Head Warden, checking his Longworth traps, long after other folk have gone home.

Wicken has been odonatologically well-recorded both by Norman Moore and Adrian Colston, who have already produced an excellent guide, *The dragonflies and damselflies of Wicken Fen*, available from the National Trust Visitor Centre.

In short, we have found a delightful, immensely practical venue for our work, possibly with even more visitor-visible margins than Woodwalton. And we managed to stay together as a team despite the distances involved.

SUMMER 2004?

Best news of all, I'm proud to say that the National Trust want us back at Wicken, and have asked us to run 50% more safaris. So, in the short term, through courses and safaris, we shall continue to provide a hands-on educational service to the general public, ramming the message home that dragonflies are beautiful, fascinating and in trouble, and that almost everyone can help.

We'll be sharing a stand again with the British Dragonfly Society at the Rutland Bird Fair, 15th/16th/17th August, as we have since they joined us there in 2001. This went very well last year. It gives us access to legions of birders. Dragonflies are at their most active and colourful when the UK bird scene is fairly quiescent, so it's an obvious opportunity.

THE FUTURE?

We have not lost sight of the success of the Biomuseum at Ashton and we are still convinced of the need for a Dragonfly Centre. We remain in discussion with the British Dragonfly Society's board with a view to some type of joint venture, clearly preferably within striking-distance for our team. We are also continuing to explore possibilities with the National Trust. There is just a chance that a small building might become available at Wicken at some point in the future, which we might be able to use as a base. One way or the other, we feel that any proposed site would need to be close to a river and easily accessible to the public. We've shown we can dig ponds, build observation platforms, attract dragonflies and get people to come, but we can't – yet – do rivers.

Chapter 34

SUNDAY, JULY 26TH, 2009

It's the Grand Opening of the Dragonfly Centre at the National Trust Nature Reserve, Wicken Fen. Visitors are starting to flood in.

We've won our spurs all right. We've continued to work here, running Dragonfly Safaris and courses every summer. Adrian Colston and his successor Chris Soans have been as good as their word. The little fenman's cottage in Lode Lane – the one mentioned in the 2004 newsletter – has been restored. Only months ago it was a total wreck, with daylight showing through the walls and huge holes in the floor. Today it looks immaculate, red-tiled and cream-washed, with a raised dragonfly demonstration pond right outside and a model garden pond close by. Inside, there are brand-new interpretation boards and well-lit display cabinets. We're launching a partnership between the Dragonfly Project, the British Dragonfly Society and the National Trust. And, this time, it's the National Trust who've done all the fundraising. Wonderful.

Here's Pam Taylor, the British Dragonfly Society's hard-working president, here are crowds of people, here are the fund-providers (including old friends from Anglian Water and the Environment Agency), here are all the volunteers that have stuck together for twenty years, here are the newer faces that have joined us since we started at Wicken, here are almost all the previous volunteers from the old days at the Sanctuary and the Biomuseum (including the Oily Rag team and the Tractor team).

Here's sledgehammer-wielding Mick Parfitt, now a Dragonfly Project Trustee. Here's Kari. Here's my daughter Catharine, now with my granddaughter, Penny.

And here's Chris Packham. He's a much bigger star now, but he's as brilliant, knowledgeable and supportive as ever. Despite the grey clouds, the day is a rip-roaring success, literally hundreds of people learning about dragonflies. And this time Henry Curry and I remember the ribbon.

BANK HOLIDAY MONDAY, AUGUST 31ST, 2009

It's been the last day of the Dragonfly Safari season here at Wicken Fen and, after a farewell drink, all the volunteers have set off home. I'm alone, standing on one the picnic tables right up at the top end of the overflow car park. It's the highest spot in Wicken, good for cellphone reception, and I've just rung Kari in Scotland. The sun has already set, and in the gloaming I look down at the little Dragonfly Centre nestled below. We've really done well, sure, but what we want now is for the BDS to add 'Raising Public Awareness' to their existing aims of 'Study' and 'Conservation'.

I toy with idea of going into Ely for a solitary final pint at the Cutter, but the thought of being alone among all those noisy Bank Holidayers is too much. So I hop off the table, walk down to the car, drive back to the National Trust Visitor Centre, park, and amble down to the edge of Wicken Lode in the quietness. I pause at the spot where we always take visitors, where the Red-eyed Damselflies linger on the pads of the yellow and white waterlilies. A Brown Hawker, crepuscularly foraging, moves back and forth over the placid water, a fluttering silhouette. I don't understand why, after all this time, such a sight still thrills me but it does.

In the west, the sky is full of streaked cloud; in the east it's clear and starlit, with the moon three quarters full, shining brightly. I stroll down to the junction of Monk's Lode and Wicken Lode, and as my shoes crunch along the gravel cycle-track I catch the cool cut-glass smell of the river, and pass through pockets of air that have been heated in sheltered spots by the sun, and now waft past my face like warm silk.

We've done it. But I miss Ashton. And I miss Miriam, gone now, too.

MONDAY, NOVEMBER 29TH, 2011

It came as a surprise, a few days ago, to get a call from the BBC's *Springwatch Christmas Special* team. Would I come down to presenter Chris Packham's house in the New Forest for a few minutes' filming? They want to reprise a sequence we'd done last summer, involving ultra-slow-motion film of dragonflies in flight. Oh, and a few words about the interaction between hobbies – the birds, that is – and dragonflies. Of course I agreed, but I'm home in Perthshire, and this is winter ...

'Don't worry,' said the fixer, 'we'll arrange all the flights and so on. What about Wednesday the 1st of December? Fly you from Edinburgh to Southampton? BBC car into the New Forest? Stay locally, then fly you back to Edinburgh Thursday morning? OK with you?'

The whole of Scotland then promptly got blanketed in snow. So, another phone call from the BBC: they're worried about the Scottish snow heading south, could I fly down earlier?'

This morning, the weather's very bad and even worse towards Edinburgh. But I'm not going to give up, so I drive through twenty miles of hurtling horizontal snow to Pitlochry station. Come wind or whatever, the Inverness-to-London 'Highland Chieftain' battles daily over Slochd and Drumochter summits and stops at Pitlochry en route south. I've checked and it's running.

I join the little group of determined folk on the platform and we wait for well over two hours for the delayed Chieftain. No staff on the station, no warm waiting room, no loos, but we make the best of it, chatting encouragingly to each other, and we applaud the train driver as the Chieftain pulls in.

As we board, we're met with a great waft of Dunkirk spirit, led by the train guard whose regular triumphant announcements on progress keep passengers smiling though the further long hold-ups and crawls towards Edinburgh Waverley. Eventually we make it and out I go to Edinburgh airport and, by 4.00pm I'm checked in, sipping coffee in the departure lounge, ready for the flight to be called. Sudden announcement: no more flights; runway closed.

So downstairs, to join a mile-long queue, and finally come face-to-face with a flight-reorganizer who is surprisingly calm considering he must already have dealt with about a thousand irritated customers. I rebook a flight for 7.00am the next morning and ring the BBC.

'Don't worry,' they say, 'we don't need you till tomorrow afternoon.'

Next morning I arrive at the airport once more; but it's quiet, too quiet. The sotto voce comments of the ground staff reveal that there's little hope of getting the runway clear.

So, back into Edinburgh and on to the next train heading south. It's worryingly empty; do other southbound travellers know something I don't? Do they know that, at Warrington, it will freeze up? Because it does. Anyway, four trains later, at 3.30pm, I reach still-snow-free Southampton and make my way by taxi to the filming location.

The BBC Springwatch team are delighted to see me and ply me with food and drink. They really are a lovely lot, as keen on wildlife and wildlife issues offscreen as on. But, between takes, they can be diverted: back in the summer, it was vintage aircraft with Chris; here in the New Forest it's motorbikes with Martin Hughes-Games. I do my few minutes with Kate Humble and Chris. Then we all go off for a Chinese meal, and Chris delivers me to my night's accommodation – which is down a long single-track road, miles from anywhere.

My return flight is still booked for the Thursday and the BBC have been unable to change it, so I spend Wednesday relaxing, recovering and making darn sure a cab can get me to Southampton airport in time for my 9.00am flight next morning.

At 3.30am on Thursday morning I get up and look out of the window. I see a foot of snow, more in places, and it's still snowing. There's no question that a Southampton taxi will get anywhere near here. So at 4.45am I set off on foot into the darkness, heading for the Southampton-Fawley fuel refinery road, five miles away.

If any road is to be kept open it'll be that one. There's an obvious roundabout at – nice name – Dibden Purlieu. I'll get the cab to meet me there; it's booked for 7.00am.

Yes, it's snowing, yes, it's pitch dark, yes, it's murderously cold, yes, it's a damn long walk through deep snow, but I think of Robert Falcon Scott and plough on through the silence, dragging my suitcase behind me.

Just before 6.00am, very pleased that my Fife-made walking shoes are still keeping my feet dry, I've covered well over three miles when headlights shine from behind me, illuminating the driving snow. I haul my case into a drift at the side of the road and wait as a four-wheel drive pick-up murmurs past. It doesn't stop. I swear at it. As if in response, it stops, reverses carefully and comes back.

'What you doin'?' asks the driver, as snow whips through his half-opened window into his face. I explain my plan.

'Get in,' he says, 'I'm headin' for the petrol station at Dibden.'

I climb aboard, and he saves me two miles of slog. We arrive at the petrol station. All the lights are on, and despite the blizzard, the staff are setting out stuff on the forecourt.

'Sorry, we're closed,' says the man in charge. 'We don't open till seven.'

My saviour mutters angrily, climbs back into his cab and drives off into the snow and darkness in search of a properly-open petrol station. Still white from head to foot from my trek, I stand in his tyre tracks. I turn to the man in charge.

'Mind if I pop in and get warm?'

'Sorry, mate.'

'Eh? You won't let me?'

'Sorry, mate. Security.'

He tries to brush past me. I stand right in his way and put my face very close to his.

'I can't believe you just said that. Can't you see ... bloody blizzard ... freezing ...'

He dodges round me and nips inside. Before the automatic doors can hiss shut again, I follow him in, and find his staff have witnessed the encounter. They glare at him and mutiny; I'm brought tea and chocolate bars.

The cab eventually arrives. We set off.

'Never seen it like this,' says the driver. 'Nothing like this in the twenty years I've been doing this job.'

He repeats 'Never seen it like this' at least fifteen times, before falling silent and switching on Radio Southampton.

'We've never seen it like this,' says the DJ.

'There,' says the driver triumphantly, jabbing a finger at the dashboard.

We reach the airport and pull up. A man in a bright yellow work jacket waves his broom at us and makes slicing gestures across his throat; we deduce that the airport is closed. I go in and make sure, then walk across the road to the train station and get lucky once more. By six o'clock that evening, I'm in the Café Royal bar in Edinburgh having a drink with Kari.

Four days for a few moments' filming? Was it worth it? Yes. Anything to raise public awareness of dragonflies.

SUNDAY, JULY 8TH, 2012

It's a shockingly wet Sunday afternoon at Wicken Fen, so wet that no one at all has come to be taken on a Dragonfly Safari. So we sit in the Learning Centre and play with the TV-Microscope link. Kari is now a full-time artist with a studio in Edinburgh. She's already had three one-woman shows of her spectacular beeswax abstracts, but she still manages to come down to Wicken with me from time to time. Today she's extracted a lily pad from the dipping ponds and she and Henry Curry are examining the tiny circular incisions made by a damselfly, egg-laying in the under-side of the leaf. Each egg has been slipped into a tiny hole, drilled by the damselfly's ovipositor. It looks almost as if someone's been doing a little sewing. Jerry Hoare, a relatively new – and very keen – volunteer distracts Henry about cameras for a moment, leaving Kari sitting, gazing idly at the image of the lily leaf on the TV screen. Suddenly, she straightens up and shouts, 'Look at that! Look at that! Bloody parasitic wasp!'

We crowd round, and there on the screen is a thin black wasp drumming with its antennae on an egg. It turns round, slips its own ovipositor into the damselfly egg, then moves on, drumming for signs of the next egg; and repeats the operation again and again. We're shocked. We're even more shocked when we look at the leaf itself and can't see anything. Then Henry notices a tiny speck of dust. It's the wasp. On the screen it looked the same size as a normal wasp, but this one is truly minute. It's so small we think we've got it and bottled it, then Kari tells us it's still on the leaf. No. It's another wasp.

We open Philip Corbet's tome, *Dragonflies: Behaviour and Ecology of Odonata*, and learn that these minute wasps can parasitize up to 90% of damselfly eggs on a given leaf. Jerry and Henry set to work to film what's happening and Kari gets the wasp we've captured ready to send off to the Natural History Museum. In the absence of preserving fluid she uses vodka.

This is certainly the first time this sort of parasitic activity has been filmed, and news comes back from the NatHist that our specimen is possibly a new species, temporarily named *Anagrus, near ustulatus*. Henry says he thought Anagrus was a small town on the Mongolian steppes, not far from …

He shows the film to the Annual Indoor Meeting of the British Dragonfly Society in November.

FRIDAY, MAY 24TH, 2013

I'm sitting in the fleeting sunshine in a deckchair in my cottage garden in Perthshire, feeling reflective.

Last autumn, around the time that Henry showed *Anagrus near ustulatus* to the Annual Indoor Meeting, the British Dragonfly Society trustees came to a decision; they adjusted the Society's aims to include 'Raising Public Awareness of Dragonflies'. It's something we'd been gently agitating for, ever since we started at Ashton. Previously the Society had concentrated on 'the Study and Conservation of Dragonflies' and left ' Raising Public Awareness' to us.

So BDS members have now taken on the responsibility that we as a team at Ashton, Woodwalton and Wicken shouldered for twenty-three years. The Dragonfly Centre at Wicken thrives, often manned now by new volunteers.

Many of the Dragonfly Project volunteers are already hard-working, highly contributive members of the BDS: Henry Curry is its secretary. Lynn takes care of its gift shop and membership administration. Mick Parfitt is a trustee. Other dragonfly victims, who have come on our courses or been otherwise indoctrinated whilst we've been at Wicken, have also become prominent members of the BDS. I'm a strong supporter – I've been to every BDS Annual Meeting since 1987 – but, from experience, I know I work best independently. BDS member Peter Mayhew, the young man who worked with us back in 1990, is now Senior Lecturer in Biology at York University.

The Dragonfly Project can now pass the baton to the BDS and the work will go on. In our time together as a volunteer team, we've learned so much about ourselves, learned skills and achieved results we could hardly have dreamed of. We've had far more triumph than tragedy. It's been a good time.

And what about our aim, all those years ago, of raising public awareness?

We've clocked up some impressive statistics: 3,500 visitors to Ashton Water Dragonfly Sanctuary, 1991–1994; 22,000 visitors to the National Dragonfly Museum, 1995–2001. We never even counted all the talks we gave countrywide, nor the number of people who came to see us at Wicken, but we certainly took over 1,000 people on half-day Dragonfly Safaris, and 400 participants attended our one-day dragonfly courses. We also lost count of the times we appeared on prime-time national and local TV and radio.

In 1990 it was relatively hard to find information about drag-onflies, and harder still to spot dragonfly-related products in shops. When we started our little gift shop, our range was pretty small. Lynn and her helpers had to work hard to locate items to sell. Now, there's an excellent selection of general-user dragonfly handbooks, and natural history film-makers nowadays can hardly resist popping a few shots of dragonflies into their documentaries. There are more dragonfly mugs, purses, cards, bookmarks and so on than any single shop can possibly stock. The same goes for dragonfly jewellery. Dragonfly designs now appear regularly on retail textiles, from Liberty scarves, through Marks and Spencers shirts to Gap boxer shorts. Even the Royal Family wear dragonfly cuff links and brooches. Things have come a long way from Kari and Berit's little range of dragonfly T-shirts and sweatshirts.

We don't claim credit for all of this, but we're very proud that our work for dragonflies with thousands of visitors – at the Sanctuary, at the Biomuseum, at Woodwalton, at Wicken Fen, in talks, in television documentaries, on radio programmes – has certainly made a significant contribution.

Granddaughter Penny heard the news that I'd be pulling back from Wicken from daughter Catharine while sitting in their car. She burst into the house, flung her arms around me and said, 'You *can't* give up dragonflies, Grandpa.' I hugged her. 'No, sweetheart,' I said, 'they're in my blood.'

It's true. My love of dragonflies is undiminished. My heart still leaps at the sight of them. I continue to derive huge joy from showing people how astonishing and how beautiful they are. Whenever Kari and I come to a pond we invariably stop, me to scan the surface, she to bend over and search for exuviae in the bankside vegetation. We've come a very long way from those sunny days by the Grand Union Canal at Denham.

BANK HOLIDAY MONDAY, AUGUST 26TH, 2013

Kari and I are staying in the Lamb Hotel, Ely. It's been a busy weekend so far. On Saturday, the volunteers arrived at Wicken to begin our last ever weekend as The Dragonfly Project. While I ran a one-day introductory course, the others took visitors out on safaris. The weather wasn't kind, and on our foray into fenland under lowering skies my class only managed to see a solitary Blue-tailed Damselfly and a glimpse of a Migrant Hawker, thus demonstrating the influence of a disappearing product to the very last.

Of course Wicken is still a brilliant place to show people the various sorts of habitats that dragonflies like, so our trip wasn't wasted, but I was reminded why we'd needed the Mill originally:

we had a roof over our heads and we spent the day mostly indoors discussing the life-cycle of dragonflies, how they behave and how to identify them. The group went away happy and converted, three participants joining the BDS on the spot.

Earlier in the day there'd been a panic over finding live dragonfly larvae in the dipping ponds to show in our glass tanks. We usually rely on Ralph Sargeant, one of most loyal local helpers. Ralph, whose face, beard and clothes would need no adjustment to fit into the nineteenth century, has worked on the fen his entire life and, though retired, still shows up daily. His knowledge of the fen is encyclopaedic, his ability to predict the weather is uncanny, and his guddling technique when hunting for larvae in the dipping ponds is unmatched. Except by one person. Ralph had arrived, downcast, with a single tiny damselfly larva. So Kari, armed with a sieve, disappeared only to reappear much later with several decent-sized ones. She grinned at Ralph. 'Takes a local to find them, you know.' For once Ralph was speechless, but his clear blue eyes twinkled at her.

On Sunday, I'd promised to make myself available for Sarah Blunt from the BBC's Natural History Unit in Bristol. Sarah and I go back a long way, 1992; she was one of the first BBC people to visit the Sanctuary. The weather perked up and – it's almost always the case when BBC people are around – the dragonflies showed off. Sarah and I just felt so lucky to be in such a gorgeous place doing what we enjoyed that several takes were spoiled due to laughter and sudden stories. But we got the job done in time for a sandwich lunch in the sunshine.

Mick Parfitt and Jerry Hoare had agreed to take out the afternoon safari, Henry Curry was at the controls of the TV-Microscope link, and Lynn Curry and Sue Parfitt were manning the gift shop, so I found myself with little to do. They could manage perfectly well without me. As it should be.

I walked out alone along the boardwalk in the sunshine, past the ancient four-sailed wind pump, over the bridge and into the clearing to the left. A Brown Hawker was gliding up and down over the reeds, its coppery wings glinting in the sunlight. A

Migrant Hawker jinked over my head, darted up to catch something and vanished into the trees, and a Common Darter landed on the upright trunk of a long dead tree. As I gazed around in the quietness, it began to sink in that this was the last weekend.

I didn't know how to feel. Sad? Yes, a bit. But as Kari says, nothing is for ever. Happy? Yes, a bit. I won't be committed to coming to Wicken all the way from Perthshire at least six times every summer as I have for the last eleven years. Now I can carry on publicizing dragonflies in other ways. Proud? Yes, a bit. We've done an awful lot.

For once, none of us especially wanted to have our evening drink before leaving. We all knew tomorrow was going to be a very big day, our official 'Handing on the Baton' party.

Kari and I came back to the hotel to find a woman, her back to us, explaining something complicated to Gemma, the receptionist. Gemma raised her eyes to us as if to say '*You* can answer this one.' And there was Carol Bouchard, flown in all the way from New Mexico, specially for tomorrow. The rest of the evening was spent collecting other friends arriving on delayed trains from Scotland. We gathered in the lounge around a circular table that steadily acquired more arrivals, more chairs and more wine.

And so to this morning, Bank Holiday Monday: I've been asked to lead the last ever safari. So, on the dot of eleven, twenty-odd people gather outside the Learning Centre. Mick Parfitt is my tail-gunner. I don't remember who invented that title for the person who brings up the rear of a Dragonfly Safari and makes sure no one gets left behind or falls in. Anyway, no one has ever fallen in.

We set off for the dipping ponds, pausing to look over the vast sedge fen and considering the extraordinary value of Wicken for dragonflies. No sooner at the ponds than Common Darters begin to oviposit right in front of us, a Brown Hawker glides to and fro, a Blue-tailed Damselfly perches daintily for all to bend over and take a look at, and a Southern Hawker puts in a brief electric lime-green-and-blue flash of an appearance. We march about looking at different sorts of habitat and then set off down the boardwalk, coming to a stand at one of the 'windows' in the dykes that the National Trust have cleared specially for visitors to see dragonflies in action.

I walk round to the other side of the dyke in order to make sure everyone can see what I want to show them. Chris Slaney, one of the most generous of our volunteers over the years – light-boxes, video recorders, projectors, etc – hops excitedly off the boardwalk in front of the group, camera in hand, to point out an Emerald Damselfly. It's hiding in the vegetation close to the water surface. As he leans forward he slips and falls right in. These dykes are narrow but deceptively deep. Chris's heavy backpack starts to pull him under. There's a moment when we're all watching a man sinking swiftly down deeper into the ooze, gasping, about to drown, before Mick and new volunteer Kevin dash down the bank, grab his flailing hand and haul him out. He's soaked in peaty water, black with mud from head to foot, but laughing with relief. Kevin takes him off to the Centre, and I do my best to continue.

We return to the Learning Centre, I hand over to Henry Curry to give the last larva demonstration, and walk into a storm of party questions. Who's going to open the fizzy? When shall we serve the food? Where's the beer? Lynn and the others have already taken a great deal of trouble to convert the Centre into a party venue. The food is beautifully laid out on long tables, Kari has nipped round to make sure it all looks colourful, the drinks are on another set of tables, and up on the wall are seventeen letters from friends and supporters that haven't been able to come today. The beer is hidden over in the Visitor Centre; it's Dragonfly Amber Ale. I spotted it in Oddbins in Edinburgh, bought three bottles, liked it, and arranged with the Fallen Brewery in Kippen for forty-eight bottles to be delivered here. On a screen, a slide-show steadily works through a massive collection of photographs from the Sanctuary, the Museum, Woodwalton and Wicken.

Just under a hundred guests arrive, including my daughters Anna and Catharine, my granddaughter Penny and my niece Jacqueline. And here's Iona Twinn, far removed from her larval little-terror stage, metamorphosed into a colourful, sensible, intelligent adult, a boon on our stands at recent Bird Fairs. The afternoon passes in a whirl. There are prints of all the photographs, too; people pick them up, smile, and take them across to other guests to share memories and laugh. Only seven of the key original volunteers from the Mill twenty years ago are missing when we take a group photograph.

Once the party's in full swing, we pause the slideshow at an image of tubby, elderly, John Wainwright, tree-planter extraordinaire, sitting happily among a small group of us at a table in the Museum tearoom garden. I call for silence.

'I have two toasts,' I say. 'One is to John Wainwright, whose bequest has helped us to keep going. When we learned of his generosity we swore we'd have a party. This is it!'

We raise our glasses, then, 'The second is to us, what we've done, and how we've shoved dragonflies up the agenda. So, to us, and to the future!'

That's all I'd planned, but, as the clapping subsides, Henry Curry suddenly steps forward, shouts, and insists on another toast, to me. He says I'm the person responsible for everyone being here and for everything we've achieved. It's not true, and from him of all people, my trusty second-in-command and dear friend for the last twenty-two years, but I'm too overcome to speak.

I wonder what would have happened if a dragonfly hadn't landed on my shirt back in 1985? I guess I'd have continued at Canning, working at something I mostly enjoyed. Mostly. I'd have retired by now and have a fairly fat pension. I'd probably do what most people with successful careers behind them do: time with grandchildren, membership of local societies, a hobby or two, gardening, cruises, frequent holidays in sunny spots.

What have I got instead? Less money, certainly. I stopped what's considered to be 'real' work at forty-six, after all, so that's only to be expected. No expensive holidays and definitely no Bentley. But, while so many others have spent that time in offices, I've had twenty years of doing what I really want to do. I don't want to denigrate work in offices; many people get real satisfaction from their commercial lives. I was truly lucky to get the break I did, and it couldn't have been done without Kari's support, or the amazing context of Ashton. Have I repaid the good fortune I was so conscious of back in those extraordinary days? I'm not sure, but if it hadn't been for Miriam and Ashton, I dare say Kari and I would never have come to where we are, nor influenced so many other lives. But it was still a risk, and a big one.

It's been an astonishing twenty-odd years. I feel I've developed in ways I never could have, had I remained working, week in week out, for an organization.

Quite apart from being able to follow various interests to a depth that might not otherwise have been possible, and spending time with and learning from all the people I met at Ashton, meeting men like Philip Corbet and Norman Moore, and spending days and days with Miriam, I've found I can write in a way that people enjoy reading.

I've really changed. I have a deep sense now of the importance of the natural world, something I hardly noticed when I was bound up in my career. The word 'conservation' really means something to me and I have a profound unease about the direction we humans seem to be drifting.

I've also gained something totally personal: a passion, a passion for dragonflies that will never die until I do, linked to the desire to tell others about these extraordinary beasts. My passion means I need never retire, can never retire. And Kari's the same: in her art, she's found a lifelong calling, but her interest in dragonfly larvae is undimmed.

It's very hard to say why I feel so deeply about dragonflies, but, to me, looking at one of these astonishing insects is like looking up at a star. I have a sense of wonder. I feel very small in front of an example of a life-form that's been around for so many millions of years. For them, my existence – our existence – is pretty much irrelevant. They will survive, whatever we do.

I'm mindful of the 17th century Dutch artists who produced those wonderful, elegant flower paintings and included insects in their work. Hidden among the petals and the stems, each type of insect had its own symbolic meaning. For those painters, dragonflies symbolized 'the resurrection of the contemplative soul'. Yes.

Further Reading and Resources

Things have changed since the 1980s. Nowadays there is a plethora of books and information on dragonflies. Here are a few recommendations:

Steve Brooks and Richard Lewington's *Field Guide to the Dragonflies and Damselflies of Great Britain and Ireland*, Revised edition, British Wildlife Publishing, 1997. I carry this, stuffed in my waistband.

Two other excellent field guides:

Dave Smallshire and Andy Swash's *Britain's Dragonflies: A Field Guide to the Damselflies and Dragonflies of Britain and Ireland*, 3rd edition, Princeton University Press, 2014.

Klaas-Douwe B Dijkstra and Richard Lewington's *Field Guide to the Dragonflies of Britain and Europe*, British Wildlife Publishing, 2006.

Other books, some of which are out of print but worth hunting down:

David Chandler and Steve Cham's *Dragonfly*, New Holland Publishers, 2013. Straightforward text, brilliant photos, in print.

Philip Corbet, Cynthia Longfield and Norman Moore's *Dragonflies*, Collins New Naturalist Series, 1960. The one that started it for me.

Bob Gibbons's *Dragonflies and Damselflies of Britain and Northern Europe*, New edition, Hamlyn, 1994. Good photos.

Cyril Hammond's *The Dragonflies of Great Britain and Ireland*, 2nd revised edition, Harley Books, 1985. Lovely illustrations.

Philip Corbet's *Dragonflies: Behaviour and Ecology of Odonata*, Harley Books, 1999. The bible for dragonflies. And his earlier book: *A Biology of Dragonflies*, Quadrangle Books, 1963.

Georg and Dagmar Rüppell's *Jewelwings*, Georg Rüppell, 2006. Phenomenal photographs.

Dan Powell's *A Guide to the Dragonflies of Great Britain*, Arlequin Publications, 1999.

Peter Miller's *Dragonflies*, 2nd revised edition, Richmond Publishing, 1995. Good for student projects.

Jill Silsby's *Dragonflies of the World*, CSIRO Publishing, 2001.

Another excellent resource is the British Dragonfly Society's website – www.british-dragonflies.org.uk – which also sells several of the above books. The Society itself has 1,500 lively members, a splendid Annual Indoor Meeting, a terrific magazine, and is well worth joining.

The two main international organizations are: the Worldwide Dragonfly Association – ecoevo.uvigo.es/WDA/dragonfly.htm⊠; and the Societas Internationalis Odonatologica – www.odonatologica.com

An indispensible tool for spotting adult dragonflies is a pair of close-focusing binoculars. I use Pentax 'Papilio', 6.5x21, perfectly good for longer-range stuff too.

Acknowledgements

Sorry, but there just wasn't enough room to fit you all in, you volunteers who gave such significant amounts of your lives to promote dragonflies. You know who you are, and how much thanks you truly, truly deserve. But I'd specially like to thank those who encouraged me whilst I worked on the book: Kari de Koenigswarter of course, because it wouldn't have happened without her and her constant love and support; Frank Woods, my writing buddy and comrade-in-arms, who has read and commented on every word; fellow-writer Linda Cracknell, source of endless sympathy and sound advice. Also: Andrew Callander, Henry Curry, John Gilliatt, Jamie Grant, Victoria Gray, Mike Hill, Berit de Koenigswarter, Charlotte Lane, Hamish and Malize McBride, Catharine Mackenzie Dodds, Nick Mould, Chris Packham, Polly Pullar, Kevin and Jayne Ramage, and Sigrid Rausing.

Particular thanks, too, to Sara Hunt, my publisher, for believing in the book and seeing it through; to Laura Jones for wading through it and making valuable suggestions; and to Craig Hillsley for his astonishing editing abilities. Without him there might have been several diplomatic incidents, and the book would be pocked with little confusions. I accept full responsibility for any remaining mistakes, or unintentional nonsense.